An Exposition
of the Four Gospels

An Exposition
of the Four Gospels

Volume 4
The Gospel of John

Herschel H. Hobbs

BROADMAN PRESS
Nashville, Tennessee

Copyright 1968
by Baker Book House Company

ISBN for Four-volume Set: 0-8054-1370-7
Item Code: 4213-70
Library of Congress Catalog
Card Number for this volume: 68-23454

PHOTOLITHOPRINTED BY CUSHING - MALLOY, INC.
ANN ARBOR, MICHIGAN, UNITED STATES OF AMERICA
1977

Dedicated
to Archibald Thomas Robertson
whose massive mind was exceeded only
by his great heart in his interpretation
of the New Testament

CONTENTS

IX. The Raging Storm

X. The Rainbow of Assurance

INTRODUCTION

This is the third volume of a projected four designed to give An Exposition of the Gospels. The first two volumes deal with Matthew and Luke respectively. The fourth will be concerned with Mark. Since these three Gospels — Matthew, Mark and Luke — have a common approach to the life of Jesus they are known as the Synoptic Gospels. But John has a distinctive approach. Matthew and Luke largely follow the framework of Mark, at the same time each adding material peculiar to itself. Since John's approach differs from the others, it seems appropriate to deal with this Gospel before proceeding to Mark.

In the previous volumes the Introduction has dealt with critical matters only slightly. However, in this work it seems necessary to deal with such more in detail. For there is no other Gospel which has been the center of controversy as has the Fourth Gospel. Some years ago B. W. Bacon referred to the critical problems growing out of this Gospel as the most unsettled, most living, and most sensitive in the field of New Testament criticism. W. F. Howard refers to it as the most fascinating problem in the area of Biblical studies. However, it is not the author's purpose to consider at length even these problems. For the student who is interested in them there is a vast available literature. The present purpose is to delve into critical matters only to an extent necessary to a general understanding of such.

The Date of the Fourth Gospel

It is generally agreed that this was the last of the four Gospels to be written, and that it was probably written in Ephesus. However, even this has not been accepted without dispute. In 1922 C. F. Burney suggested that it was originally written in Aramaic, and therefore was the first one to. be written. But this theory gained practically no support among either Greek or Aramaic scholars.

9

However, at the other extreme were those who insisted that it was written as late as A.D. 170. It is significant to note that the trend in modern scholarship is to date it much earlier, even during the last quarter of the first century. One of the most significant evidences in this regard was the discovery of the John Rylands Fragment of the Fourth Gospel. Three leading papyrologists, Bell, Kenyon, and Schubart, agree in dating it during the first quarter of the second century (A.D. 98-117). Schubart strongly suggested a date around A.D. 81-96. Even if the later date be accepted, one must allow time for the copy of the Gospel whence came this frament to have circulated from Ephesus to as far as Egypt. This would suggest a date somewhere during the last quarter of the first century for the writing of the original.

Furthermore, the discovery of the Dead Sea Scrolls has shown that the thought patterns of the Fourth Gospel are similar to those existing in Palestine around A.D. 70. The Gospel is definitely Hebrew, not Greek, in nature. So an early date for this work seems to be more strongly established today than at any time since the rise of Higher Criticism.

It would appear, therefore, that a date sometime during the last quarter of the first century is most likely. We would place it about A.D. 80-90, probably the latter date.

The Authorship of the Fourth Gospel

The problem of authorship has also been the center of much difference. Whereas other possible authors have been suggested, the greater emphasis has been placed upon John the Apostle and an Elder John of Ephesus. At best, however, this *elder* is a somewhat vaporous person. Some who hold to this authorship suggest that he wrote down the events as he received them from John the Apostle. Even if this were true, the Gospel still would reflect the eyewitness experiences of the Apostle himself.

However, as Dods says, it is certain that by the last quarter of the second century the Fourth Gospel was accepted by the church as the canonical work of the Apostle John. In support of this position one may cite Ignatius, Irenaeus, Eusebius, Polycarp, Theophilus of Antioch, the Muratorian Canon, and the *Diatessaron* of Tatian. This last was a harmony of the four canonical Gospels which opens with a portion of the Fourth Gospel. Even heretical writings of the period make reference to the Apostle John as the author of this Gospel (Heracleon). One of the earliest references to this Gospel was by a Gnostic teacher, Basileides of Alexandria,

Egypt (*ca.* A.D. 125). He is quoted by Hippolytus as saying, "This is that which is said in the Gospels, 'That was the true light which lighteth every man that cometh into the world'" (cf. John 1:8). This does not name the author, but it does show that the Gospel existed and was in use by that date. And Dods refers to uses of it even prior to Basileides. He concludes that "already in the earliest years of the second century the Fourth Gospel was an authoritative document." This in itself suggests an apostolic authorship.

The internal evidence of the Gospel itself strongly suggests the Johannine authorship. This evidence reveals that the author was a Palestinian Jew, an eyewitness to the ministry of Jesus, and, by implication, that he was the Apostle John.

That the author was a Jew is evidenced by his Hebraistic style, his knowledge of Hebrew and Aramaic, and his familiarity with Jewish thought and life. His style of Greek is very simple, suggesting one who was only familiar with conversational Greek. Unlike Paul he shows no knowledge of Greek literature, and does not use the finer points of precise Greek expression. His habit of inserting Greek translations of Aramaic words and of explaining Jewish customs indicates that he is a Jew writing for Greek readers.

Furthermore, the author was a Palestinian Jew. At least his background was Palestinian, even though at the time of writing he may have lived outside of Palestine.

For instance, he is thoroughly familiar with the topography of Palestine. He shows a knowledge of Jerusalem prior to its destruction in A.D. 70. This is true not only of the temple area, but, as will be seen later, of the exact location of the pool of Bethesda. His references to distances (e.g. 11:18), to obscure places, to the brook Cedron, and to the garden beyond, all reveal a familiarity beyond that of a tourist or of one who had read travel books. Also it appears that the author quotes from the Hebrew scriptures rather than from the Septuagint which was used by Jews of the Dispersion.

Likewise, the author shows evidence that he was an eyewitness of the ministry of Jesus. This suggests that he was one of the Twelve. Also he was one of Jesus' intimates, suggesting that he was one of three (Peter, James, John) whom the Synoptic Gospels describe as being an inner-circle closest to Jesus among the Twelve. The author never names himself. In Chapter 21 he is identified by the Ephesian elders (vv. 20-24). The disciples mentioned in this event include Peter, James, and John (the sons of Zebedee).

Since Peter is clearly mentioned by name he is eliminated from consideration. James died soon after Pentecost. So this leaves only John. This fact, along with further internal evidence, plus the abundant external evidence, points clearly to John the Apostle as the author of the Fourth Gospel. And the more that we learn of this Gospel the more plausible this identification becomes.

The Historical Value of the Fourth Gospel

Perhaps here as nowhere else the storm of criticism has raged. Some have rejected the historical value of the Fourth Gospel on the basis of a late date of writing and a non-apostolic authorship. But as previously noted this position becomes more untenable with the passing of time and the rising flood of knowledge concerning this Gospel and its relation to the closing years of the first century.

Another basis of questioning the historical value of this Gospel is to view it as merely a polemical work aimed at refuting certain schools of thought which opposed the deity of Christ and His Messianic claims. One such group was the John the Baptist movement which would make him, not Jesus, the Christ. Some see a Jewish-Christian controversy as the occasion for the writing of this Gospel. Others would make it merely a philosophical dissertation on the Logos. Still others view it as a polemic against Gnosticism.

It may be granted that all of these elements are present in the Gospel. But do these things necessarily militate against its historical value? Who could better answer these schools of thought than one who was an eyewitness to the glory of Him who was the only God-begotten? By merely recording the facts he shows that Jesus, not John, was the Christ. And as for the Jewish-Christian controversy, the author simply relates that such a controversy existed even between Jesus and the Jewish leaders during His ministry. The other three Gospels record the same. Indeed, without John's record we would be largely at a loss to understand this element in the Synoptics. How, without John's record of Jesus' Jerusalem ministry, could we comprehend the deep-seated enmity of the Jews during Passion Week? Even the *Jewish Encyclopaedia* in an article on "Jesus" admits that the controversies between Jesus and the Jewish leaders indicate that Jesus was familiar with the rabbinic lore and style of debate.

As for the Logos concept, if John's Gospel were merely a philosophical dissertation on this idea it is strange that the word *Logos* referring to Christ does not appear in the book after 1:14.

The Hebrew nature of the Gospel strongly suggests another purpose in John's use of *Logos*. This position has been strengthened by the discovery of the Dead Sea Scrolls. And later it will be shown that a more reasonable origin of John's *Logos* idea may be offered than to see it simply as Grecian in nature.

Admittedly, John is a powerful polemic against Gnosticism (cf. Colossians). But in no sense should this be a refutation of its historical value. As in previously cited cases, no better answer to this philosophical system could be offered than historical facts to which the author was an eyewitness. The strong emphasis of this Gospel on "witness" or on first hand knowledge argues not only for its historical value but also for its apostolic authorship.

Increasing knowledge is a good answer to prejudice. As in so many other debated issues concerning Scriptural historical accuracy, so it is true with John. Wherever archaeology has thrown light upon these matters it has substantiated the Bible. And John is no exception. Luke is a primary case in point. The proved historical accuracy of Luke and Acts lends credibility to the other Gospels. There is nothing in John that contradicts Luke. Indeed the two Gospels corroborate each other. The historical accuracy of John stands more strongly today than ever before in the history of Biblical criticism. And there is no valid reason to fear but that this will continue to be increasingly true in the future.

One cannot help but wonder if the storm which has swirled about John is not due more to a prejudice against the deity of Jesus than to an honest desire to learn more about the background of this Gospel itself. For while the other Gospels clearly present Jesus' deity, it is more definitely emphasized in John than in any of the others. So long as John stands so long will the Gospel testimony that Jesus is the eternal God made flesh stand. And in every case the emergence of new knowledge authenticates both.

The Thought Environment of the First Century

A study of this environment shows how timely the Fourth Gospel was toward the close of the first century. Briefly, therefore, let us examine the atmosphere into which it was sent forth.

First, let us look at the idea of a John the Baptist Movement. It is evident from the New Testament itself that such a movement continued after the earthly life of Jesus (cf. Acts 19:1 ff.). Certain early Christian writings other than the canonical scriptures tell of such a movement which sought to set up John the Baptist as a rival messiah to Jesus.

In this light one can better understand certain elements in the Fourth Gospel. The author's stated purpose to show that Jesus, not John, is the Christ (20:31) made it quite likely that he would point out their true relationship. However, this does not argue for fabricated events on the part of the author. To the contrary it argues that he would be careful to cite true history which could not be questioned. Rather the author selected actual events and words spoken by John himself as showing his own concept of Jesus as the Christ. And if we admit that Andrew's companion (1:40) was the author of this Gospel, it is understandable that he would recount things which he had heard his former teacher say about Jesus. Added to these would be reports as to how John had said that he must go on decreasing but that Jesus would go on increasing.

Second, there is the idea of the Logos. That this idea was prevalent in the first century is evident to any student of the thought element of this period. Basically the idea was of Greek origin. But it had also become a great subject of Philo's thought. And he dealt with it largely through the allegorical method in vogue in Alexandria, Egypt. Therefore, some interpreters of John have tended to relate John's use of *Logos* to either one or the other. And since Philo used the allegorical method, some have attempted to find this same method in John's interpretation of Jesus. The claim, therefore, was that John's picture of Jesus was wholly unreal. He was called a mere imitation of the Stoics and Philo.

However, there were those who insisted upon the Hebrew nature of this Gospel. These found John's source of the Logos not in Greek philosophy or in Philo, but in the Old Testament use of the Hebrew *Memra,* or Word *(Logos)*. They held that *Memra* was personified in the Targums. *Wisdom,* said they, is personified in Proverbs. J. Rendel Harris suggested that all of the distinctive phraseology in the Prologue could have come from Proverbs 8. E. A. McDowell noted that if we substitute *sophia* for *logos* and say "In the beginning was Wisdom, and Wisdom was with God, and Wisdom was God," it would make a good transition from Proverbs 8 to John 1:1.

If one should try to harmonize these various positions he would be inclined to label John's Gospel as a literary freak. On the one hand it is called a thoroughly Hellenistic book; on the other hand it is seen as the most Jewish of all the Gospels. Obviously it cannot be both. In recent years archaeology has given strong evidence to the latter position, so that today we are justified in emphasizing the Jewish nature of the Gospel.

However, there is an element of truth in the Greek flavor of the Fourth Gospel. It was written in a Greek environment long after the destruction of the Jewish nation, and for primary readers who were familiar with Greek culture. This would include the Greek idea of the Logos. And since Philo had sought to bridge the gap between Greek philosophy and Hebrew theology, it is possible that these readers were somewhat familiar with his literary works. One author has questioned whether or not John had ever heard of Philo and the Alexandrine philosophy. This is a little difficult to accept. But, even so, a passing or popular knowledge of both the Greek and the Philonic ideas would suffice for John's purpose.

It is entirely possible, therefore, that against the background of such knowledge John used these ideas of the Logos as a spring board from which to present his own idea of the Logos. And in so doing to present the Logos as the eternal Christ who was incarnated as Jesus of Nazareth. And as will be shown later he did not necessarily relate this term to Hebrew *Memra* or Wisdom. Since the Logos means an open, spoken manifestation, he went back to the beginning of the Biblical record and related the term to God's spoken word as evidenced in the account of creation. It is quite clear that John presented the Logos as a Person, something that was not done by Greek philosophers, Philo, the Targums, or other Hebrew interpretations of *Memra* or Wisdom. Thus, while he adapted his language to the broader thought environment of his day, John's concept of the Logos is his own.

Third, let us note the Gnostic philosophy. This philosophy ante-dated Christianity. Thus it should not be classified as a product of Christian speculative theology. A. T. Robertson (*Paul and the Intellectuals*) says that it was the product of oriental syncretism. It is not purely Jewish, neither entirely Persian nor Babylonian. Rather it is a "syncretism of Persian dualism, Babylonian astrology, Hellenistic speculation, primitive magic, and certain elements of Judaism."

Basically Gnosticism was concerned with the origin of the universe and the existence of evil. It regarded God as entirely good, and matter as absolutely evil. A good God could not create evil matter. To explain the origin of the universe they postulated a series of emanations (called *aeons,* spirits, or angels) which came between God and matter. This series of *aeons* came out of God in a descending chain. Each possessed a portion of deity, but each less than the one which preceded it in the chain. The *fulness* (*plērōma*) was the sum-total of deity in God. But this *fulness* was disseminated throughout the chain. The last *aeon,* called the Demiurge, had enough of deity to be able to create, but so little as to be able to create evil matter.

When this philosophy came into contact with Christianity, they were faced with the Person of Christ. Where did He belong in their system? Some placed Him at the center of their "chain," while others placed Him at the end of it. But all agreed that He was the one who created evil matter. In any case it struck at the very heart of the Person of Christ. At best it made Him a demi-god, almost a demon.

Furthermore, these Gnostics were divided into two schools of thought with respect to Jesus Christ. The Docetics (from *dokeō,* I seem) said that Christ did not have a real flesh and blood body. He only *seemed* to have one. Thus they denied the humanity of Christ. They had no place in their system for an incarnation of God. So they said that Christ was neither born, nor did He die. His body was only an illusion.

The Cerinthian Gnostics (from their leader, Cerinthus) denied the identity of Jesus and Christ. Thus they denied the deity of Jesus. According to their position the *aeon* Christ came upon Jesus at His baptism and left Him on the cross (cf. John 1:32; Matt. 27:46). So they also denied both the birth and death of Christ.

It is not surprising, therefore, to find the New Testament strongly opposing such a system (cf. Colossians, I and II John). While the incipient Gnosticism of the latter half of the first century was not as elaborate as that of the second century, nevertheless it was as Paul called it, a "philosophy" characterized by "empty deceit" (Col. 2:8). And if left unanswered it would play havoc with the Christian gospel.

We would be surprised if the Fourth Gospel had ignored this philosophy. And if there is a polemical nature in it, it is aimed at Gnosticism more than at anything else. This is evident from the outset. The Prologue is a series of rapid-fire blasts at every tenet of it. It declares that rather than Christ being a created being He is eternally God Himself. In Him is resident the "fulness" or the sum-total of deity (cf. Col. 2:9). He is the Creator of every single part of the universe, and is the Source of all Life and Light. And He became Jesus of Nazareth, a flesh and blood man, to be the revealer of God and the intermediate Agent of all grace and truth brought to mankind. And it is against this tremendous background that John presents his historical proof that Jesus is the Christ who is God revealing Himself and providing redemption for lost men through His death on the cross and His bodily resurrection from the dead.

And having completed his account he says that "these are written, that ye might believe that Jesus is the Christ, the Son of God; and that believing ye might have life through his name" (20:31).

The Purpose of the Fourth Gospel

The author's clearly stated purpose is found in the above quotation (20:31). And, of course, this overrides all other purposes. It is evident in his dealing with the various thought-problems which have been discussed above. But his very selection of material suggests the secondary purpose of supplementing the other three Gospels.

Many years ago the writer prepared his doctoral thesis on the question "Does the Author of the Fourth Gospel Consciously Supplement the Synoptic Gospels?" Even a casual comparison of this Gospel with the Synoptics shows that John does supplement them. The problem of my thesis was the word "consciously." Is there evidence that John did this consciously and with deliberate design? The conclusion reached was in the affirmative.

John certainly could have had access to the other Gospels by the time that he wrote. And he was not without precedent in supplementing their accounts.

Matthew supplements Mark, and Luke supplements both of them. Even the Acts and the Pauline Epistles supplement one another. And there was need for adding material omitted by the Synoptic Gospels. This is seen in John's Prologue, the Jerusalem ministry, the clear relation between Jesus and John the Baptist, certain items of chronology, and additional details which help to clarify the Synoptic narratives.

The omission from John of certain important events found in the Synoptic record suggests that John assumes his readers' knowledge of that record. A comparative study of these four Gospels in the Greek text suggests that John may have had the Synoptic Gospels before him as he wrote his own.

If the reader cares to do so, he will find a most interesting study of certain connectives used by John. One of these is *tote*, a demonstrative adverb of time. From Homer down it has been rendered *then*, or *at that time*. In the Fourth Gospel it is used in most cases to indicate that a certain thing took place immediately following some other event (7:10; 8:28; 12:16; 13:27; 19:1, 16; 20:8). Perhaps the one exception to this usage is found in John 10:22 (see p. 160).

The other connectives are *meta touto* (after this) and *meta tauta* (after these things). The former is rarer in John's Gospel than the latter. The singular form suggests *after* a shorter period of time, while the plural form suggests *after* a longer period of time. *Meta touto* seems to refer to a single preceding event in John. But *meta tauta* seems to refer to a succession of events. But in either case they seem to be used by John to relate his account to the Synoptic Gospels. This is especially true of *meta tauta* where John seems to use it as an indication that he is at that point inserting into the record a body of material not found in the Synoptics. These instances will be pointed out *in loco*.

The Pattern of This Volume

This volume is designed to give a simple exposition of the Gospel of John. In so doing each verse is brought under consideration. The basic English text used is the King James Version. Where others are followed the version used is identified. The Greek text followed is Nestle's *Novum Testamentum Graece*. At times the author has made his own translation of given verses. Where it seems helpful the force of various Greek verb tenses is noted.

The bibliography for such a work as this could be almost endless. References are made to a few works not included in the bibliography. In order not to make the citations burdensome, we have quoted certain basic volumes later without footnotes. But these volumes are listed along with others in the following bibliography.

William Barclay, *The Gospel of John,* 2 Volumes, Westminister, Philadelphia, 1956

J. H. Bernard, *The Gospel according to John,* 2 Volumes, *The International Critical Commentary,* Scribner, New York, 1929

F. L. Godet, *Commentary on the Gospel of John,* 2 Volumes, Zondervan, Grand Rapids

Marcus Dods, *The Gospel of St. John,* Volume I, *The Expositor's Greek Testament,* Eerdmans, Grand Rapids

Herschel H. Hobbs, *The Crucial Words from Calvary,* Baker Grand Rapids, 1958; *The Gospel of John, A Study Guide,* Zondervan, Grand Rapids, 1967; *The Holy Spirit: Believer's Guide,* Broadman, Nashville, 1967; *Preaching Values from* the *Papyri*, Baker, Grand Rapids, 1964; *The Life and Times of Jesus*, Zondervan, Grand Rapids, 1966; *An Exposition of the Gospel of Matthew*, Baker, Grand Rapids, 1965; *An Exposition of the Gospel of Luke*, Baker, Grand Rapids, 1966

G. Campbell Morgan, *The Gospel According to John*, Revell, Westwood, N.J.

A. T. Robertson, *Epochs in the Life of the Apostle John*, Revell, New York, 1935; *A Harmony of the Gospels*, Broadman, Nashville, 1950; *Word Pictures in the New Testament*, Volume V., "John," Sunday School Board of the Southern Baptist Convention, Nashville, 1932

B. F. Westcott, *The Gospel According to St. John*, 2 Volumes, John Murray, London, 1908

The author of the Fourth Gospel had the happy faculty of expressing the profoundest truth in the simplest language. This volume is sent forth with the prayer that it has violated neither of these grand elements of this greatest of Gospels. If even one person through reading it comes to believe that Jesus Christ is the Son of God, and believing, finds life in His name, then it will not have been written in vain.

Herschel H. Hobbs

First Baptist Church
Oklahoma City, Oklahoma

I
The Eternal
and the Historical

John 1:1-5, 9-18

The Eternal Christ

Each of the four Gospels was written to specific readers and for a specific purpose. And in each case these dual ideas are reflected in the manner of approach used by the author. Matthew, writing for Jewish readers, began by giving the legal genealogy of Jesus. Mark wrote for Roman readers who were primarily concerned with what Jesus did. Therefore, he plunged immediately into the ministry of John the Baptist and subsequently into that of Jesus. Luke, with Gentile readers, particularly Theophilus, in mind, began by setting forth his method of research and writing. But John wrote in a later Greek environment, probably in Ephesus, and in the thought environment of an incipient Gnosticism. Thus he began with a summary statement as to the eternity of Christ who became Jesus of Nazareth.

His primary purpose was to refute the Gnostic position concerning Jesus Christ in showing that He was God the eternal Christ who lived among men in a flesh and blood body, and who died and rose again as the Saviour of men. His stated purpose in writing was to the end that his readers "might believe that Jesus is the Christ; and that believing ye might have life through his name" (20:31). That which he succinctly summarized at the close he also summarized more at length at the beginning. This beginning is called the Prologue to the Gospel (1:1-18).

The Word of God (1:1-2)

"In the beginning." Immediately we are introduced to the vast scope of the Evangelist's mind with regard to his Gospel. Mark began his account on the banks of the Jordan river. Matthew takes us back to Abraham. Luke in his genealogy looks back to the creation, to "Adam, which was the son of God" (3:38). But John sweeps back behind creation into the eternities. "In the beginning," whenever that was.

Furthermore, we are reminded of the Hebrew character of this Gospel. It seems that with deliberate design John began his Gospel

23

with words which would set the reader's mind back to the opening verse of Genesis. Like Moses, he does not argue the point. He simply declares it. "In the beginning."

And what about "in the beginning?" "In the beginning was the Word, and the Word was with God, and the Word was God. The same was in the beginning with God" (1:1-2). One who is familiar with Gnosticism sees that with one tremendous statement He drove his sword into the very heart of that philosophy. Gnosticism said that Christ was a created being, the last in a long series of such beings and one who was almost bereft of deity. But John says that the Word (Christ) was in the beginning before creation, that He was equal with God, and that He was God Himself. Thus he declared the eternity of Christ, His equality with God, and His oneness with God.

How did John come to choose "Word" as his designation of the Christ? The Gospel of John has long been regarded by some as being primarily Hellenistic in nature. It was natural, therefore, to regard the author's choice of *Logos* (Word) as being related to Greek philosophy. Basically the word *logos* is from *legō,* to speak or to express an opinion. But *logos* itself carries the idea of an open expression, the spoken word or manifestation of the one speaking. Thus it involves the idea of revelation. However, in Greek thought it came to mean even more. For instance, Heraclitus used it for the principle which controls the universe. To the Stoic philosophers it represented the soul of the world. Marcus Aurelius used it to express the germinative principle in nature. All of these ideas may be seen in John's use of *Logos.*

All the while there were those who insisted upon the Hebrew nature of the Fourth Gospel. So they sought to relate John's choice to the use of *memra* (Hebrew for "word") or to the Old Testament emphasis upon *wisdom* or the Wisdom of God (cf. Prov. 8). It should be noted, however, that while the Old Testament almost personified these ideas it never quite does so.

Some sought to combine the Greek and Hebrew positions, and thus to explain John's choice by Philo's usage of *logos.* He sought to harmonize Hebrew theology with Greek philosophy. In so doing he used the word *logos* almost thirteen hundred times; he almost personified it, but not quite.

But does any one of these positions, or even a combination of them, really explain the basis of John's choice of *Logos?* Keep in mind the meaning of *logos* as the spoken word, an open manifestation or revelation of the speaker. Furthermore, recall the similarity of John's opening words to those found in Genesis 1:1. To these things add the fact that the Dead Seas Scrolls show that the thought patterns of this Gospel are in harmony with those which were current in Palestine in the latter half of the first century. We may conclude, therefore, that John's Gospel is Hebraic, not Grecian in nature. In the light of these things it is reasonable to expect that the author's choice of *Logos* is entirely Hebraic.

Now let us examine Genesis 1. In so doing we discover that each new phase of God's creative act is introduced by the words "And God said" (1:3, 6, 9, 11, 14, 20, 24, 26, 29). Here then is repeatedly the spoken word, the open manifestatioon, the revelation of God, the *logos* of God. It would seem, therefore, that on this basis John chose the word *Logos* to depict Him who is God's open manifestation, His supreme revelation. So he says, "In the beginning was the *Logos*." John uses this word four times in the Prologue to refer to deity which he identifies as Jesus Christ (1:14-17). And while he does not so use it again in the Gospel, it is clear that the *Logos* is always present in the person of the Son of God (cf. I John 1:1; 5:7; Rev. 19:13).

Note that in John 1:1-2 the verb "was" appears four times. The Greek form is *ēn*. It is the imperfect form of *eimi,* our verb "to be." It expresses the idea of essential existence or, in this case, of eternal being. The imperfect form expresses continuous action in past time. So that actually John says, "In the beginning always was the Word, and the Word always was with God, and the Word always was God. The same always was in the beginning with God."

In these words John makes three declarations about Christ. In the first place, He is eternal. He *always was* in timeless existence. There never was a time when the Word was not. Rather than being a created being, He always was before creation. And He existed not merely as a principle or an idea; He was a Person.

In the second place, Christ is equal with God. "The Word always was with God." The Greek phrase rendered "with God" is *pros ton Theon,* face to face with God. This entails both equality and intimacy. In ancient times if one entertained two guests of equal rank they must be seated on an equal basis. If one were tall and the other short, the latter was seated on pillows so that when he looked at the former their eyes met on an even line. Neither must look down upon or up to the other. They saw eye to eye. They were *pros,* face to face, with each other. They were equal. So when John said that the Word was *pros ton Theon* he meant that they were equal. So Christ was not a lesser created being of God. He was equal with God.

In the third place, Christ was God. "The Word was God." In the Greek text this is even stronger. For "God" is placed before the verb, not as the subject but for emphasis. Literally, "The Word was God Himself." Verse 2 is simply added to emphasize the threefold thought in verse 1.

Therefore, Christ is not simply the least of a series of created beings coming out of God. Eternally He is God, is equal with God, yea, is God Himself.

The Creator-Christ (1:3)

As the eternal God Christ is the Creator (cf. Gen. 1:3 ff., "And God said"). "All things were made by him; and without him was not anything made that was made" (cf. Heb. 1:2). Here John employs another word for *being*, "was made" *(egeneto)*. This is the aorist form of *ginomai*, to become or to come into being. Whereas *eimi* (vv. 1-2) expresses eternal being, *ginomai* denotes something which once did not exist but which came into being. So Christ created or brought into being the universe. "All things" *(panta)* may be rendered "the universe in its several parts." Thus Christ created the universe from atoms to suns. "By him" really is "through [*dia*] him." So Christ is the intermediate Agent in the creative act.

John adds emphasis to this truth when he says, "And without him was not anything made that was made." Literally, "And apart from him came into being not even one thing which has come into being." Not even one atom exists except through His complete creative act.

It is of interest to compare John's statement with that of Paul in Colossians 1:15-17. Paul also was writing to refute Gnostic philosophy. He refers to redemption through the blood of God's Son (v. 14), thus answering the Docetic Gnostics who denied that Christ had a real flesh and blood body, and the Cerinthian Gnostics who separated the *aeon* Christ from the man Jesus. He was real flesh and blood, and He died on a cross. Then Paul says, "Who is the image [exact manifestation] of the invisible God, the firstborn [Lord] of every creature [all creation]: for by [*en*, in the sphere of] him were all things [*ta panta*] created; that are in heaven, and that are in earth, visible and invisible [planets to atoms] . . . all things [*ta panta*] were created [stand created, perfect tense] by [*dia,* through] him and for [*eis,* unto] him."

Note that Paul uses *panta* with the definite article *ta.* This means the universe as a whole. So whereas John sees the universe in its several parts, Paul views it as one vast expanse. Both agree that Christ is the Creator of the universe. But note Paul's use of prepositions *(en, dia, eis).* Thus he declares that Christ is the Sphere in which creation took place or its Source; He is the intermediate Agent in the creative act; He is the Goal toward which all creation moves. As if this were not enough he adds, "And he is before all things [*pantōn,* any single part of the universe], and by [*en,* in the sphere of] him all things [*ta panta,* the universe as a whole] consist [holds together]" (v. 17). It is Christ who holds the universe together as a cosmos rather than to have a chaos.

For centuries men thought in terms of a *geocentric* universe. Since Galileo they have regarded it as *heliocentric.* But modern knowledge makes even this view untenable. We now know that ours is but one solar system centering in its sun. Some astronomers hold that there are at least twelve quadrillion solar systems, each centering in its own sun. A quadrillion is a one followed by fifteen zeros. So in what or in whom does the entire universe center? Almost two thousand years ago Paul said that it centers in Christ. Thus we may think in terms of a *Christo-centric* universe. The more we know about the universe the greater is our concept of Christ!

Thus both John and Paul combine in answering the Gnostics. They declare that Christ is God of very God, that He is the Creator and the center of the universe; and in so doing they refute the Gnostic claim that matter is essentially evil. It is the result of the creative act of God in Christ who is absolutely good and who pronounced that His creation is also good (cf. Gen. 1:10, 12, 18, 21, 25, 31).

The Source of Life and Light (1:4-5, 9)

Furthermore, John declares that Christ is the source of life. "In him was life." Here John returns to his use of "was." In Christ always was life.

"Life" renders the Greek word *zōē.* Usually in John this word refers to spiritual life as opposed to *bios,* the manner of life. But his usage here may be understood to mean the very principle or essence of life both natural and spiritual. Thus the source of all life in the universe is Christ. Here John denies the claims of rank materialism. Back of the natural universe is spiritual life. This is the insistence of such scientists as Eddington and Jeans. Life cannot be reckoned only in physical terms. There is a spiritual meaning which pervades all things. And men cannot ignore this fact with impunity.

A further truth is that "the life was the light of men." In the Greek text both "life" and "light" carry the definite article. So either may be considered as the subject of the verb. It is just as true to say, "And the light was the life of men." Christ is both Life and Light to men. John's emphasis at this point is upon the pre-existent Christ. But his Gospel clearly shows that this dual truth applies also with regard to the Incarnation.

The Gnostics were fond of using the words "light" and "darkness." So John, taking note of that fact, says "The light shineth [present tense, keeps on shining] in darkness; and the darkness comprehended [aorist tense, apprehended] it not" (v. 5). The picture here is that of darkness chasing light as night chases the day. The darkness of evil keeps on chasing the light of life. But not once has it overtaken it or seized it to extinguish it. This is suggestive of the cosmic struggle between God and Satan, a struggle which went on during Christ's earthly ministry and beyond. The assurance is that Satan will never destroy the Light/Life. It keeps on shining despite the evil efforts of darkness.

One of Satan's favorite tricks is to present substitute lights posing as the Light. But John says that by contrast Christ "was the true Light, which lighteth every man that cometh into the world" (v. 9). "The true Light" carries the double definite article. So "The Light the true" as opposed to any false light. A. T. Robertson (*Word Pictures,* later) says, " 'The Light the genuine,' not a false light of wreckers of ships, but the dependable light that guides to the harbor of safety." Marcus Dods (*Expositor's,* later) comments, "The designation [the true Light] . . . means that which corresponds to the ideal; true not as opposed to false, but to symbolical or imperfect." Even so, any less than the true light would be a false one.

This "true Light" is the one "which lighteth every man that cometh into the world" (v. 9b). This statement causes some difficulty in interpretation. As it reads above it could imply universalism. Or that "every man that cometh into the world" receives this Light. Verse 9 has been called the Quaker text. The Quakers interpret it to mean that every man has his day of visitation from

God, and that God gives to every man of His grace. In either case this verse is made to teach universal salvation. But since such is contrary to the overall teachings of the New Testament, there must be another meaning.

Suppose that we try a literal translation. "There was the Light the true, which lights every man, coming into the world." West-cott translates it thusly. "There was the light, the true light which lighteth every man; that light was, and yet more, that light was coming into the world." In either case the meaning seems to be that Christ is the true Light, the only source of light to man. And that Light, which always has been, is now coming into the world in incarnate form. This does not mean that every man will receive this Light. It is offered to every man. But each man must receive it personally if it is to light his life. And as we shall pres-ently see, not every man did/does receive Him.

The Tragedy and the Triumph (1:10-13)

"He was in the world, and the world was made by him, and the world knew him not" (v. 10). Actually this verse contains a play on ·the word *kosmos* rendered "world." Literally, "In the cosmos he always was [*ēn,* imperfect, as in v. 1], and the cosmos through him came into being [*egeneto,* aorist, point action], and the cosmos did not any time know [acknowledge, aorist] him." Obviously the first two uses refer to the pre-incarnate state. The first is eternal. The second refers to the point of creation. To what does the third *kosmos refer?* One could interpret it as "world." But in the light of the foregoing, and verse 11, it seems more likely to refer to the cosmos or universe. Though Christ eternally was in the cosmos and created the universe, still it did not acknowl-edge Him as its Sovereign.

Even before the Incarnation the universe was out of joint. Satan made a false claim to sovereignty in it (cf. Matt. 4:8-9). The purpose of the Incarnation was to refute this claim. In Romans 8 Paul says that Christ's redemptive work will avail for both the natural and the spiritual universe. So prior to the Incarnation the entire cosmos was in an unredeemed state. It did not acknowledge Christ as its Creator and Lord.

The earth itself was included in this rebellion. For "he came unto his own, and his own received him not" (v. 11). This is seen in the two words "own." The first is a neuter plural *(ta idia),* "his own things." This same idiom is found in John 19:27 with

reference to John's "own home." Some would see *ta idia* as referring to Israel as a nation. While others see the second "own"
in this regard. A more natural way to look at *ta idia* would be
to see the earth as Christ's "own home" or the place where He
chose to dwell in His Incarnation. So He did come and dwell
upon the earth.

But "his own received him not [did not welcome him]." Here
"own" is a masculine form *(toi idioi),* referring to people. Does
this refer to Israel as a people? Certainly as a group they did not
receive Him. Does it refer to His "intimates," as some see it? There
were those within His own family circle who did not believe
in Him until after His resurrection. But do either of these positions satisfy the context?

John seems to be thinking in much broader terms than would
be involved in either Israel or Christ's immediate family on earth.
True, the Gospel records His rejection by the Jews. But is not
John thinking in terms of the planet earth *(ta idia)* and the in-
habited world *(toi idioi;* cf. John 3:16)? The planet did not refuse
to receive Him. But for the most part its inhabitants did and
still do. John is presenting Christ as the universal Saviour offered
to all men, not merely as the Saviour of the Jewish nation. So
while He chose the earth as His temporary home, for the most
part those who also lived on the earth did not choose Him. This
is the *tragedy.*

However, there is also the *triumph.* "But as many as received
him, to them gave he power to become the sons of God, even
to them that believe on his name" (v. 12).

The word "but" sets this group apart from *toi idioi* in verse 11.
For among the inhabitants of the earth there was a small minority
which did welcome Him by believing in Him as the Christ, the
Saviour. And to as many as did so He gave "power" to become
God's children *(tekna).* The word "power" renders *exousian.* This
word is composed of *ek,* out of, and *ousia,* being; so "out of being."
It is the power which is resident in one by nature of his being
(cf. Matt. 28:18). So it is expressive of God's very nature. This
word may also be translated as "right," "privilege," or "authority."
Any one of these makes sense here. But in substance John says
that all who received Christ by faith in Him, to them He imparted of the very nature of God or God's very being. So that they
became children of God. Thus they received through Him the
right, privilege, and authorization as children of God.

And how do men become the children of God? John makes

three distinct negative statements. Literally he says, "Which not out of bloods [plural], neither out of the will of the flesh, nor out of the will of men, but out of God were begotten." The words "out of" *(ek)* refer to the source of this new relationship.

It is not "out of bloods." It is not out of ordinary physical generation. Why did John use "bloods?" Robertson suggests that it could mean the blood of the father and the mother. Godet and Meyer see this as referring to the various parts out of which blood is composed. Westcott holds that it connotes the element which in various measures forms the body. Marcus Dods, while uncertain, suggests that John is speaking of one's family lineage. A person's family relationships, his ancestors, have no part in his becoming a child of God. Thus, in measure, he agrees with Robertson. Certainly John is saying that one does not become a child of God by the accident of physical birth (cf. Matt. 3:9).

Again, it is not out of "the will of the flesh" or out of sexual desire. Furthermore, it is not out of "the will of man." Robertson sees this as "the will of the male" *(andros)*. But this would make it simply a continuation of the previous thought. The Greek text calls for three separate negatives. We agree with Marcus Dods in that it is not merely a matter of human purpose. Of himself a man cannot become a child of God simply by determining to do so. Not by an act of his will alone, namely through good works, can he change his nature. Alas, how many seek to do so! A man may become a gentleman, a good citizen or father thereby. But he cannot thusly become a child of God.

What then is the source of this being "begotten?" It is "out of God." God alone can impart to a man of His nature. And He does so on grounds of His own choosing. It is a spiritual generation or regeneration wrought by His grace through Christ, and is given to those who "believe on his name." No other person can claim to be a child of God or to call Him "Father" in the true sense of the word. God is fatherly in His nature; He longs to be the Father of all men; but He is Father in truth only to those who become His children through faith in His Son. And this nature God offers to all men through

The Incarnation of the Word (1:14)

"And the Word was made flesh, and dwelt among us, (and we beheld his glory, the glory as of the only begotten of the Father,) full of grace and truth."

To grasp the full significance of this tremendous verse let us combine it with verse 1. "In the beginning always was the Word, and the Word always was equal with God, and the Word always was God Himself . . . and the Word became flesh. . . ." Note the change in verbs from "was" *(eimi)* to "became" *(ginomai)*. The eternal Word or Christ *became* what He had never been before. He became flesh. Robertson points out that "flesh" is without the definite article. Therefore, it cannot mean that the flesh became the Word, but that the Word became the flesh. John clearly means that the Word became Jesus of Nazareth. We often say that Jesus was God. True. But this is an even more tremendous statement. *God became Jesus of Nazareth!*

Now this does not mean that He ceased to be the Word. He continued to be every whit God, but God accommodating Himself to the conditions of human existence apart from sin. At the same time He did not simply indwell a man. He became flesh. Thus in one statement John avows both the deity and the humanity of Christ. He answers the Docetic Gnostics by declaring that He had a real body of flesh. He answers the Cerinthian Gnostics by stating that Christ did not simply come upon a man. He became flesh. The Spoken Manifestation of Genesis 1 became the Jesus of history.

One is justified in seeing John 1:14 as the Fourth Evangelist's account of the virgin birth. Certainly John was aware of the accounts in Matthew and Luke. It is his purpose to supplement them where desirable. And at other points he makes contacts with their accounts as he relates his own story. This seems to be one of these points. Certainly John 1:14 does not make sense apart from the virgin birth. For how else could the eternal Christ become flesh?

Now John says that He "dwelt" among us. This word renders a verb meaning to pitch a tabernacle or tent. It suggests temporary dwelling, but one which spans the normal course of one's life. In this regard John says that "we beheld [saw with their own eyes] his glory, the glory as of the only begotten of the Father." These words should not be limited to any one phase of Jesus' life, such as the Transfiguration. They include the sum-total of the Word's sojourn as flesh. Particularly John is thinking of Jesus' ministry from Jordan to the Ascension (cf. I John 1:1-3). But it involves everything from His birth through His ascension.

The Christ who tabernacled among men was "full of grace and truth." These consisted of the moral qualities which dwelt in Him and which out of His fulness He bestowed upon others. "Grace" is one of the great words of Paul. But it appears in John only here and in verses 16-17. However, "truth" is one of the key words in John's Gospel. And it may be said to involve the idea of "grace" also.

The Fulness of the Incarnation (1:16-17)

"And of his fulness have all we received, and grace for grace."

This is the only time that the word "fulness" *(plērōma)* appears in this Gospel. But it is used of Christ repeatedly in Paul's writings. It was a key word in Gnostic philosophy. To them it expressed essence of deity. But in their system it was distributed among many subordinate, created beings called *aeons*. They regarded Christ as the lowest of these beings and so one possessing the least amount of deity. But John says that the "fulness" was resident in Him.

Perhaps the greatest statement in the New Testament concerning the deity of Christ is found in Colossians 2:9. In verse 8 he warns his readers against being carried away as booty by Gnostic philosophy characterized by empty deceit. Then he says of Christ, literally, "For in him and him alone is permanently and abidingly at home all the essence of deity [*plērōma*], the state of being God, in bodily form."

This is implied in John 1:16. And John says that all who received Christ received of His fulness. They received of His nature (cf. 1:12). Whereas Christ *is* the Son of God, those receiving Him *become* sons of God.

And this experience is through "grace for [*anti*] grace." Grace at the end of grace, or grace following after grace. Like manna in the wilderness, a new supply of grace for each day, each experience.

So often people hesitate to receive Christ lest they be not able *to hold out.* Here is the answer to such an attitude. God does not give a new Christian a ton of grace, telling him that it must last until he reaches the end of life. He gives grace after grace in an unending supply. One is saved by grace, and he is kept saved by grace. To paraphrase an old song

> My Father, this I ask of Thee,
> Knowing that Thou wilt grant the plea;
> For this, and only this, I pray,
> Grace for today, just for today.

Grace for each trial and each task,
What more, my Father, should I ask?
Just as I need it day by day,
Grace for my weakness, this I pray.

John then adds the comment, "For the law was given by [through] Moses, but grace and truth came [egeneto] by [through] Jesus Christ." Or "through Jesus Christ became [came into being]." When God revealed His law He did so through a man. When He revealed His grace and truth He became man.

Note that here for the first time in this Prologue John identifies the *Logos* become flesh as in the person Jesus Christ. So Christ became Jesus of Nazareth that He might reveal His grace and truth. "And of his fulness [essence of deity] have all we received."

The Divine Exegete (1:18)

No man at any time has seen God with his eyes. As Paul says, He is the "invisible God" (Col. 1:15). This does not mean that He is visible but has not been seen. It means that He is incapable of being seen. He is Spirit. But "the only begotten Son . . . hath declared him" (John 1:18). "Hath declared" renders a verb *(exēgeomai)* meaning to lead out, to draw out in narrative, to recount. From it comes our word "exegete." So Jesus Christ is the Divine Exegete. He exegeted God for us. In Him in flesh we see the complete revelation of God. "He that hath seen me hath seen the Father" (John 14:9).

What a glorious ending to this Prologue to John's Gospel. The eternal Christ became flesh that in Him we might see who God is and what He is doing. He is seen as the Redeeming God opening the way whereby all men may be saved. And this truth in embryo as found in John 1:1-18 is unfolded throughout the remainder of the Gospel of John.

John 1:6-8, 15, 19-36

The Messenger and the Message

The overall significance of the Prologue to the Fourth Gospel is that the eternal Christ entered into time as Jesus of Nazareth. And His coming was for the purpose of providing redemption for men from their sin. Even in the midst of the glorious song of the eternal, the historical note is heard. For the author takes note of the messenger who would herald the coming of Christ into the world. Who is this messenger?

The Identity of the Messenger (1:6)

"There was a man sent from God, whose name was John."

Now, of course, this John was not the apostle John, the son of Zebedee. For his name never appears in the Gospel. This was John the Baptist whose ministry is given in all four Gospels. Matthew and Mark simply relate his ministry. It is to Luke that we are indebted for the record of his supernatural birth (1:55 ff.). John assumes a knowledge of this account.

But John says more than merely to record his existence. He says, "There came to be" (egeneto, historical aorist). This suggests the idea of appearing, as though he suddenly burst upon the scene. It reminds one of Elijah suddenly appearing before Ahab to announce the extended drought upon Israel. He truly came in the spirit and power of Elijah (Luke 1:17).

His name well portrays his mission. For "John" is the Hellenized form of Jonathan or Joanan meaning a "Gift of God." He was one having been sent "from God" or "from alongside God" (para Theon). He was born as a man through natural generation. And yet the age of his parents made it a supernatural birth. Thus, while his was not a virgin birth, it was contrary to the ordinary working of the laws of genetics. Therefore, in a very real sense, he was a Gift of God. He was sent to prepare the way for the coming of Him who is God's greatest Gift to a lost world.

35

The Mission of the Messenger (1:7-8, 15)

The mission of John the Baptist was "for a witness" (v. 7). Thus his mission is stated generically. He did not come to start a John the Baptist movement. His coming was that he might bear witness concerning another. Thus his mission is stated specifically. He had been born for this purpose (Luke 1:17). And all of his training and power was directed to this end. He was "to bear witness of [*peri*, concerning] the Light," of Him who is the Light of Life of men (John 1:4). And it was to the end that "all men through [*dia*] him might believe." Thus he was the intermediate agent sent from God to point away from himself to another.

This is the first use in this Gospel of the word "believe" (*pisteuō*). In this sense it means "come to believe" (ingressive aorist). This is one of the great words of this Gospel, appearing one hundred times. The Synoptic Gospels use it by comparison only thirty-four times. Which shows the great emphasis which John places upon believing. Yet the word *pistis* (faith) does not occur in this Gospel. The word *pistos* (believing) is found in it only in the author's statement of his purpose in writing (20:27). Nevertheless, the preponderance of the verb form shows that this is a Gospel of faith.

The verb (*pisteuō*) may also be rendered to trust or to commit. This latter meaning is given in John 2:24. And since the English word *believe* has come to carry such a great intellectual connotation, the sense of the Greek word may better be found in *trust* or *commit*. Of course, one must believe intellectually. But that belief must evolve into an act of the will (trust, commit) if it is to become a means of grace. So John's mission was to enable men to come to believe not only about but in the Christ, and thus to trust or commit themselves to Him.

Even after John the Baptist's death there is evidence that there continued to be a movement which gathered about his mission and work (cf. Acts 19:1 ff.). We cannot be certain that this movement continued until the end of the first century. But it certainly continued for more than twenty years after his death. At any rate the author of the Fourth Gospel is careful to point out that the Baptist was not the Christ, and that he did not intend to perpetuate his own ministry. It was to give place to the ministry of the Christ.

The first of these notes is sounded in John 1:8. "He was not that Light, but was sent to bear witness of that Light." In the Greek text the emphasis is upon the negative particle. "Not was that one the Light, but in order that he might bear witness concerning the Light." He was a light (John 5:25) as, indeed, are all believers (Matt. 5:14). But he was not "the Light." While some even from the beginning thought that John might be the Christ, the author is careful to point out his true relationship to the Messiah.

This truth is reiterated in verse 15. Here the author records his first words as spoken by the Baptist. Having asserted the fact of the Incarnation he reports John the Baptist as testifying to Him. "He that cometh after me is . . . before me: for he was before me." In historical time John came before Jesus as His forerunner. But Jesus "is become" *(gegonen,* effective perfect) "before" *(emprosthen)* John. This word "before" used with "become" *(gegonen)* means higher in rank. Though John preceded Him in the sequence of time events, Jesus exceeded him in rank. This was evident in subsequent history. But it was also an eternal truth. This is seen in "for he was before me." Here the eternal "always was" is used with "before" *(prōtos)*. Christ was eternally before John in sequence as well as in rank of importance.

John the Baptist occupies an important place in God's redemptive purpose. Jesus Himself said of him that "there hath not risen a greater than John the Baptist: notwithstanding he that is least in the kingdom of heaven is greater than he" (Matt. 11:11). John stood on the shoulders of all who preceded him as messengers of God. He was the forerunner of the Christ. But a greater privilege than being the forerunner is that of believing in Christ, for him as well as for us.

The Fidelity of the Messenger (1:19-28)

In all of human literature, outside of Deity Himself, there is no greater example of fidelity than that which is found in John the Baptist. He was faithful to his mission and to Him whom he proclaimed.

When the Baptist came preaching in the wilderness of Judea, multitudes came to hear him. It had been four hundred years since a prophet had appeared in Israel. The famine concerning the word of God, a famine predicted by Amos (8:11 ff.), had been fulfilled with a vengeance. The literature of the interbiblical period reveals the longing in men's hearts to hear some word from God. The Jews detected the note of God's voice in John's preaching. So from everywhere they flocked to hear him.

When word of this phenomenon reached the ears of the "Jews"*
in Jerusalem, they sent a deputation to inquire as to the meaning of it. A group of priests and Levites came to him asking,
"Who art thou?" (v. 19). Literally, "You, who are you?" John's
subsequent answer shows that he understood this to mean, "You,
are you the Christ?" Had John been made of lesser stuff he might
have been tempted to point to himself as the long-awaited Christ.
Others had assumed such a role. So caught up in this wave of
enthusiasm, a man of selfish interest might have sought to capi-
talize upon it for himself. But not John.

If the delegation had put their question in an emphatic form,
John's answer was even more so. For "he confessed, and denied
not; but confessed, I am not the Christ" (v. 20). His emphasis is
seen first in the verb forms used. "Confessed," "denied," and
"confessed" are all aorist tenses. Without hesitation he emphatically did these things. Positively, negatively, and then again positively he disavowed any claim to Messiahship. This emphasis is
further seen in the fact that "I" *(egō)* is both written out and is
contained in the verb "am." The Jews had asked, "You, who are
you?" So John said, "I, I am not the Christ." In effect, he said,
"I am not now and never will be the Christ."

The Jews were set back on their heels by this forthright answer.
So with less emphasis they asked, "What then? Art thou Elias" or
Elijah (v. 21)? They believed that Elijah would return to earth
before the Messiah appeared (Mal. 4:5 f.). Later Jesus will say
that John is Elijah in spirit (Matt. 17:10-12). But here John
tersely replied, "I am not." He simply meant that he was not
Elijah in person. So the Jews tried another question. "Art thou
that prophet?" Moses had said that there would come a prophet
like himself (Deut. 18:15). Indeed, following the feeding of the
five thousand the people thought of Jesus as such a prophet
(John 6:14). Some hold that they only saw Jesus as the prophet
who would precede Christ (cf. John 7:40). This latter verse could
be so understood. But in the light of John 6:14-15 it would seem
that in that case the Galilean Jews equated the prophet with the
Christ. However, in John the Baptist's case with a blunt "No"
he flatly denied that he was that prophet.

So the Jews from Jerusalem then asked John who he was (v. 22).
They must have some answer to carry back to the rulers in

---

*This term in the Fourth Gospel is used primarily to refer to the Jewish
religious leaders.

Jerusalem. Therefore they simply asked him a blanket question. "What sayest thou of thyself?" "Just who are you?" they asked.

In reply John quoted from Isaiah 40:3. "I am the voice of one crying in the wilderness" (v. 23). Note how he subordinated himself. He did not say, "I am John the son of Zacharias." He ignored the marvelous circumstances of his birth and the destiny prophesied for him. He did not even say that he was a man. He said, "I am a voice." How humble he was! No claims made for himself. He was just a *voice* crying in the wilderness. And what was he crying? "Make straight the way of the Lord, as said the prophet Esaias." Thus he declared himself to be the forerunner of the Christ. Christ is the *Logos* or Word. John is the *phōnē* or the Voice heralding the coming of the Word.

The reference in Isaiah 40 follows Jehovah's call for one to comfort His people, to speak to the heart of Jerusalem (Isa. 40:1-2). So the One to bring this comfort, to speak to sad hearts, is on His way. The King is coming. And John goes before Him to "prepare the way of the Lord" (Isa. 40:3). He is to fill in the low places, to level down the rough places, and to make a straight highway in human hearts, that they may be ready to receive the King.

Parenthetically the author notes that this delegation inquiring of John was "of the Pharisees" (v. 24). They were Pharisees sent by the Sanhedrin, the religious ruling body of the Jews. This body was composed of both Pharisees and Sadducees. But the Sadducees were the ones who were in the seats of power. The high priest was a Sadducee.

These two principal parties among the Jews were poles apart in their respective positions. The Sadducees were realists. They were for the *status quo* in politics since they under the Romans enjoyed a certain amount of political power, especially in civil and religious matters. Usually they were men of wealth and affluence. Theologically they were more liberal than the Pharisees. They accepted as Scripture only the five books of Moses. They denied the resurrection of the dead; and they also denied the existence of angels.

The Pharisees, on the other hand, were strongly nationalistic. They bitterly hated the Romans, and looked with contempt upon all Gentiles. As for theology, they were conservatives. They accepted all of the Hebrew Scriptures, believed in angels and in the resurrection of the dead. They were the self-appointed interpreters of the Scriptures, were strongly ritualistic, and were the custodians of their multitude of traditions and rote rules of conduct which they had devised within the basic framework of the Mosaic Law. While some Pharisees appear in a good light, as a body they were opposed to Jesus. At times they joined with the Sadducees in opposition to Jesus. It was a coalition of these two groups which finally brought Jesus to His death.

Returning to the inquiry of the Pharisees, we note that they turned from John's identity to a question as to his authority. Since John was not the Christ, Elijah, or the prophet, asked they, "Why baptizeth thou then?" (v. 25). Apparently John's claim to be a "voice" did not impress them. Nothing has been said hitherto in this Gospel about baptism. The details of such are found in the other Gospels. But assuming a knowledge of this, the author simply states the question. The Jews were familiar with proselyte baptism applied only to Gentiles who became Jews in their religion. But here was one who was baptizing Jews. He treated them just like they had been Gentiles. Furthermore, John's baptism was based upon repentance and a willingness to be a part of the coming kingdom of God. John had even challenged the Jewish concept that every descendant of Abraham was already in God's kingdom (Luke 3:7 ff.). So here was something new. And the delegation wanted to know by what authority John was doing this. Was his authority from heaven, or had he merely assumed it on his own?

John did not answer their question directly. Instead he used it as the occasion to declare the office and person of Christ. "I baptize you in water." Since the pronoun "I" is written out, it is emphatic. "I on my part baptize you in water." This emphasis plus the mention of "in water" sets up a contrast. There is someone else who will baptize in another element. And while the author does not mention this other baptism, it is clear from the other Gospels what he means (cf. Matt. 3:11; Mark 1:8; Luke 3:16). There comes another who will baptize in the Holy Spirit and fire. The author assumes a knowledge of this on the part of his readers.

"There standeth one among you whom ye know not" (v. 26). "Among you" or "in the midst of you" comes first in the sentence, and so is emphatic. Right now in their very midst is the one in whose authority John was baptizing. But, of course, they did not know Him. From John 1:32-33 it is evident that John had already baptized Jesus. So he knew the Christ's identity, but the Pharisees did not yet "know" of whom he spoke. But John knew His identity and that He would soon be revealed to all who would hear and heed Him. But, alas, the Pharisees, while they will become acquainted with Him, will never *really know Him*. This is the meaning of the word "know" *(oidate)*. But though they do not know Him John continues to identify Him.

He says that He is the one "coming after me ... whose shoe's [sandal's] latchet I am not worthy to unloose" (v. 27). "Is preferred before me" is not found in the best manuscripts. The Jewish Talmud says, "Every service which a servant will perform for his master, a disciple will do for his Rabbi, except loosing his sandal thong." But John says that he is not even worthy to perform so menial a task for the Christ. Thus he exalts Him beyond any other person on earth. The Baptist, though receiving the plaudits of the multitudes and being honored (?) even by an inquiry from the Sanhedrin, is unworthy of doing this humble service for the One whom he proclaims.

But such an exalted claim for Christ was wasted on the Pharisees. For apparently they did not press the matter further. After all, what interest would the Jewish leaders have in One about whom they did not know? However, no man can ignore Jesus. The Sanhedrin will learn this truth. They, as every other man, will have to answer the question as to what they will do with Jesus, the one called Christ.

The Evangelist closes this incident by noting that these events took place "in Bethany beyond Jordan." The King James Version reads "Bethabara." But present-day scholarship agrees that "Bethany" is the correct reading. It was located on the eastern side of the Jordan river. Hence the designation to distinguish it from the Bethany near Jerusalem. Literally, it is the place "where was John, baptizing."

So John the Baptist stood as tall and sturdy as an oak. He refused to bend before or stoop to the desire for personal popularity. He proved faithful to his commission to point away from himself and to Jesus. This was not the last time that he would do so.

The Message of the Messenger (1:29-36)

At this point the Evangelist begins a series of references to time and to a sequence of events. These are important to him for they mark the beginning of a shift of interest from John to Jesus.

It was the day following the Baptist's encounter with the Jewish delegation (v. 29). By comparing the Fourth Gospel with the Synoptics we know that following Jesus' baptism He had spent forty days in the wilderness where He had been tempted by Satan (cf. Matt. 4:1-11 and parallels). So this event must have come about six weeks after Jesus' baptism. During this time the Baptist had continued his ministry. Now on this day he sees Jesus again coming toward (pros) him. It is natural that Jesus would do so, since in John He found a kindred spirit.

Seeing Jesus John probably pointed Him out, saying, "Behold the Lamb of God, which taketh away the sin of the world" (v. 29). This statement has been the subject of controversy among the scholars. Some see it as evidence of a late date for this Gospel. They hold that the Baptist, a product of his own people, could not have had such a concept of the Messiah. But even Strauss, one of the most outspoken critics, admitted that "a penetrating mind like that of the Baptist might, even before the death of Jesus, gather from O.T. phrases and types the notion of a suffering Messiah." This declaration of John clearly reflects Isaiah 53. And since he had identified himself as a "voice," showing his thought patterns as being centered in Isaiah 40, it is not surprising to hear him make a statement which finds its greatest meaning in Isaiah 53. Apparently he was thoroughly versed in this great prophecy of the Suffering Servant. And while his later inquiry from prison reveals a confused mind with respect to the Messiah of judgment as revealed in the Minor Prophets and the Suffering Servant of Isaiah, there is no reason to deny to him a knowledge of the latter with respect to Jesus. Indeed, Marcus Dods suggests a lengthy discussion of this matter between Jesus and John following the former's baptism.

In his subsequent remarks John relates his understanding of Jesus' true identity to his experience at Jesus' baptism. It takes little imagination, therefore, to find in divine inspiration the source of John's clear understanding of Jesus' role. Thus we must not limit John's prophetic understanding by that of the rabbis or of the popular expectation of a political-military Messiah.

John calls Jesus the "Lamb of God." And that figure clearly suggests sacrifice, whether one relates it to the paschal lamb or to other lambs used in sacrifice. The purpose of the Lamb of God was to bear away the world's sin. And every Jew hearing the Baptist would relate such a ministry to sacrifice. Note also that He is not to take away the sin of the Jews only, but of the world. Thus He is presented as the Saviour of all men. And He is to take away the "sin," not merely the "sins" of the world. This suggests that His saving work is related to the basic cause of man's separation from God, his sinful nature which expresses itself in man's *sins*. The word for sin is *harmatia*, a missing of the mark. All men have missed the mark of God's righteousness and glory. Therefore all men need a Saviour from sin. The message of John is that Jesus Christ is such a Saviour.

Then the Baptist repeats his statement about Jesus which is recorded in John 1:15. Only here "of whom I said" actually should read "on behalf of [*huper*] whom I said." He spoke this not only about Jesus but on His behalf.

Prior to Jesus' baptism John says that He did not *really know* (*eidein*) Him. He had predicted His coming and had described Him before he met Him (cf. Matt. 3:11-12; Mark 1:7-8; Luke 3:15-18). Whether Jesus and John had met before the former came to the latter for baptism, we cannot say with certainty. Since they were related through their parents (cf. Luke 1:36), in all likelihood they had known one another as children. It is possible that they had not seen each other for some years. But, even so, the word "knew" (*eidein*) implies that while John may have known Jesus as a person, he did not know of His mission.

Jesus was identified to John as such at His baptism. The purpose of the Baptist's ministry was to reveal to Israel the presence of the Messiah (v. 31). God had revealed to John that the Christ would be the one upon whom he should see the Holy Spirit descending (v. 33). And he "bare record" or "witness," saying, "I saw the Spirit descending from heaven like a dove, and it abode upon him" (v. 32; cf. Matt. 3:16; Mark 1:10; Luke 3:22). The words "bare witness" might well be called John's affidavit to this fact. Actually he recognized Jesus as the Christ even before he baptized Him (cf. Matt. 3:14 f.). But the promised sign was God's evidence of this truth. And John, in effect, takes an oath that he actually saw the sign with his own eyes. This is evident in the verb used. *Tetheamai* is a perfect tense of completeness. The verb is that whence comes our word "theatre." So as a viewer John saw the Spirit descend upon Jesus. It would seem that only John and Jesus saw it. But there is no question in John's mind but that he saw it.

So in verse 34 he repeats his statement recorded in verse 32. Only here he used the word which means to see with the natural eye and to retain the vision of what is seen (*horaō*). The perfect form *(heōraka)* repeats the emphasis of certainty. The perfect form of "bare record" *(memartureka)* adds emphasis and means that he has fully witnessed to the fact that "this is the Son of God" (v. 34).

The author injects a second note of time in verse 35. For "the next day" after John had borne this witness, he saw Jesus walking along (v. 36). With John were two of his disciples. So once again John says, "Behold the Lamb of God!" Imagine one pastor telling two of his members to leave him to follow another! This is, in effect, what John did. He pointed away from himself to Jesus. Such was his fidelity to his mission and to Jesus that he takes the second place. In all things Christ must be pre-eminent.

Insofar as the record shows this could have been the last time that John saw Jesus. If so, it is a fitting finale to his work. For he fully bore witness to men that Jesus is "the Lamb of God."

II
The Year of Obscurity

John 1:37-51

The Beginning of the Harvest

Out of the many who had submitted to John's baptism, there were those who apparently had attached themselves to him as his "disciples." They were *mathētai* or learners. They were his *pupils.* References are made to John's disciples elsewhere in the Gospels (cf. John 3:25; Matt. 9:14; 11:2; Mark 6:29). There is no reason to believe that John sought to perpetuate his own movement. It is natural that his work would continue so long as he lived and was free to preach. But always he pointed away from himself and toward Jesus. The record shows that some of Jesus' first disciples came out of that group which had attached itself to John.

When Jesus returned from His temptation experience in the wilderness, He was ready to begin His own public ministry. And He was helped on His way by John himself. As has been seen he pointed to Jesus as "the Lamb of God" (1:36). And two of his disciples left him to follow Jesus. And thus Jesus' harvest of souls began. And this harvest involved several things.

The Reward of a Transferred Allegiance (1:37-39)

Literally, "And two of his disciples heard him speaking, and they began to follow Jesus" (v. 37). They did not simply forsake John. But at his own word they found a greater allegiance.

One of these disciples was Andrew; by implication we may identify the other as John the beloved disciple, the author of the Fourth Gospel. He is thus identified since the name of this outstanding apostle does not appear in this Gospel. He is often referred to as the one whom Jesus loved. The natural inference is that John the beloved disciple is that person.

As Jesus walked along He heard their footsteps behind Him. Suddenly "turning" (aorist participle, v. 38) He saw them following. Jesus says to them, "What seek ye?" These are the first words of Jesus given in this Gospel. And what a challenge they contain. He did not ask, "Whom seek ye?" but, "What seek ye?" What was their purpose in following Him? Were they seeking Him out of curiosity, or for what He could give to them? Marcus Dods notes that this is Jesus' first use of the "fan" (Matt. 3:12) as He sought to separate the wheat from the chaff. Our Lord never courted popularity or numbers as such. He sought men, and still does, who will follow Him in spirit and in truth.

This abrupt inquiry astonished the two men, as indeed it may all of us. At the moment they did not have the answer. So they simply asked, "Rabbi ... where dwellest thou?" Note that they called Him "Rabbi." It was an honorable title among the Jews. It means "my greatness." As an address it resembles "Your majesty," although its immediate reference was to a *teacher*. This John notes as he translates the term for the benefit of his Gentile readers (v. 38 b), but showing the basic Hebraic nature of his Gospel. Here the word "Master" is *didaskale,* or teacher. It is of interest to note that Luke, also writing to Gentiles, does not use the term "Rabbi." Matthew uses it with reference to Jesus only twice, and these by Judas (26:25, 49). Mark uses it twice in one verse (14:45) from the lips of Judas. He places it in Peter's mouth on two occasions (9:5; 11:21). John records that the disciples at times called Jesus "Rabbi" (1:38, 49; 9:2; 11:8). But before the end of Jesus' ministry they usually called Him "Lord" (*kurie;* cf. 13:6, 25; Matt. 26:22).

It is natural, however, that Andrew and John would on this initial occasion address Jesus as "Rabbi" (cf. also 1:49). For that was what He was to them at the moment. And their inquiry as to His abiding place had reference to His present stopping place, not to His permanent home. Some see in this inquiry the desire for a quiet interview. Others suggest that they wanted to know where they could find Him for a future visit.

But whatever their reason Jesus brought the matter to a head. He said, "Come and see" (v. 39). Literally, "Come, and ye shall see." It was a simple reply. But it carried tremendous meaning and promise. It was an invitation to inspection. The Christian gospel is not afraid of honest inquiry. But in a broader sense this is the challenge for all men to come to Jesus and to find in Him the answer to all of their spiritual needs.

The writer recalls that this was the text for his first sermon. He called it "God's Universal Invitation to Humanity." The topic was an imposing foundation. He may have built a chicken coop on top of it. But the tremendous invitation is an abiding challenge.

In essence Jesus said that they should seize upon the present

opportunity without delay. Jesus is always *at home,* and the
latch string is always out. There is no time like the present.
Today is God's day. *Tomorrow* and its delay are the devil's day.
So "Come, and ye shall see."

"And they *came* and *saw* where he dwelt" (v. 39, author's
italics). These two aorist verbs show their immediate response to
Jesus' invitation. And they "abode with him [*par' autōi,* alongside
him] that day" (v. 39). And what a day it was! These two eager
men sitting alongside Jesus, listening to His words. And when
they departed they knew that He was more than just another
"rabbi." He was the Christ for whom all of Israel had hoped
and prayed.

It was an unforgettable experience. For more than a half-
century later John remembered the exact time of day when he
first came to Jesus. "It was about the tenth hour" (v. 39). This
time element introduces a debated issue about this Gospel. Did
John use Roman time or Jewish time? If Roman time, this could
mean ten o'clock in the morning. But if Jewish time, it would
be four o'clock in the afternoon. A. T. Robertson, along with
many others, holds to the Roman time. However, many others,
including Marcus Dods, hold to Jewish time. The current trend
is to hold to this position. Since the Dead Sea Scrolls tend to show
that John's Gospel is true to the Jewish thought environment of
this period, it is a natural trend.

But if one holds to this view he runs into difficulty as to the
time of the crucifixion. John 19:14 places Jesus before Pilate at
"about the sixth hour." According to strict Roman time this would
be 6:00 A.M. or about sunrise. But if one follows Jewish time this
would mean noon. Mark 15:25, obviously using Jewish time, places
the crucifixion as beginning at 9:00 A.M. Obviously to follow
Jewish time in John poses a time problem. Marcus Dods explains
this discrepancy by suggesting that both Mark and John *guessed*
as to the time by the sun, since no sun dial was available. But this
leaves much to be desired. Is there a better explanation available?

It is true that officially the Romans figured the civil day, by
which legal documents were dated, as from midnight to midnight.
But the hours of each day usually were also reckoned from sunrise to sunset. Becker points out that on Roman sun dials noon
is marked VI. Now it would be expected, therefore, that even
if John had followed Roman time, in setting time generally he
would have figured it from the Roman sun dial. But even if he
followed Jewish time that would have corresponded with the

Roman sun dial. On the other hand Pilate's Roman court would have figured the time of Jesus' trial by the official method. Thus "the sixth hour" would have been 6:00 A.M. Assuming that in this instance John used the court's timetable, then his "sixth hour" would be 6:00 A.M., and would be in harmony with Mark's time note. So instead of being a conflict, John's time reference shows the work of an eyewitness to the trial of Jesus who set the time with exactness in keeping with legal procedure.

If this be accepted as an adequate explanation of this time problem, then there is no reason why, following the Hebraic nature of this Gospel, we should not say that "the tenth hour" in John 1:39 is 4:00 P.M. If one sees a conflict with the statement "and abode with him that day," it may be resolved by noting that "that day" (tēn hēmeran ekeinēn) is simply an accusative of extent of time. It could mean "the rest of that day," or until sunset.

But whether one considers that they spent six hours with Jesus or two, the fact remains that it expresses the impression which the visit made upon the Apostle John. As indeed all such hours spent in fellowship with Jesus should do for us. Andrew and John left their teacher to follow the Teacher. And this transfer of allegiance remained to bless them all the days of their lives.

The Result of an Experience (1:40-42a)

John clearly identifies one of these two men as Andrew (v. 40). He is further identified as "Simon Peter's brother." Since Simon at this moment was not called *Peter,* it is obvious that the author is writing from the perspective of later years and for readers who were not familiar with Andrew. But Simon Peter would be known to the people of Asia Minor (cf. Peter's epistles, I Peter 1:1). So John tells of the relation of Andrew to Simon Peter. John does not point out that they were fishermen. This fact was related in the Synoptic Gospels (cf. Matt. 4:18; Mark 1:16; Luke 5:1 ff.). But he is careful to point out that they were of Bethsaida (1:44). The Synoptic record shows Peter as living in Capernaum; he apparently established residence there when Jesus chose this city for His base of operations in Galilee (cf. Matt. 4:13).

But notice what Andrew did. "He first findeth his own brother Simon" (v. 41). Literally, "This one finds first [*prōton*] the brother the own" or "his own brother." What is the meaning of "first?" Some strong manuscripts read *prōtos* (adjective). If this be followed it means that Andrew was the first one to find his brother, implying that John also found his brother James. Marcus Dods accepts this reading. But Westcott and Hort and Nestles accept the reading *prōton*. A. T. Robertson follows this reading also. *Prōton* is an adverb. It means that the first thing that Andrew did, before doing anything else, he sought out his brother Simon to share his experience with him. This seems to be the proper reading, but it does not necessarily mean that John did not do the same.

Before Andrew did anything else, he sought out his brother in order to tell him the good news. He did not even pause to eat his evening meal. This mission towered above all others in his life, as indeed it should for every follower of Jesus.

Of interest is the fact that according to the record Andrew was the first person (after John the Baptist?) to receive Jesus as his Saviour and then to seek out another to whom he might witness. Thus he stands at the head of that long line of believers who through the centuries have done likewise.

Andrew may not have been as prominent or as talented as his brother. But he had one spiritual gift, and maybe only one, which he surrendered to Jesus. He brought men to Jesus. This seems to be the emphasis that John places upon him. Except for one mention of the home of Andrew (1:44), 'every other time that John mentions him he is bringing someone to Jesus (1:40 f.; 6:8 f.; 12:22).

The fact that Andrew *found* his brother suggests that he did so after a search. Somewhere in all the crowd he found his brother. And what did he say to him? "We have found the Messiah" (v. 41). Note the added interpretation of "Messiah" as "Christ." For the benefit of his Greek readers John gave the Greek equivalent (Christ) of the Hebrew "Messiah." He and John had made the greatest discovery of the ages. The One for whom all Israelites had been looking, they had found Him. In fact, the sense of "we have found" is "we have seen." Imagine the excitement in Andrew's voice. "Simon, John and I have actually seen the Messiah!"

Note that Andrew did not go into a theological discussion. To be sure his words involved a whole system of Hebrew theology. But he merely told his experience. He had had an experience with Christ, and he shared it. This is the very essence of Christian witnessing. The Christian is to be neither a prosecuting or defense attorney, nor a judge or jury. He is to be a witness, telling only what he has experienced. The word "found" is *heurēkamen*. The perfect tense means "we have really found the Messiah!" The first person of this form is *heurēka,* whence comes the English word "eureka," "I have found." So as Dods says, this exclamation from Andrew's lips is the greatest of all *Eurekas. Eureka!* I have found Him! Have you? If so, you should tell it to others.

"And he brought him to Jesus" (v. 42). Robertson suggests that this means that Andrew had to overcome some resistance on Simon's part. If so, he persisted unto the completion of his purpose. Perhaps, using the words of Jesus, he insisted, "Come, and you shall see." Dods suggests that since it was late at night this may have occurred on the following day. But the aorist tense of "brought" suggests an immediate action (cf. also v. 43). He had no rest himself, neither did he allow any to his brother, until he had brought him to Jesus. Would that all Christian witnesses were as persistent!

So based upon Andrew's experience Simon also came to Jesus. It is ever thusly. One leads another. And Simon came to have this experience for himself. While not stated, it is certainly implied in the following words and in subsequent history.

Looking back at Andrew certain things are apparent. He made a great discovery. He found the Christ. His discovery generated in his heart a great enthusiasm. He *first* findeth his own brother. He rendered a great service. He brought him to Jesus. This service was rendered to one close to him. It was the result of his own spiritual experience which he shared. Andrew was not as talented or as prominent as his brother. But when the Lord gives out the victors' crowns, Andrew along with Peter will receive a crown. His crown will contain as many jewels as that of Peter, plus one. For, you see, he brought Peter to Jesus. Andrew's is the perfect example of a one-talented man who dedicated his talent to Jesus. And from Jesus he has heard the "well done."

The Prophecy of Achievement (1:42b)

When the two brothers came to Jesus He "beheld him." Literally, "Beholding him." The basic verb *(emblepō)* is the verb to look, with the prefix which gives it intensive meaning. Thus it means to gaze earnestly, to look attentively or searchingly upon someone. All of these thoughts may be understood in Jesus' look. He searched Simon's heart as He looked upon him.

And as He searched what did he see? He saw a man with a great heart but an impulsive nature. He saw one who was prone to make mistakes. But they were mistakes of the head, not of the heart. Evidently the name "Simon Barjona" was associated with one who was as unstable as mud. But Jesus saw more. He saw that this man under His patient guidance and power could be transformed into a fit instrument for His use. It is even possible that Jesus saw the longing in Simon's heart. He wanted to be more than he was. He may have been fretting under his reputation for instability. More than anything else he wanted to be known as a solid, dependable rock.

At any rate this is exactly what Jesus told him he would become. It is possible that Jesus had known Simon heretofore. If so, this could explain his understanding of his nature and desire. Or it could be that He had only now come to know Simon, having been introduced to him by Andrew. Nevertheless, Jesus called him by name. "Thou art Simon the son of John [Simon Barjona, Simon son of John. Matt. 16:17; Simon Johnson]: thou shalt be called Cephas" (v. 42). Again John interprets for his Greek readers. The Aramaic *Kēphās* he translates with the Greek word *petros,* a stone. Simon is not now a stone, but he will become one. This prophecy Jesus declared as fulfilled in Matthew 16:18. "Thou art Peter." *Su ei Petros.* "You are a stone." He is not the *petra* (feminine gender) a ledge rock or foundation rock. He is a *petros* (masculine gender), a smaller stone broken off of the *petra* and partaking of its nature. Christ is the *petra* of His Church; Peter and all others like him who partake of His nature are *petroi,* the material of which the superstructure is built upon the foundation.*

So when Jesus first saw Simon he told him that following Him he would become what he wanted to be. Is this not also true of all men? The equation of life reads: Man as he is, plus Christ, equals what man can be. It was true of Simon Peter. It can be true of any man who is willing to pay the price of faith and complete dedication to God's will.

The Response to a Challenge (1:43-45)

"The day following" (note the time sequence, fourth day since 1:19) Jesus began His return journey to Galilee, probably to Nazareth. (This is John's first mention of Galilee.) And what stirring memories Jesus carried with Him: the preaching of John the Baptist, the phenomena accompanying His baptism, the temp-

---

*For a further discussion of Matthew 16:18 see my *An Exposition of the Gospel of Matthew,* Baker, 1965, pp. 216-219.

tation experience, and the winning of His first disciples. Now He must begin His own ministry. Since He was of Galilee it is natural that He would begin there. And while John will record very little of the Galilean ministry, this note of Jesus' return there shows his knowledge of the Synoptic accounts.

As Jesus traveled along He "findeth Philip" (v. 43). Again this suggests the result of a search. Did Andrew and Peter bring Him to Jesus? Or did Jesus search him out? At any rate when Jesus found him He said, "Follow me." The present tense reads, "Follow me, and keep on doing so." This was no simple invitation for Philip to be a traveling companion on the journey to Galilee. It was a command (present imperative), a direct challenge to Philip to become a disciple of Jesus. "Keep on following me," Jesus commanded.

John notes that Philip was of Bethsaida, a fellow-townsman of Andrew and Peter (v. 44). So evidently they knew each other. Many Jews had adopted Greek names, especially those of Galilee. Andrew and Philip were two such people.

No specific reply of Philip is given. But his actions spoke louder than words. For "Philip findeth Nathanael" (v. 45). Again, the suggestion of a search. Philip, now a disciple of Jesus, kept up the work. One winning one. First it was Andrew finding Simon; then perhaps John finding James; then likely Andrew and Peter finding Philip, their fellow-townsman, and now Philip finding Nathanael. And so the gospel spreads. Nathanael is a Hebrew name meaning "God has given." In the Synoptic Gospels he is probably the apostle called Bartholomew. The name Nathanael does not appear in the Synoptics, and Bartholomew does not occur in John. John 21:2 tells us that Nathanael was from Cana. It was common then as now for a man to have two given names.

Finding Nathanael Philip said, "We have found him, of whom Moses in the law, and the prophets, did write, Jesus of Nazareth, the [a] son of Joseph" (v. 45). It is of interest that Philip calls Jesus "a son of Joseph." Despite Jesus' virgin birth (recorded in Matthew and Luke) He was known in His earthly relationship as Joseph's son. This is natural since Jesus grew up as a part of his family. For that matter Joseph, though not Jesus' real father, was His foster-father. So this reference in no sense militates against Jesus' virgin birth. The author already has referred to Jesus as "God-only begotten" (1:18). And no one can read this Gospel without knowing that Jesus is uniquely the Son of God (cf. 3:16). Robertson suggests that Philip called Jesus "a son of Joseph" merely to attract Nathanael's attention. Nevertheless Philip responded favorably to Jesus' challenge. And forthwith he shared his experience with another.

The Realization of a Dream (1:46-51)

The response of Nathanael left much to be desired. Literally, "Out of Nazareth is it possible anything good to be?" (v. 46). Note the emphatic position of "Nazareth." Out of all possible places can anything good be from there? Since Nazareth was so near to Cana, Nathanael's scornful attitude could be attributed to small town rivalry. However, Nazareth seems to have had quite a bad reputation. On a principal trade route, it probably attracted a polyglot of people. And such would be conducive to making it a town which attracted evil. But no matter how bad the town may have been, earth's fairest flower had grown up in its midst.

Philip did not argue the point. Instead he challenged Nathanael. "Come and see" (v. 46). An imperative (come) followed by an aorist (see) expresses double urgency. One demonstration of God's grace outweighs a thousand arguments.

Nathanael was willing to be convinced. So he arose and went with Philip. As he approached Jesus, Jesus said, "Behold an Israelite indeed, in whom is no guile!" (v. 47). The word "guile" renders *dolos,* meaning deceit or bait as for a fish. It comes from the verb connoting to catch with bait. This same Greek word *(dolos)* is used in the Septuagint (Greek translation of the Old Testament) in Genesis 27:35. Isaac speaks to Esau concerning Jacob. "Thy brother came with subtilty [*dolos*], and hath taken away thy blessing." So "guile" is suggestive of Jacob. In effect Jesus said of Nathanael, "Behold an Israelite indeed, in whom is no Jacob." Israel, of course, was the name given to Jacob, the trickster or supplanter, after he had surrendered himself to God's will (Gen. 32:28). Israel was one who had persevered with God. So Nathanael was one who persevered but sought to achieve his goal without resorting to trickery or deceit.

Nathanael recognized that Jesus had correctly diagnosed his character. But "whence knowest thou me?" (v. 48). Had Philip told Jesus about Him? Anticipating such a question Jesus said, "Before that Philip called thee, when thou wast under the fig tree, I saw thee" (v. 48). It was probably about noon, and Nathanael was resting under the fig tree. Its foliage was such that it provided not only shade but privacy. Yet Jesus "saw" *(eidon)* him.

This verb carries not only the idea of physical sight but of perception. So Jesus not only had seen him under the fig tree; He also had seen into his innermost thoughts.

It was this latter idea which evoked from Nathanael, "Rabbi, thou art the Son of God; thou art the King of Israel" (v. 49). This was a great confession, especially from one who so recently had scorned the idea. Philip had said, in effect, that Jesus of Nazareth was the Messiah. And Nathanael now went all the way, calling Jesus both "Son of God" and "King of Israel." At first thought the latter title may seem anti-climactic. But in Psalm 2 both "king" and "Son" are used as Messianic titles. Philip had implied Nathanael's knowledge of the Scriptures (v. 45). So evidently he had Psalm 2 in mind when he made his confession of faith in Jesus.

Jesus, in turn, noting that Nathanael's faith was then based upon His perception of him, promised even more. "Verily, verily, I say unto you [note the solemn declaration], Ye shall see heaven open, and the angels of God ascending and descending upon the Son of man" (v. 51). "Hereafter" (KJV) is not in the best manuscripts.

Thus ends the account of the interview. But what does it mean? As we study this passage certain things hang together. Nathanael, a rather cynical man, is resting under a fig tree. When he approaches Jesus he is met with a statement as to his character, a statement growing out of Jesus' perception of him which designates him as a true Israelite possessing none of the traits of Jacob. This is followed by his confession and Jesus' promise that, believing in Him, Nathanael shall see "heaven open, and the angels of God ascending and descending upon the Son of man" or upon Jesus Himself.

How may we relate these various items? Nathanael was an idealist, a dreamer in the best sense of that word. He was familiar with the great episodes in the Scriptures where God had seemed to be so near and so real. He longed to have such an experience himself. But like so many of his contemporaries he despaired of ever seeing it come to pass. It had been so long since God had so revealed Himself to His people. And Nathanael's despair had made him cynical.

Then he heard about John the Baptist. He had heard him preach. In the Baptist's preaching he detected the note of divine authority. And this had sent a thrill coursing through Nathanael's being. Now he is on his way back home. The excitement is over.

At noonday he is resting under a fig tree. And as he rests he muses. How wonderful had been these recent days! Heaven had seemed so near. It was as though heaven had opened and God had spoken. Almost it was like the experience of Jacob so long ago yet not so far from where Nathanael was now. Under the deep shade of the fig tree he mused about Jacob's night experience. Heaven had opened, a ladder had come down, and he had seen the angels of God ascending and descending upon the ladder (Gen. 28:12). Jacob had called the place where this happened Bethel, the house of God. Said he, "Surely the Lord is in this place; and I knew it not . . . this is none other than the house of God, and this is the gate of heaven" (Gen. 28:16-17).

So Nathanael mused. But then he came back to the present reality. He longed to see such a thing in his day. But, alas, such was impossible.

It was probably at that moment that he heard Philip calling to him. "The Messiah, you say? Jesus of Nazareth? Nothing like that could happen now. And surely not someone from Nazareth!" Yet reluctantly he did as Philip said. He would go and see.

Suddenly he heard Jesus' words. "Behold an Israelite in whom is no Jacob!" So Jesus not only knew him, but He also knew what he had been thinking. His soul overflowed with joy. Here is the Messiah, the Son of God, the King of Israel! It has happened *here* and *now!*

And in effect Jesus said, "Nathanael, you want to experience that which happened to Jacob. You want heaven to come down to earth. You want to know that God is with you. Well, Nathanael, you will see something better than that which Jacob saw. Not a ladder, but Me. In Me God is here in this place. In Me you truly find the gate of heaven. I am the true Bethel. For I am God's house. In Me God is dwelling among you as flesh."

The realization of a dream! Once again we see the heavenly equation. Nathanael as he is, plus Christ, equals what Nathanael wants to be. Will you permit this equation to solve the hopes and dreams of your life?

John 2:1-11

The Beginning of Signs

By the time that Jesus arrived back in Galilee He had acquired probably six disciples. Upon His word and that of John the Baptist they had accepted Him as the Christ. But apart from those evidences they had no further assurance that He was who He claimed to be. The event related in this passage, therefore, is of great importance. For in it is seen the first of certain "signs" which John records as proving the deity of Jesus and which thus affirm the faith of those who believe on His name (John 20:30-31). Certain definite things with reference to Jesus' nature are inherent in this present passage.

The Social Nature of Jesus (2:1-2)

Whatever may have been the background of John the Baptist's experience, he definitely was an ascetic. While he sought to redeem society, he himself had little or no concourse within it.

But Jesus was of an entirely different nature. He was a social being. One can hardly think of the Baptist being invited to a social dinner. Even less can one conceive of him accepting such an invitation. But Jesus was a popular figure on the *banquet circuit*. It is strange that some of the contemporaries of both of these men should condemn them for their positions. Because the Baptist held himself aloof from such things he was called insane. Because Jesus participated in them He was called "a man gluttonous, and a winebibber, a friend of publicans and sinners" (cf. Matt. 11:16-19). It has been pointed out, however, that "a friend of sinners" may also be rendered "sinners' friend." So that a criticism may become a compliment. Jesus went where people were that He might lead them to where He wanted them to be.

The first recorded social affair attended by Jesus was a marriage feast in Cana of Galilee (2:1). Of interest is the fact that on a sarcophagus now located in the Lateran Museum there is a representation of this occasion.

The location of Cana is not certain. It is identified as "Cana of Galilee" to distinguish it from another Cana in Judea. However, there are two sites in Galilee which are suggested as this Cana. One is a village called Kefr Kenna, located about three and one-half miles northeast of Nazareth. The other is called Khirbet Kana, some eight miles due north of Nazareth. Each has had its champions. Present-day scholarship seems to favor the latter location. But from the standpoint of distance from Nazareth, either could fit the account in John 2:1.

John says that "on the third day a wedding [marriage festival] took place in Cana, the one of Galilee." What "third day" was this? Following the references to time in John 1:29, 35, 43, it is natural to figure this third day from verse 43. This would allow enough travel time to put Jesus in this vicinity. He probably went directly to Nazareth. Arriving there He learned of the wedding feast to which He was invited. Almost immediately, therefore, He and His disciples walked the three and one-half or the eight miles to Cana.

John notes that Jesus' mother "was there." The imperfect form "was" (ēn) suggests that she had been there for some time, probably having gone to Cana before Jesus arrived back in Nazareth. After all, she did not know when He would return. So even though both had been invited, she had gone on alone.

While John notes that "the mother of Jesus was there," he does not record her name. Indeed, he never mentions her name in his Gospel, probably because it was well known from the Synoptic records. It should be noted that no mention is made of Joseph's presence. Of course, he does not figure in the story. Even so, in all probability he had died several years previously. Tradition says that he died when Jesus was about sixteen years of age.

The fact that Jesus was "invited" suggests that He was accustomed to attending such functions. And since "was called" is a third person singular, it means that only Jesus, not His disciples, had received an invitation. They probably were given a door invitation when they appeared along with Jesus.

The word rendered "marriage" is gamos. This was not a wedding ceremony as we regard it. It was the marriage feast or banquet connected with the marriage festivities.

Among the ancient Jews marriage consisted of three things. First, there was the contractural arrangement. This usually was handled by the parents or by other agents. It might even be done in the childhood of the two parties. When the girl reached a marriageable age, she could either accept or deny this arrange-ment. If she accepted it she was bound to it. Second, there was the bethrothal. This was more than our engagement but less than our marriage. However, the betrothal might last as much as a year. Immorality on the future bride's part was punishable by death. Third, there was the marriage itself, after which a couple lived as man and wife. While marriage was most sacred among the Jews, the events connected with the marriage seem to have been more social than religious. This was the culmination of all that had gone before. Therefore, it was a time of great rejoicing. The marriage feast is used in the New Testament as a symbol of joys in heaven.

The marriage feast (gamos) was usually an extended affair lasting seven days. Different guests may have been invited for different days. But it was considered an insult to a friend not to invite him to the feast. A common saying was "He who does not invite me to his marriage will not have me to his funeral." To refuse such an invitation was also a grave insult (cf. Matt. 22). We can see, therefore, why Jesus after a hard journey of three days would respond to the invitation from a friend in Cana.

The New Relationship (2:3-4)

Sometime after Jesus arrived at the feast an emergency arose. "When they wanted wine" should read "when the wine failed" or "was lacking" (v. 3). Why was this true? Some suggest that it was due to the unexpected arrival of six additional guests along with Jesus. However, this would not make so great a strain on the supply of refreshments. More likely this was the closing day of the feast. And the supply had been exhausted.*

At any rate when Jesus' mother became aware of the situation, she came to her Son. "They have no wine," said she. Why did Mary come to Jesus instead of going to the ruler of the feast? She may have wanted to avoid embarrassment to the ruler and to the bridegroom. However, the fact that she came to her Son suggests that she felt that He could remedy the situation. Since the death of Joseph she had come to lean on her eldest son. Furthermore, she was aware of Jesus' divine nature. So her words could have been a

---

*We must avoid being detoured into such issues as to whether Jesus drank wine or why He made wine, so as to lose the lesson of this passage.

subtle hint that He should use His power to relieve this social
emergency.

Jesus replied, "Woman, what have I to do with thee? mine hour
is not yet come" (v. 4). Literally, "What [is it] to me and to you,
woman?" Does this mean "This is not our concern?" Neither of
them was the host nor hostess. In isolation this could be the sense
of this answer. But in the context it takes on a broader meaning.
For, as Sir William Ramsay says, this Gospel is written on the
broad plane of eternity. John was a mystic. And it is often
necessary to look underneath the surface event in order to catch
his deeper meaning. This seems to be the case in this instance.

Two things suggest the key to John's and Jesus' meaning: the
word "woman" and the statement "Mine hour is not yet come."

Some see in the word "woman" (gunē) a note of disrespect on
the part of Jesus toward His mother. However, one immediately
asks, "Could He who exalted all womanhood speak thusly to His
own mother?" Of interest is the fact that only twice in John's
Gospel does Jesus speak to His mother (cf. 19:26). And in both
cases He addresses her as "Woman" (gunē). Surely in so tender a
scene as Calvary He would not have spoken disrespectfully.

What is the significance of this term? It did not involve disrespect. To the contrary it was a term of respect. In the Greek
tragedies it was constantly used in addressing queens and other
women of distinction (Marcus Dods). And Godet notes that in
Dio Cassius a queen (Cleopatra) is so addressed by Caesar Augus-
tus. No, gunē was a term of respect. But it also involved the idea
of separation. Both of these thoughts are involved in Jesus' use
of the word in addressing His mother. He respects her as His
human mother. But gently He reminds her of the new relationship which He now bears to her.

She is no longer to know the relationship of mother-Son. Jesus
is the Christ. And He has entered into this role. He is not her
Son to be commanded. He is her Saviour to be believed. Later He
will say that His mother, brethren, and sisters are those who
believe in Him (Matt. 12:48-49). His relationship to her and
others is no longer genetical but spiritual.

In His dealing with this delicate matter Jesus has shown us how
we should regard His mother. Surely we should respect her memory.
We should show honor to the one whom God selected to be the
mother of His Son. However, this does not justify the exalted position to which she has been elevated by some. Her Son never so
exalted her. And neither should we.

But what does Jesus mean by "Mine hour is not yet come?" Repeatedly John records Jesus referring to "mine hour" (2:4; 7:30; 8:20; 12:23, 27; 13:1; 17:1). Always it referred to His death. It involved His manifestation as the supreme expression of God's redeeming love.

But why did Jesus use this expression to His mother at this time? Was it because He detected in her statement to Him the suggestion that He should perform a miracle, thus showing this group that He was the Christ? Doubtless she knew of what had happened to Him in recent weeks. So why not begin to show His powers? It could have been Satan's wilderness temptations all over again. And that from His well-meaning but misguided mother! A similar situation obtained when Jesus' half-brothers suggested that He should show Himself in Jerusalem (John 7:3 ff.). Jesus refused to go at the moment. There He said almost the same thing that He had said to His mother in Cana. "My time is not yet come: but your time is always ready" (7:6, 8). Later, at a time and in a manner of His own choosing, Jesus did go to Jerusalem (7:10). He was moving in a divinely given schedule, and no one, not even His mother, who believed in Him, or His half-brothers who were unbelievers at the time, would hasten Him unduly.

So Jesus gently but firmly reminded His mother of this fact. Godet quotes Luthardt. "Here for Mary is the beginning of a painful education." Then Godet adds, "The middle point of this education will be marked by the question of Jesus, 'Who is my mother, and who are my brethren?' (Luke viii.19 f.). The end will be that second address: *Woman* (xix:26), which will definitely break the earthly relation between the mother and the son. Mary feels at this moment, for the first time, the point of the sword which, at the foot of the cross, shall pierce through her heart" *(in loco)*. But Jesus made this first pricking of the sword as painless as possible. He gently but firmly reminded her of this new relationship, as He pointed her to His "hour" when He fully would manifest God's redeeming love.

This suggests the central truth of the Incarnation. Though Jesus was mindful of men's physical, social, and intellectual needs, these do not comprise the heart of His mission. His ministry in these matters was but a contributing factor to enhance the grand portrait of God's redeeming love seen at Calvary. Jesus is not in the business solely of meeting social emergencies. Their solution should come out of His ministry, but they should never become its center. For His "hour" points to a cross.

The Provision for a Need (2:5-8)

That Jesus is concerned as to social needs is evident in that which followed this brief exchange with His mother. How Mary knew that Jesus would meet this need we are not told. Evidently by some look, gesture, or move she knew that He would do so. At any rate she said to the servants of the house, "Whatsoever he saith unto you, do it" (v. 5). Note, however, that she no longer suggests a course of action to Him either by direct word or by implication. Instead she told the servants to respond to His bidding.

At such feasts as this several containers of water were kept available for purposes of ceremonial purification. For the benefit of his Greek readers John explains their use (v. 6). Perhaps they were kept in the courtyard adjacent to the banquet hall. On this occasion there were "six waterpots of stone ... containing two or three firkins [*metrētas*] apiece." This Greek word simply means a measure containing about eight and one-half gallons. So each pot would hold between twenty and twenty-five gallons. Thus the six waterpots would hold something over one hundred and twenty gallons. The natural conclusion is that all ,of this was involved in the miracle which Jesus was about to perform.

Jesus told the servants to "fill" the pots. The word "fill" means to fill full (v. 7). This is emphasized by the added words that they filled them "up to the brim" or "to the top." Then Jesus told them to "draw out now, and bear unto the governor of the feast" (v. 8). The "governor" or "ruler" was usually a chief servant whose duty it was to superintend all the arrangements in connection with the feast. This would include the setting up of tables and couches as well as preparing the food and refreshments. He also tasted the food before it was presented to the host or guests. It is evident that he was not involved when Jesus performed the miracle.

When did the water become wine? Godet says that it occurred between verses 7 and 8. But A. T. Robertson suggests that the liquid was still water when it was taken from the pots, and that it became wine while being carried to the ruler. We cannot be certain although verse 9 suggests that Robertson is right. The point is that Jesus did this. And it provided for the need of all who were present. Yes, Jesus is concerned with the natural needs of men. But He provides for them in keeping with the greater purpose of His being.

The Best for the Last (2:9-10)

The ruler of the feast tasted of the product which Jesus had produced miraculously (v. 9). He did not know its source. Parenthetically John notes that the servants knew. At least they knew that water had been poured into the pots. Perhaps they also knew that they drew water out. And now it is wine. This definitely was a miracle on the part of Jesus. There is no point in debating whether or not this was real wine. The Greek word *oinos* normally denotes the fermented juice of the grape. The ruler's appraisal of it in verse 10 suggests that it was wine of the best quality. However, this does not merit the claim that either Jesus or the Bible supports the present-day liquor interests with their ravages upon humanity. Jesus' concern for man's welfare militates against any such idea.

Having tasted the new supply of wine, the ruler of the feast called to the bridegroom. "Every man at the beginning doth set forth good wine; and when men have well drunk, then that which is worse [inferior]: but thou [in contrast to the custom] hast kept the good wine until now" (v. 10). Naturally at the beginning of a feast the host would serve his best. But as the festivities continued, if necessary, he would augment the supply with that of inferior quality. The words "have well drunk" are debatable as to meaning. Basically the verb *methuskō* means "cause to become intoxicated" (cf. Eph. 5:18). Marcus Dods so interprets the word here. However, he cites the Revised Version reading: "when men have drunk freely." He comments, "And if the word does not definitely mean 'when men are intoxicated,' it at least must indicate a condition in which they are unfit to discriminate between good wine and bad. The company then present was not in that condition, because they were able to appreciate the good wine; but the words of the architriklinos unquestionably imply that a good deal had already been drunk." A. T. Robertson follows the reading "when men have drunk freely." Arndt and Gingrich give this as the possible rendering in John 2:10. And this most likely is the sense intended by John. The guests were not drunk. But the wine already imbibed would affect the sensitivity of their taste buds. However, we agree with Robertson who says, "The verb does not mean that these guests are now drunk." Dods also agrees that verse 10 shows that certainly the ruler of the feast, and probably the guests also, while having drunk freely had not reached the state where they could not appreciate this good wine.

In this context *methuskō* definitely does not mean that they were intoxicated.

Even so, is John primarily interested in the relative quality of the wines? It appears that we are justified in looking beneath the surface of this story to see a hidden, mystical meaning. If so, then John is saying that the revelation of God in Christ is the "good wine" as opposed to the first wine that now is lacking, namely, the Old Testament revelation, and particularly the wine of Judaism. The new "good wine" supplies the lack of the former wine. Just so does God's revelation in Christ supply the lack of His revelation in Old Testament patterns. In a sense there is a kinship between this incident and Jesus' teaching about putting new wine in old wineskins. "And no one puts new wine into old wineskins; else the wine and skins perish: but new wine in new skins." In other words the old forms of religious expression cannot contain or express the new. If you try to pour the new truth of Christianity into the old forms, both shall be lost. The new revelation must be expressed in new forms. This is suggestive of the new wine of Jesus' spiritual ministry, the new life in Him, coming out of, and replacing, the old water pots of the ceremonial cleansing of Judaism.

One difference is noted between the language of Mark and John. Mark speaks of "new [*neos*] wine," new in contrast to the old. John speaks of "good [*kalos*] wine." The emphasis here is upon quality: the beautiful, good, useful wine. Thus in His Son God has kept "the good wine until now." He saved the best for the last.

The Purpose of the Signs (2:11)

John closes this incident by noting that "this beginning of miracles [*sēmeion*, signs] did Jesus in Cana of Galilee, and manifested forth his glory; and his disciples believed on him." His word for miracles is *sēmeion*, coming from the verb *sēmainō*, to give a sign (12:33; 18:33; 21:19). John uses this noun form seventeen times. Four times in the King James Version it is rendered "sign" (2:18; 4:48; 6:30; 20:30). Thirteen times it is "miracle" (2:11, 23; 3:2; 4:54; 6:2, 14, 26; 7:31; 9:16; 10:41; 11:47; 12:18, 37). The sense in which it is used throughout is that which shows forth the miraculous power or deity of Jesus Christ. Lightfoot calls *sēmeion* a "visible pointer to the invisible truth about him."

In 20:30 John indicates that he has selected certain *sēmeia* as showing that Jesus is the Son of God, that those who believe in

Him may have life in His name. So in a sense this Gospel may be called a book of signs. C. H. Dodd refers to John 2 — 12 as "The Books of Signs." The word "sign" does not appear after 12:37 until 20:30 where it is used in the sense of a summary. Some scholars point out seven (the perfect number) signs as the framework about which John builds his Gospel: the changing of water into wine; the healing of the nobleman's son; the healing of the lame man at the pool of Bethesda; the feeding of the five thousand; Jesus walking on water; the giving of sight to a blind man; and the raising of Lazarus. Robertson adds an eighth, Jesus' word about raising the temple. It should be noted, however, that only three of these works are specifically called "signs." Also the word "signs" is used several times in a general sense. Certainly Jesus' bodily resurrection was a "sign" (cf. Matt. 12:38ff.). Yet it is not so labeled by John. Granted that John is a "Book of Signs"; however, this title should not be limited to certain chapters or to those specific events that are so labeled, or even to seven or eight specific things. The entire Gospel is a "Book of Signs." For Jesus' every word and deed was a "visible pointer to the invisible truth about him." Indeed, John 1:14 says, "And we beheld his glory, the glory as of the only begotten of the Father." This statement and John 20:30 form two parenthetical marks enclosing the whole of the earthly ministry of Jesus (chap. 21 added later by John).

But John does say that the changing of water into wine was the first of specific signs performed by Jesus (but note His baptismal sign, 1:32f.) which manifested His glory (cf. John 1:14). And because of this "his disciples believed on him" (2:11). They had already accepted Him as the Christ. This "visible pointer" only served to confirm their faith. It will be so throughout the Gospel. Jesus' "signs" will increase the faith of His friends and will increase the hatred of His enemies.

John 2:12-25

The Lord of the Temple

After the event in Cana Jesus probably returned to His home in Nazareth. Whether the "sign" was reported in His home town is not stated. It would be natural to suppose that after the exciting events which began with His baptism He might wish to retire to the comparative quiet of familiar surroundings for a time of meditation. Then He would be ready to launch forth into a public ministry.

The Visit to Capernaum (2:12)

"After this he went down to Capernaum, he, and his mother, and his brethren, and his disciples: and they continued there not many days."

Here we note the first use of *meta touto* ("after this," see "Introduction"). This does not mean that Jesus went directly from Cana to Capernaum. The presence of Jesus' "brethren," not mentioned as being at Cana, implies that this journey began at Nazareth. The significance of "after this" is that John is about to begin an account which is not found in the Synoptic Gospels (2:13 — 4:42; except 4:1-4; Matt. 4:12; Mark 1:14; Luke 3:19-20; 4:14). A. T. Robertson in his *A Harmony of the Gospels* calls the period beginning with Jesus' baptism (Matt. 3:13ff.) through His return to Galilee (John 4:43-45) "The Year of Obscurity." The greater portion of this year is recorded only by John. His use of *meta touto* serves to introduce his account of Jesus' first visit to Jerusalem during His public ministry. John records four such visits prior to the last one. A section found only in Luke (9:51 — 18:14) gives a Judean ministry. But were it not for John's record, it would appear that Jesus made only one such journey, the last. Therefore, we would be at a loss to explain the strong opposition to Him in Jerusalem on this visit, and the growing opposition in Galilee, for that matter. Hence the added importance of this Gospel in understanding the life of Jesus. And the author's use of the phrases *meta touto* (after this) and *meta tauta* (after these things) is vital to this understanding.

Returning to the text, John notes that Jesus and His company made a brief visit to Capernaum. "They continued there not many days" (v. 12). Therefore, this can hardly correspond to references in Matthew 3:13 and Luke 4:31. But this is John's way of identifying Jesus' ministry with this city (cf. 6:24).

Capernaum was an important city located on the northwestern shore of the sea of Galilee. In all probability it was located on the site of modern Tell Hum which is little more than ruins today. Its most imposing ruin is that of a synagogue which probably dates back to about A.D. 200 or later. In all likelihood it stood on the site and was shaped much like that of the synagogue which was there in Jesus' day. It was an imposing structure of white limestone, facing southward toward the Galilean lake and toward Jerusalem. Synagogues in Palestine usually faced toward Jerusalem. The idea was to offer prayers toward the sacred city (cf. I Kings 8:38).

When Jesus began His Galilean ministry, after having been rejected by Nazareth, He used Capernaum as a base of operations. It was ideal for this purpose. Why He made this brief visit to this city at this time is not told. It could have been for any one of many personal reasons. But one wonders if, even at this early date, the Lord was not contemplating the possibility of later locating there.

The First Passover (2:13)

"And the Jews' passover was at hand, and Jesus went up to Jerusalem." Probably this was in the spring of A.D. 27. This was the first of three passovers, possibly four (5:1), mentioned in this Gospel. Thus this mention of the time element is important. If we had only the Synoptic record, it would appear that Jesus' ministry was only a little over a year in length. But, following John, it was at least two and one-half, and probably three and one-half years in length.

Note that John calls it the "Jews' passover." In the Synoptics it is simply called the "passover." But since John wrote for Greek readers long after the destruction of the Jewish nation (A.D. 70), for the information of his readers he points out that this was a Jewish festival. And since it commemorated the deliverance of Israel from Egyptian bondage, it was the principal religious feast of the Jews. Its principal observance was in Jerusalem. This, in part, explains why Jesus made this long journey to attend it.

The feast was "at hand," or was near. So Jesus and His disciples (no mention is made of His family on this journey) "went up" to Jerusalem. The words "went up" are significant. They journeyed southward or *down* geographically. But the author is speaking topographically. Since Jerusalem is located in the mountains twenty-five hundred feet above sea level, any approach to the city except from the south, is *up*. *Went up* is especially true when one remembers that the area around the Dead Sea near Jericho is twelve hundred and ninety-three feet below sea level. This little detail is important from the standpoint of authorship. It suggests one who is familiar with the topography of Palestine.

So, perhaps following the usual route used by Jews traveling from Galilee to Jerusalem, Jesus and the disciples crossed the Jordan river eastward, then went southward through Perea, crossed the river again westward just opposite Jericho, and thence to Jerusalem. This was done to avoid passing southward through Samaria (cf. 4:4). Thus Jesus came to the first Passover during His ministry.

The Bazaars of Annas (2:14)

Upon His arrival in Jerusalem Jesus entered the temple area *(hieros)*. This was the temple built by Herod the Great, and was the pride of every Jewish heart. As one approached it from the east over the Mount of Olives, especially in the morning, its white marble structure overlaid with gold plates on the east, looked like a sea of white emblazoned with golden fire. Josephus likened it to a snow-covered mountain. The temple area was composed of many courts: the Court of the Gentiles; the Court of the Women; the Court of Israel; and the Court of the Priests. East of this last court were the porch, the Holy Place, and finally the Holy of Holies. This last was the temple proper *(naos)*. This was separated from the Holy Place of sacrifice by a heavy veil or curtain. Within the Holy of Holies God was said to dwell in mercy with His people. Only the high priest might enter the *Naos,* and that once each year on the Day of Atonement. Most of Jesus' temple ministry took place in the Court of the Gentiles. Since He was not a priest He never entered into the Court of the Priests, and certainly not into the Holy Place or the Holy of Holies.

The incident under consideration took place in the Court of

the Gentiles. It was in this area that Gentiles were permitted to enter. But at each door leading beyond that into the Court of the Women were posted slabs of stone bearing a warning, some in Greek, others in Latin (Josephus), that Gentiles were forbidden to go beyond that point. To do so incurred the penalty of death. One of these stones has been recovered and is now in the Museum of the Ancient Orient in Istanbul. A piece of another such inscription has recently been found. The one complete stone carries the wording: "No foreigner may enter within the balustrade and enclosure around the Sanctuary. Whoever is caught will render himself liable to the death penalty which will inevitably follow" (cf. Acts 21:28 f.; Eph. 2:14).

When Jesus entered into the Court of the Gentiles He found a scene more fitting to an oriental bazaar than to a temple of God. For He "found in the temple those that sold oxen and sheep and doves, and the changers of money sitting" (v. 14). This scene was the result of what had begun as a service to the worshippers. It was inconvenient for them to bring the animals and doves from their homes. This was especially the case with those who came from great distances, some even from outside Palestine. So an arrangement was made whereby they could purchase them at the temple. Also each one was required to pay annually the half-shekel temple tax. It must be paid in that specific coin. Up until a certain date this tax could be paid in one's place of residence. After that date it must be paid at the temple. So "money-changers" (*kermatistas*) were there for the purpose of providing the required coins. For instance, the shekel would have to be exchanged for two half-shekels. Or Roman or other foreign coins had to be exchanged for the Jewish coin. A charge was made for this service.

But what had begun as a service had become a racket. Exhorbitant prices were charged for the animals and doves and for the service of exchange. The profits were supposed to go into the temple treasury. But much of it was finding its way into private pockets. Since Annas, the former high priest, and his sons were in charge of this, this supposed service had come to be called "The Bazaars of Annas."

One can imagine the scandal all of this had produced. Due to these abuses the people had come to despise worship in the temple. Like attracts like. And one tradition says that the thievery in the name of worship even had led thieves to use the temple area as

the place to gather in order to plot their crimes (cf. Matt. 21:13).
The house of prayer for the nations (cf. Mark 11:17; Luke 19:46)
had become a den of robbers. Had a Gentile entered the Court
of the Gentiles for prayer, this scene would have driven him from,
not to, the worship of Jehovah.

It is easy, therefore, to understand Jesus' indignation over such
a scene. Had He acted other than He did, it would have been
surprising indeed.

The Cleansing of the Temple (2:15-17)

Therefore, Jesus "made a scourge of small cords" (v. 15). The
word for "cords" (schoinion) means small ropes. So with this whip
Jesus drove or cast them out of the temple area. That is, He drove
the animals out, and overturned the tables of the money-changers.
The word for "tables" means "bankers' tables." Some see a problem in Jesus using a whip on the animals. However, this seems
to be straining out gnats. But it is not specifically said that He
whipped them. Merely shaking the whip at them would have
sufficed.

Having cleared the area of animals Jesus said to the dove-
sellers, "Take these things hence" (v. 16). Since the doves probably
were in cages this was necessary. And then He added to all, "Make
not [stop making] my Father's house an house of merchandise"
(v. 15), or an emporium. All of this recalled to His disciples the
Scripture "The zeal of thine house hath eaten [shall eat] me up"
(v. 17; cf. Ps. 69:9). Psalm 69 was a Messianic psalm. So the
disciples recognized Jesus' act as that of the Messiah exercising
authority over the temple. This then was also a "sign" to them as
to Jesus' office as the Christ. According to the Synoptic record Jesus
similarly cleansed the temple on Monday prior to His death
(Matt. 21:12-13; Mark 11:15-17; Luke 19:45-46). Some students
see this as the same one related by John, with the probability
that John erred in placing it at the beginning of Jesus' ministry.
However, there is no real reason why both cannot be true. John
is recording a phase of Jesus' ministry omitted by the Synoptics.
And there are sufficient differences in the two accounts to warrant
holding that they are separate events. The sense of greed is strong.
And there is no reason not to suppose that after the first cleansing,
the Bazaars of Annas were once again set in operation. It is also
easy to see why the Christ would begin His ministry by asserting
His authority over the temple.

The Challenge to Authority (2:18)

If Jesus' act strengthened the faith of His disciples, it had another effect elsewhere. News of this action came to the "Jews" or Jewish religious leaders. Therefore, they came to Jesus with the challenge, "What sign showest thou unto us, seeing that thou doest these things?" Jesus' act had interfered with their profitable enterprise. However, they were technically within their rights in making this challenge.

According to their teaching apart from themselves only a prophet, the Messiah, or God Himself had authority over the temple. Jesus had assumed such an authority. So they held it to be their duty to ascertain His claim to authority. A "sign" to them would be some tangible evidence that Jesus had this authority. Certainly they did not recognize this Galilean as a prophet (cf. John 7:52). Most assuredly they did not attribute deity to Him. So their challenge involved whether or not He claimed to be the Messiah. This is the first of many confrontations between Jesus and the Jewish leaders.

But for reasons of His own He avoided any open admission that He was the Christ. Among the Jews this term was highly nationalistic. They thought in terms of a political-military Messiah. An admission at the time that He was the Messiah would have misled the people as to His true nature. It also would have served to bring the wrath of Rome down upon Him. And His "hour" was not yet come.

The Answer to the Challenge (2:19-22)

In reply to the challenge of the Jewish leaders Jesus said, "Destroy this temple, and in three days I will raise it up" (v. 19). Marcus Dods sees this statement as intentionally enigmatical. In a sense it was a parable intended to reveal truth to the faithful and to hide it from the hostile. In response to the Jews' demand for a "sign" Jesus gave one which they, because of their critical attitude, would not understand. Even the believing disciples had not yet advanced in faith to be able to comprehend it (cf. 2:22). The Jewish rulers did not understand it either then or later. At Jesus' trial they used their gross misunderstanding of it as a charge against Him (cf. Matt. 26:61).

But what did Jesus actually say? He said, "Destroy this temple." The word "destroy" is an imperative form. Robertson calls it a permissive imperative. He did not order them to destroy it, but rather suggested permission to do so. "Destroy this temple, if you will." He used the word *naos* for "temple," not *hieros* which referred to the entire temple area. While *naos* at times was used to refer to the entire temple area, in its restricted sense it referred to the Holy of Holies. In pagan temples it was used in this sense to refer to the place where the image of the pagan deity stood. Jesus apparently used the word in this strict sense. Let them destroy this *naos*, the dwelling place of God, and He would raise it up in three days.

It is thusly that we discern the true sense of Jesus' words. Let them destroy His body, the *naos* in which the Father dwells, and in three days He will raise it up. Therefore, His reply is the equivalent of the "sign" given to the Pharisees about Jonah (Matt. 12:38-40).

Whether by accident or by design the Jews interpreted Jesus' use of *naos* to refer to the entire temple structure. For they said, "Forty and six years was this temple [*naos*] in building, and wilt thou rear it in three days?" (v. 20).

This was a matter of history. Herod the Great was a great builder. Compared to Solomon's temple the one built under Zerubbabel left much to be desired. Even this temple had been ravaged by pagan conquerors through the years. So that about the middle of his reign Herod proposed to build a new and more glorious temple. His stated reason was religious. But the Jews distrusted him, thinking that he wanted to do away with the temple altogether. It was not until he had shown good faith by gathering all of the material for the new temple that they agreed for him to proceed. A thousand priests were trained to serve as masons and carpenters. Ten thousand workmen were used in the task of building. Finally Herod's subjects permitted him to begin construction in 20-19 B.C. It took eighteen months to complete the temple proper or the *naos*. Eight years were required to complete the cloisters and courts. However, various projects of construction continued. It was not completed until A.D. 64 during the time of Agrippa II, just six years before it was destroyed in A.D. 70. Large Herodian stones from this temple may still be seen in the structures in Jerusalem.

Construction was actually going on when Jesus spoke His words. And since this was in the spring of A.D. 27, this would mean "forty and six years was this temple in building" up to this point. Obviously this made Jesus' claim seem ridiculous to them.

The claims of Jesus always seem so to those who view them only through the natural eye. But when rightly understood and viewed through the power of God they make sense indeed. Even so Jesus spoke of a miracle. The Jews asked for a "sign" and received one. It was God's supreme "sign" as to the deity of His Son. The Jewish rulers did not understand it at the time. And when it became true for all to believe they refused to accept it (cf. Matt. 28:12-15).

The disciples themselves did not understand Jesus' enigmatical words at the moment. But the time came when they did comprehend. For speaking retrospectly John says, "But he spake of the temple of his body" (v. 21). The Jewish rulers did effect the destruction of "this temple." And God did raise it up in three days. And His followers did believe (v. 22).

The Reserve of Jesus (2:23-25)

The Jewish rulers demanded a "sign," and received one that would be given at a future date. Jesus never worked miracles on demand or in response to unbelief. Nevertheless throughout this Passover week He continued from time to time to do "signs" ("which he did" is an imperfect tense, "which he kept on doing"). And "many believed on his name" (v. 23) because of them. "But Jesus did not commit himself unto them, because he knew all men" (v. 24). "Men" is not in the Greek text. "He knew all."

Why this reserve on the part of Jesus? Why did He not "commit" Himself to these who "believed in [eis, on] his name?" The reason hangs on the words "believe" and "commit." Actually they translate the same Greek verb (pisteuō). This word means to believe, to trust, or to commit. It might be only an intellectual acceptance of facts or it might be wilful trust and commitment on the basis of the facts. For instance in Acts 8:13 Simon Magus "believed" as it is said of others (8:12). It is evident, however, from the context that Simon was not saved. He "believed" the miracles which Philip performed. But he did not trust in or commit himself to Jesus whom Philip was preaching.

So here the people "believed" on Jesus' name because of His "signs." They believed the "signs" as coming from one who could do such things. But it was only an intellectual belief devoid of trust or commitment. Therefore, in effect, Jesus knowing this superficial faith, did not commit Himself to them. They *believed* on Jesus, but He did not *believe* on them. The imperfect tense shows that He "kept on not trusting himself unto them."

Jesus is looking for wilful trust and commitment, not merely

intellectual acceptance of the facts of the gospel. Because of this
He held Himself in reserve from these *surface believers*. For "he
kept on not having need that anyone should witness concerning
men: for he himself [and no other] kept on knowing what kept on
being in man." These three imperfect forms show the absolute
knowledge of Jesus as to man's nature. In the final analysis He
and He alone decides the genuineness of one's faith. Anything
less than full trust and commitment cannot pass His judgment.

John 3:1-21

The Unparalleled Teacher

It is of interest to note that whereas Jesus is mentioned repeatedly as preaching, and at times preached to great multitudes, the Gospels never refer to Him as a *Preacher*. But repeatedly He is called the *Teacher*. Some of the richest things which fell from His lips came in a pupil-Teacher relationship. And one of His greatest lessons is taught in the passage under consideration.

The Teaching Situation (3:1-2)

Apparently Jesus remained in Jerusalem throughout this passover week. It has been noted that many "believed" on Him because of the "signs which He kept on doing." One such person was Nicodemus. As important a figure as he was in Jesus' ministry, he is mentioned only by John.

Nicodemus was a Pharisee (v. 1). As we study the life of Jesus we are prone to think of this sect, numbering never more than six thousand, as a bad lot. And insofar as the Gospel record goes, this was for the most part true. But there certainly were exceptions as is seen in Gamaliel and Paul. Nicodemus was such an exception (cf. 7:50; 19:39). His Greek name means "conqueror of the people." Whether he ever conquered anyone else or not, he certainly won a victory within himself.

Apparently Nicodemus was a Pharisee who possessed their virtues but few, if any, of their vices. It would appear that he was not altogether a prisoner to their system. He was a godly man who believed the Scriptures. He was a righteous man. And he was one whose mind and heart were open to new truth as revealed of God. In short, he was one of the fairest flowers of his nation. While it is not stated, tradition holds that he was a man of wealth (cf. 19:39). Furthermore, he was a man of position and influence. He was "a ruler of the Jews," meaning that he was a member of the Sanhedrin, the highest ruling body among his people (cf. 7:50 f.).

Nicodemus "came to Jesus by night." Actually in the Greek

76

text the word is not "Jesus" but "him" *(auton)*. The thought of
Jesus is brought over from the closing verses of Chapter 2. By implication Nicodemus may have been one of those who had believed
Jesus' "signs" but who had not yet believed in Him (cf. 3:2,
"signs") .

But why did he come "by night" (cf. 7:50) ? Various reasons
have been suggested. Years ago Koppe suggested that he came to
spy on Jesus. But the tone of his visit negates this idea. Meyer
saw in this night visit Nicodemus' desire to ask Jesus how he might
be saved. However, as a Pharisee he would feel no such need,
thinking that he was already in the kingdom of God. Of course,
the most broadly held view is that he came by night to avoid
publicity. He did not want to endure the criticism of his colleagues.
One facet of this position is that as a ruler of the Jews he did not
want to enhance Jesus' stature by it being known that he had
called on Him. However, this seems to be contrary to the context.
A more recent and more charitable reason is suggested, that he
came by night out of consideration for Jesus' busy schedule. The
rabbis said that the best time to study the law was at night. Or
did he come by night to insure an uninterrupted interview?
Frankly, no one can say with certainty. His subsequent conduct
seems to support the view that he wished to avoid publicity. But
there is reason in the thought that he simply came by night when
he could have a more lengthy and undisturbed visit.

Whatever his reason, he opened his visit by calling Jesus
"Rabbi" (v. 2) . This was a title of great honor among the Jews.
The least that can be said of Nicodemus is that he was a cour-
teous man. But even though Jesus was not an accredited rabbi,
he recognized him as a "teacher." He really called Jesus "My
Master," for that is one meaning of the term.

When Nicodemus said, "We know," it is natural to think that
he was speaking for others also. Was this group of "believers"
in 2:23? It would seem to be referring to a more intimate group
than this. Was he speaking for himself and Joseph of Arimathea?
Or had a group of his colleagues been discussing the report of the
delegation sent to John the Baptist? And had their thinking along
these lines been strengthened by the "signs" which Jesus had done,
including His cleansing of the temple? Whoever the "we know"
refers to, the verb used *(oidamen)* means that they had thought
through their experiential knowledge and had reached a conclusion. And what was that conclusion?

"We know that from God you have come a teacher" (v. 2) .

"From God" is in the emphatic position. This is the important thing. Jesus was not an accredited teacher of the Pharisees. But his accreditation was far greater. It was from God. This truth was avowed by the "signs" which He had done. And Nicodemus and his colleagues wished to know more. Involved is the thought that Jesus could possibly, and probably, be the Messiah.

An old adage is that a university is Mark Hopkins on one end of a log with a pupil on the other end. So here we find a perfect teaching situation. The learned, cultured, and inquiring Pharisee coming as a pupil. And this Galilean peasant as the teacher. But this Teacher was from God.

The Lesson Stated (3:3)

To Nicodemus' gracious approach Jesus responded rather abruptly. "Verily, verily [note the solemnity], I say unto thee, Except a man [anyone, tis] be born again, he cannot see the kingdom of God." "See" here carries the sense of partaking of or enjoying the kingdom of God.

Was this actually Jesus' first statement to Nicodemus? Many years ago Grotius suggested that this is an abridged report of the conversation. That prior to this there had been an extended discussion of the nature of the kingdom of God. More recently Dods suggested that Jesus perceived that Nicodemus came with some overture from the Pharisaic party. Therefore, He deliberately cut him short. The tone of the interview seems to indicate otherwise. Jesus accepts Nicodemus as an honest inquirer.

Why, then, this abrupt answer? Jesus was the Teacher. The latest methods of pedagogy are found in His teaching. A method in vogue today is called the "shock method." The teacher makes a statement designed to make the pupil think. It seems, therefore, that Jesus was simply applying the "shock method." For His words certainly were designed to produce that effect.

As a righteous Pharisee Nicodemus had never questioned but that he was a part of God's kingdom. Despite John the Baptist's harsh words to some of his colleagues this righteous Pharisee claimed a choice place in the kingdom of God. And here was this Galilean peasant Teacher telling him that unless any man, even a Pharisee, were born "again" (anōthen), he would never see the kingdom of God. The word anōthen could refer to a complete radical change from the beginning, a second natural birth, or to a birth from above. While all three meanings make sense here, the last two meanings seem to be uppermost in this interview. That was the lesson posed by Jesus to His pupil. Now what would Nicodemus do with it?

The Problem Posed (3:4)

Had Jesus said that all Gentiles had to be born again, that would have been in keeping with Nicodemus' own theology; but a Jew, a Pharisee, a ruler of the Jews? What could this possibly mean?

That Nicodemus thought of *anōthen* as referring to a second physical birth is evidenced by his reply. Literally, "How can a man be born again being old [*gerōn ōn*]? is it possible into the womb of his mother a second time to enter and to be born?" Nicodemus' use of the negative particle *mē* before *dunatai* (is possible) means that he expected to receive a negative reply.

So the learned pupil is puzzled. Furthermore, he had missed the point altogether. Jesus spoke of a birth from above. He thought of a second physical birth. One wonders if this was not exactly the response that Jesus expected, and, perhaps, desired at this point. Hence His use of *anōthen* with its possible dual meaning. This is more of the *shock treatment*. For somehow He must dislodge from Nicodemus' thinking the idea that he was already in the kingdom of God by virtue of his *first* natural birth. This was the teaching of Judaism. A Jew did not need to gain entrance into the kingdom of God. By his natural birth he was automatically in it. Thereafter, his good works were merely to make him well pleasing to God, the result being greater rewards in the kingdom.

Now Nicodemus is faced with a birth *anōthen*. A second physical birth, you say? Surely you cannot mean that. For "how?" The shock method had worked. Bewildered, the Pharisee asks for further light.

The Lesson Explained (3:5-7)

Nicodemus was now ready to have this grand truth unfolded to him. Solemnly, therefore, Jesus began to explain what He meant by *anōthen*. "Except a man [anyone, *tis*] be born [may be born] of water and of the Spirit, he cannot enter into the kingdom of God" (v. 5).

What did Jesus mean by "of [*ex* or *ek*] water and Spirit?" Bernard rejects "water and" as a gloss added later in order to bring Jesus' words into harmony with the belief in baptismal regeneration as held by a later generation. However, he admits that these words cannot be removed on the basis of the manuscripts in hand. So on the basis of including these words how may we understand Jesus' statement?

To begin with one is hardly justified to see in the reference to water the idea of baptismal regeneration. The abundant teaching of the New Testament is to the contrary. Even those passages so often cited in support of this belief lend themselves to an interpretation which is in harmony with the weight of teaching in the New Testament (cf. Acts 2:38; I Peter 3:20-21). Mention may be made of the fact that John uses "of water" in verse 3 but not in verses 5 and 7. This alone should warn against seeing in verse 5 the doctrine of baptismal regeneration. It would seem strongly that Christian baptism was not in Jesus' words spoken to His pupil.

Godet suggests that "of water" refers back to the baptism of John the Baptist, a baptism which connoted repentance and a willingness to participate in the coming kingdom. The Pharisees had rejected John and his baptism. Thus it is held that Jesus was saying that a man must have the experience symbolized in that baptism before he can be born of the Spirit. In essence Marcus Dods follows this position, adding that baptism "is only a symbol." John Calvin saw "of water and Spirit" (note the one preposition) as referring to one act, the cleansing work of the Spirit. And he has many followers today in this view. For instance, William Barclay sees "of water and Spirit" as symbolizing "cleansing" (water) and "power" (Spirit), Robertson, rejecting baptismal regeneration, mentions several views. Among them, connecting verse 6, is that of "meaning the birth of the flesh coming in a sac of water in contrast to the birth of the Spirit." One of the able New Testament scholars of today rejects this idea as unworthy of consideration. However, it seems to this writer that this view is not to be disposed of so easily. For he agrees with Robertson that someway, somehow this verse strongly suggests that Jesus is trying to separate His pupil's mind from the idea that he is in the kingdom by means of a natural birth, and that he can see the kingdom of God only through a birth from above.

However one may read "of water and Spirit" in verse 5, it is clear that in verse 6 Jesus contrasts the natural and spiritual births. "That which is born of the flesh is flesh; and that which is born of the Spirit is spirit." A natural birth produces only a natural relationship. It is the spiritual birth which brings one into relationship with spiritual things.

Looking back, what do we find? Jesus spoke of a birth *anōthen*, from above, a spiritual birth. Nicodemus countered with a birth *anōthen*, a second natural birth. Jesus, in turn, spoke of a birth "of water and Spirit." Then He clearly spoke of both a natural and a spiritual birth. It would seem, therefore, that verse 5 is the meat in the sandwich between two slices of bread (vv. 4, 6). Thus the clear contrast is between Nicodemus' *second natural birth* and Jesus' *one spiritual birth from above.* One must be born naturally before he can be born spiritually. And as the natural birth ushers one into natural relationships, so the spiritual birth ushers one into spiritual relationships.

Therefore, Jesus reiterates His statement of verse 3. "Marvel not that I said unto thee, Ye must be born again," or from above. Bernard notes that the Greek word for "marvel" *(thaumazō)* usually connotes "unintelligent wonder." The verb is an ingressive aorist form. "Do not begin to wonder unintelligently." "Ye" *(humas,* accusative plural) is a plural form, probably referring back to "we" in verse 2, and yet including all men. Jesus said to Nicodemus *(soi,* singular), "ye" must be born "from above." "Must" *(dei)* expresses a moral and spiritual necessity. So literally, "Do not begin to wonder unintelligently that I said to you, It is morally and spiritually necessary with respect to you and all others to be born from above."

The Truth Illustrated (3:8)

Jesus now proceeded to illustrate the truth which He had taught. We may well imagine that a night breeze was blowing. Ever alert to draw spiritual lessons from natural phenomena, Jesus used this breeze as a picture of what He was saying. "The wind bloweth where it listeth [wishes], and thou hearest the sound thereof, but canst not tell whence it cometh, and whither it goeth: So is every one that is born of the Spirit."

Note that here Jesus drops the figure of water. Having cleared up His pupil's problem as to His use of *anōthen*, Jesus proceeds to emphasize the "from above" or spiritual birth. From a play on the word *anōthen* He moves to a play on the word *pneuma*. For this word may be rendered as either "wind" or "Spirit." It comes from the verb *pneō*, to blow, or to breathe out, which is the word "bloweth" in this verse. So "the *pneuma* blows where it

wills [wishes] . . . so is every one that is born of the *Pneuma*." The
wind is invisible but powerful. One cannot see the wind, but one
can hear its sound, yea, even realize its effect. The same is true of
the Spirit. The wind is a mystery, and so is the Spirit. Yet we can
experience the working power of each.

Therefore, in a sense Jesus told Nicodemus that while he did
not fully comprehend the wind, even so he could not fully comprehend the Spirit. A sailor does not analyze the wind. Yet by
setting his sails properly, he uses the wind. In the same manner by
yielding ourselves to the Spirit, we receive His beneficial power.
A doctor does not fully understand all the powers involved in the
physical birth. But cooperating with all the knowledge that he
possesses, he is useful in the working of the genetical powers. In
like fashion one does not need to know the processes of God in
regeneration. But in faith yielding to them he can know the
fruits of same.

The Confused Pupil (3:9)

Still Nicodemus was puzzled. "How can these things be?" he
asked. Indeed, is not this the question which all must ask? We
are so preoccupied with mundane things that we cannot grasp
heavenly things. We are like those who can predict the weather,
but we cannot comprehend the mighty working of God within us
and around us.

The trouble with Nicodemus was that he was looking for
knowledge, when he should have been exercising faith. We can become so involved in asking questions that we do not find the
answers. Someone has said that we must be content to let God
know some things which we do not know. It was the great Hebrew
scholar, Doctor Harper, who asked why someone long before did
not tell him that he could exercise faith in Jesus, and find the
answers to his questions afterward. Nicodemus, like so many
others, was stalled on the *dead center* of spiritual ignorance. It was
his Teacher's role to swing him over to an intelligent faith.

The Patient Teacher (3:10-13)

Any teacher knows the need of patience in imparting truth for
dull minds. And each one who proposes to teach might well learn
a lesson from Jesus in this regard.

Our Lord expressed both sadness and astonishment in His reply
to Nicodemus' question. Literally, "You [*su*, note its emphatic

position, you of all people] are the teacher of the Israel, and these things you do not know?" The definite articles before "teacher" and "Israel" suggest his relation to his people. Some see this to mean a teacher among or of teachers. But the natural sense is that of one who is an accredited teacher among his people. In this sense *su* might also set Nicodemus over against Jesus as an unaccredited teacher. This unaccredited Teacher was teaching the accredited teacher of Israel things about which he had never heard. Robertson notes that "his Pharisaic theology had made him almost proof against spiritual apprehension. It was outside of his groove (rote, rut, rot, the three terrible r's of mere traditionalism)." If the teacher were so spiritually dense, what about his pupils?

Jesus continued, literally, "We are speaking that which we truly know [*oidamen*] and are bearing witness to that which we have actually seen [perfect tense of completion]; and ye are not receiving [plural verb, he and his group] our witness." In effect, Jesus said that what He was saying was not merely an academic matter. His witness was based upon a full comprehension of knowledge which had been proved in experience. Jesus had actually seen it with His own eyes. Others had been regenerated by the Spirit's power. Yet Nicodemus and the other Pharisees, on the basis of academics, were rejecting His eye witness testimony to the facts.

William Barclay tells of a former drunkard who had been born from above. In his presence someone questioned whether or not Jesus changed water into wine. He replied, "I don't know whether He turned water into wine when He was in Palestine, but I do know that in my own house and home He has turned beer into furniture!"

How many things in everyday life we accept by faith! Healing processes, the nourishment of food, the mysteries of electronics — to mention only a few. If most of us refused to experience these things until we understand them, few would ever do so. But we accept the mystery by faith, and are blessed thereby. In the Christian experience there are also mysteries which call for faith if they are to become real to us.

This is what Jesus was saying to Nicodemus. And if the pupil would not believe on the basis of earthly phenomena, how could he hope to believe the mighty workings of heaven (v. 12)? No mere man has ascended up into heaven to discover these things for himself. But Jesus has come down from heaven to reveal these things, "even the Son of man" (v. 13). "Son of man" was Jesus' favorite term of self-designation. "Which is in heaven" is not found in the best manuscripts. Jesus alone knows the mind of God. So to Nicodemus He says, as did the Father to Peter, James, and John, "Hear ye him" (Matt. 17:5).

The Lesson Personified (3:14-15)

Nicodemus had not grasped the truth embodied in the illustration of the wind. So Jesus tried again. If His pupil was not versed in natural phenomena, he was supposed to be a master in the Hebrew Scriptures. So the Teacher drew an analogy from them.

"And as Moses lifted up the serpent in the wilderness, even so must the Son of man be lifted up: that whosoever believeth in him should not perish, but have eternal life."*

Nicodemus, like every student of the Scriptures, could grasp this figure (cf. Num. 21:4-9). And for the first time there perhaps was a faint light of understanding in his eyes. The serpent part he understood. Could Jesus lead him to comprehend its application?

We have noted previously the meaning of the word "believeth" (*pisteuō*, cf. 2:23-24). But what about the term "eternal life?" This is one of John's key phrases, occurring sixteen times in John and six times in I John. Literally, it means "life of the ages" or "age-abiding life." It is that kind of life as opposed to temporal, physical life. Of course, it means spiritual life which abides in eternity. But is this all? Is it something that one will know only in heaven? Does it not also speak of the quality of life which a Christian possesses here and now? It is that state of being which may be described as *peace:* peace with God, oneself, other men, and other things. It is the positive answer to the question as to whether or not the entire universe is friendly. It is a right relationship with reality which enables one to *live all of his life here and now,* and to continue this life enhanced immeasurably unto the ages of the ages. This is what Jesus promises to all who look upon Him in true faith.

Note that Jesus says that the Son of man "must" (*dei,* a moral and spiritual necessity) "be lifted up." This latter verb is used in John to refer only to the cross (cf. 8:28; 12:32, 34). But in Acts (2:33; 5:31; cf. Phil. 2:9) it refers also to the Ascension. Barclay includes both as objects of faith. This is certainly true. But in John's Gospel the emphasis is upon the crucifixion.

---

*Some scholars see John 3:14-21 as John's comments and not as words of Jesus. We see them as Jesus' continuation of His lesson. There is no real reason to deny this.

In these verses Jesus seeks to lead Nicodemus from a quest after knowledge into an experience of faith. The Israelites were not saved from death by serpents' bites through an understanding of the material elements involved in the brazen serpent. They were saved through their faith in God's promise and power to perform. In like fashion we are saved from hell (perish), not through our full comprehension of the redeeming work of God in Christ. We are saved by grace through faith in His redeeming work as our Substitute. As with Israel and the serpent, so it is with us and the Son of man — faith.

The Lesson Applied (3:16-21)

Seeing the pale light of understanding in His pupil's eyes, Jesus sought to unveil to him the heart of the lesson which He had been teaching. The spiritual truth depicted in verses 14-15 He applied as He related it to God's purpose and His mission. The result is one of the sublimest passages in the Bible.

Why is it that those who believe in "the Son of man ... lifted up" shall have eternal life? "For God so loved the world, that he gave his only begotten Son, that whosoever believeth in him should not perish [aorist, utterly being lost in hell], but have [present, keep on having] everlasting life" (v. 16).

Who can enlarge upon this Gospel in a verse? It is called "Everybody's Text." As indeed it is. Robertson calls it the "Little Gospel." If the remainder of the Bible were lost and only this verse preserved, it contains enough gospel to save the whole human race! It tells us that God in love takes the initiative in salvation, that He saves through His Son, that this salvation is appropriated through faith in Him, and that those believing are saved to the uttermost of degree and time. And yet, probably fewer sermons are preached from this text than from any other of the more familiar ones. The reason being that when you quote it you have said it all. Explain it one may. But enlarge upon it one cannot. It is the gospel in superlatives.

It tells of the greatest reason for divine love (for), the original source of love (God), the greatest degree of love (so), the greatest emotion of love (loved), the greatest object of love (the world), the greatest relation of love (that), the greatest expression of love (he gave), the greatest gift of love (his only begotten Son), the greatest demand of love (that), the greatest recipients of love (whosoever), the greatest response to love (believeth in him), the greatest deliverance of love (should not perish), the greatest alternative of love (but), the greatest possession of love (have), the greatest quality and extent of love (everlasting), and the greatest fruit of love (life).

Then Jesus recapitulated this superlative truth in negative fashion (v. 17). God did not send His Son into the world to be its judge. The Christ does judge the world (cf. Matt. 25:31f.; John 5:27). But this was not His primary purpose in coming. He came first of all to be the Saviour of the world. His judgment is only upon those who reject His salvation. The one believing on Him "is not condemned" (v. 18). The word "condemned" is the same verb rendered "judge" in verse 17. The believer has already been judged in Christ "lifted up" on the cross. But the unbelievers have already been judged by their refusal to believe in the Son of God. The basis of their judgment is their refusal to believe in Him. And what is this judgment? That men, loving darkness (evil) better than light, would not come to Him who is Light (v. 19; cf. 1:4). Like vermin, the doers of evil hate the Light who reveals their evil in its true being (v. 20). Conversely, those who live according to truth that is in Christ welcome the Light (v. 21). They are happy for their godly deeds to be revealed. And thus Jesus ended the lesson.

Did Nicodemus understand it? The record does not say. But certainly he had been privileged to hear the greatest lesson from the greatest Teacher who ever taught. He probably had much home work to do (John 7:50 ff.). But at the end of the Session he graduated *Summa Cum Laude* (John 19:39 ff).

John 3:22-36

The Friend of the Bridegroom

Following the Passover Jesus and His disciples departed from Jerusalem. But for a time they remained in Judea (v. 22). During this time John says that Jesus "baptized." Literally, "was baptizing" (imperfect tense) or "baptized from time to time." The implication is that He won other followers, and as they believed in Him they were baptized. However, in John 4:2 the author states parenthetically that the baptizing was done by Jesus' disciples. This is the only reference to Jesus baptizing, even through others.

John introduced this section with his words *meta tauta*, "after these things." Of course, this phrase could refer back to the recent events in Jerusalem. But assuming John's designed use of the phrase, it is likely that he used it here to note that he is making contact with the Synoptic record (cf. Matt. 4:12; Mark 1:14; Luke 3:19-20; 4:14). Here mention is made of John the Baptist being put in prison, and that this fact prompted Jesus to return to Galilee. Since the Synoptics do not record the portions found in John about this recent Jerusalem ministry, it would appear that John the Baptist's imprisonment occurred shortly after Jesus' temptation in the wilderness. Luke's reference, coming before his report of Jesus' baptism, is, of course, merely inserted at that point to complete his present record of the Baptist. But John, by using the phrase *meta tauta*, shows that the Baptist's imprisonment actually came much later in Jesus' ministry. And that until that time he and Jesus had parallel ministries.

The Paralleled Ministry (3:22-25)

Mention has already been made of a possible group who still claimed to be disciples of John the Baptist, and who sought to elevate him above Jesus. This then would explain John's purpose in recording this portion of his Gospel. If we had only the Synoptic record it would appear that Jesus did not begin His ministry until after the Baptist was imprisoned. When actually

87

their ministries had run along side by side for at least many months. How great an interval intervened between Jesus' baptism and this first Passover is a matter of conjecture. But it certainly involved weeks and perhaps months.

In any case when Jesus departed from Jerusalem for a brief ministry in the rural areas of Judea, John the Baptist was still "baptizing in Aenon near to Salim" (v. 23). This location is not certain. There is a Salim east of Shechem, and a village called Ainun some seven miles to the northeast. The distance hardly fits John's description. Furthermore, it is in Samaria, an unlikely place for the Baptist to be preaching. On the other hand Eusebius and Jerome suggested a site in the Jordan valley west of the river about seven and one-half miles south of Beisan, the ancient Scythopolis. There are still many springs (seven) there located within a radius of a quarter of a mile of each other. This would fit John's language "much water there." This site was identified in the fourth century to a pilgrim named Aetheria as the location mentioned in verse 23. And this is in the general vicinity of the Baptist's ministry as recorded previously. In all probability this is the place.

So while Jesus was somewhere near this place preaching and baptizing (through His disciples), John the Baptist was still active in his ministry. And the people "kept on coming and from time to time were being baptized" (v. 23). These imperfect participles give a vivid picture of the many people coming to him, and as they accepted his message were baptized.

The author makes a pointed comment at this time. Literally, "For not yet was cast into prison John" (v. 24). Note the emphasis upon "not yet." Despite the impression which one might get from the accounts in Matthew and Mark, the Baptist's ministry continued alongside that of Jesus. One might ask as to why John would continue his ministry after he had baptized and identified Jesus as the Christ. This may have been one of the arguments advanced by John's later disciples with respect to his relation to Jesus. However, knowing that John always pointed away from himself to Jesus, it is reasonable to suppose that so long as people came to him he used his continuing ministry as a means of calling upon them to receive the Christ whom he was heralding.

It was at this time that there arose a dispute between some of the Baptist's disciples and "a Jew" (the correct text, not "Jews"). This dispute centered about "purifying," or the Jewish ceremonial washings of their bodies and eating utensils (cf. Heb. 6:2; Mark

7:4). The argument may have been about the relation of John's baptism to these rites. It appears also that in the dispute there arose a question as to the relation of John's baptism to that of Jesus. In either case this suggests busy parallel ministries of both Jesus and John.

The Alarm of John's Disciples (3:26)

Evidently John's disciples brought this problem to their teacher. At the same time they expressed alarm over the growing popularity of Jesus (cf. 4:1). "Rabbi, he that was with thee beyond Jordan, to whom thou barest witness, behold he baptizeth, and all . . . come to him." Does "with thee" mean that since John had baptized Jesus they considered Him only as one of John's disciples also? If so, their complaint bears even more weight. To them one of John's disciples was *hogging the show*. Their rabbi had baptized and witnessed to Jesus, and now He had a ministry of His own. Furthermore, "all are coming to him." Apparently John's ministry was on the wane, as more and more people gathered about Jesus instead of about John. Theirs was a jealousy of loyalty on behalf of their teacher. A mistaken loyalty, but a loyalty nevertheless. Evidently they recalled Jesus' baptism but failed to catch the significance of John's witness to Him. It is hard for one to see his cause waning while that of another is increasing.

The Answer of John (3:27-30)

Had John the Baptist been made of lesser stuff, he might have given a sympathetic ear to this report. He had faced this temptation before when the delegation from Jerusalem had come to him. This stalwart oak did not bend before the wind then; neither did he do so before that which blew within his inner circle.

His reply enhances him in the eyes of history. "A man can receive nothing, except it be given him from heaven" (v. 27). He bowed before the verdict of heaven. Heaven had given him a ministry and he had performed it faithfully. Now he steps back into the shadow of history. For Another has come to whom heaven has given a greater ministry. The fact that "all are coming to him" is not of man's but of heaven's design. "Be given" is a perfect passive subjunctive form of *didōmi*, I give. The subjunctive mode suggests a condition. The passive voice means that what is given is from another. The perfect tense connotes a finished work. The Baptist simply states a condition or possibility which evolves into a probability. In such case that which is given is from "heaven" or from God. It is a gift bestowed in the past, is still true, and will continue to be true. He is simply saying that from the beginning, even in eternity, it was given of God that what was then happening was to continue. John's ministry was not an end, but a means to an end. And that end was/is Jesus Christ and His ministry of redemption.

John then reminded his disciples of his previous witness to Jesus (cf. 1:19 ff.). He had said, "I am not the Christ, but that I am sent before him" (v. 28). He was before him in historical sequence but not in eternal being or in degree of greatness. Here again John emphasized the negative by placing "not" (ouk) at the beginning of his statement.

Why then should either John or his disciples complain? They might complain, but he is rejoicing. "He that hath the bride is the bridegroom: but the friend of the bridegroom, which standeth and heareth him, rejoiceth greatly because of the bridegroom's voice: this my joy therefore is fulfilled" (v. 29).

Jesus is the Bridegroom come to claim His bride (cf. Mark 2:19). Out of those coming to Him will come His bride. The duty of the "friend of the bridegroom" was to make the wedding arrangements, to prepare the way for the bridegroom to make possible the coming together in marriage of groom and bride. As he stands and hears the voice of the bridegroom coming to claim his bride, the "friend" rejoices greatly. His work is over. The purpose of his being has been realized. So he stands aside as "with joy he rejoices" to see the bridegroom claiming his bride.

This figure John uses to depict his relation to Jesus. Thus, "this my joy therefore is fulfilled." The perfect tense (is fulfilled) means that the cup of his joy is filled to the brim and running over. The voice of the Bridegroom may have grated on the ears of John's disciples. But to him it was heavenly music indeed.

What a lesson for everyone who seeks to serve Christ. His purpose is not to glorify himself, but Christ. Any spiritual movement built upon or about a man will fail even as he will. Only that which is built upon and about Christ will endure. For He is "the same yesterday, and to-day, and forever" (Heb. 13:8).

Finally, John made one of the greatest statements ever uttered by a man. "He must increase, but I must decrease" (v. 30). Literally, "It is morally and spiritually necessary he to go on increasing, but me to go on decreasing." The Synoptics later record John's confusion and question as to Jesus' Messiaship (Matt.

11:2 ff.; Luke 7:19 ff.) * But these words are the Fourth Gospel's closing record of John the Baptist's preaching (but cf. 10:40-42). Of John's words Westcott says, "the fulness of religious sacrifice and fitly close his work."

Thus from the Baptist's own lips this Gospel gives a final and complete answer to any who sought to carry on his work in competition with the Christian cause. And they challenge everyone who dares to speak for Christ. He must go on increasing, while we go on decreasing. To the preacher the poorest of compliments should be "What a great sermon *you* preached." And the greatest should be "What a great *Christ* you proclaim." The more of us men see, the less of Christ will they see. The less of us they see, the more of Christ will they see.

The Commentary of the Author (3:31-36)

Here unquestionably is a commentary by the author of this Gospel with respect to John's words as well as those of Jesus spoken earlier in this chapter. Truly the One sent from heaven is above all, including John the Baptist, "a man sent from God" (1:6). John was "of the earth;" Jesus is "from heaven" (v. 31). Jesus' message is a true witness or testimony. It is what He has seen and heard (v. 32). Yet men do not receive or believe His testimony. Even though crowds follow Him, He still knows their fickle nature. Only a few will truly trust Him and commit themselves to Him. But the one receiving Him puts his seal of approval upon the fact that God is true or that Jesus truly speaks God's message (v. 33).

Jesus continues to speak the words of God because God has bestowed His Spirit upon Him without limit of measure (v. 34). The Holy Spirit worked through John the Baptist. But not in the same sense or degree that He was in Jesus. In Jesus alone has God given the Holy Spirit in His fulness. For that reason Jesus can bestow the Spirit upon those who come to Him in faith (cf. 7:38 f.).

"The Father loveth the Son, and hath given all things into his hand" (v. 35). "The Son" is John's favorite designation of Jesus. And he says that out of love for the Son the Father not only gives Him the Spirit without measure; He also has given "all things" (*panta*, every single part of the universe, both natural and

---

*See my *Expositions* of Matthew and Luke for a discussion of this matter.

spiritual) into His hand both to possess and to rule. Marcus Dods comments, "God has made Christ His plenipotentiary for this world and has done so because of His love. It was a boon then to Christ to come into the world and win it to himself. There is no history, movement, or life of God so glorious as the history of God incarnate."

It is for this reason that "he that believeth on the Son hath [note the present tense, keeps on having] everlasting life: and he that believeth not on the Son shall not see life; but the wrath of God abideth [another present tense, keeps on abiding] on him" (v. 36). *Only* in the Son is there God's life; outside the Son there is God's wrath only.

The word for "wrath" is *orgē* (cf. Rom. 1:18). This word connotes God's abiding and universal opposition to sin. It appears only here in John. But it is found in Revelation six times. Altogether it is used thirty-six times in the New Testament (Matt. 3:7; Mark 3:5; Luke 3:7; 21:23; John 3:36; Rom. 1:18; 2:5, 8; 3:5; 4:15; 5:9; 9:22; 12:19; 13:4-5; Eph. 2:3; 4:31; 5:6; Col. 3:6, 8; I Thess. 1:10; 2:16; 5:9; I Tim. 2:8; Heb. 3:11; 4:3; James 1:19, 20; Rev. 6:16-17; 11:18; 14:10; 16:19; 19:15). It is found in Romans twelve times where it is contrasted with God's righteousness, or God's activity through Christ in declaring believers as justified before Him (cf. Rom. 1:16-18).

Another New Testament word rendered "wrath" is *thumos*. In contrast to *orgē* it means a sudden boiling up of God's wrath which soon subsides, such as the periodic eruption of a volcano. This word is not found in John; but out of eighteen times in the New Testament it appears ten times in Revelation (Luke 4:28; Acts 19:28; Rom. 2:8; II Cor. 12:20; Gal. 5:20; Eph. 4:31; Col. 3:8; Heb. 11:27; Rev. 12:12; 14:8, 10, 19; 15:1, 7; 16:1, 19; 18:3; 19:15). So the contrast is between a sudden outburst of God's punishing wrath on a given occasion (*thumos*) and God's abiding, universal opposition to all evil (*orgē*). John's one use of the word "wrath" is the latter.

Of interest is the fact that the word *orgē* is used by John the Baptist when he said to the Pharisees and Sadducees, "O generation of vipers, who hath warned you to flee from the wrath to come?" (Matt. 3:7). Could it be that John's only use of this word comes at the conclusion of his comments about the Baptist? It is a highly suggestive thought. If so, it is John's way of taking note of the Baptist's warning and of pointing to the Son as the only means of escape from the abiding, universal opposition of the Father to all evil.

John the Baptist's figure was that of God's *orgē* like a fire sweeping across the dry desert vegetation, with snakes and other desert creatures fleeing before it. Using *orgē* he says that this fire is everywhere and it will never be quenched. So where can you flee to find safety? Only where the fire has already burned. And where is that? At Calvary. There God's *orgē* was poured out without measure upon His Son. In Him were satisfied all of the demands of God's holy and righteous nature. And only there can the sinner find eternal security from God's abiding, universal opposition to his sin. So this security, this "life of the ages" *(zōēn aiōnion)* is only in "the Son." For upon those outside "the Son" this abiding, universal opposition of God to sin "keeps on abiding [keeps on being at home] upon him."

It is no wonder then that the Baptist kept on pointing away from himself to Jesus. It is understandable why this Gospel closes its record of the Baptist on this note. There is every reason why we should point away from self to Jesus. For salvation is not in us, in the Baptist, or in any other man. It is in the Son alone. Therefore, we must go on decreasing, but He must go on increasing. So be it, Lord!

John 4

The Master Soul-winner

Probably after several weeks of ministry in Judea, Jesus decided to return to Galilee. Combining the Synoptic accounts (Matt. 4:12; Mark 1:14) with that of John we learn the reasons for Jesus' decision. Word came to Him that Herod Antipas had arrested John the Baptist. Josephus says that he imprisoned him in his fortress of Machaerus east of the Dead Sea. This was a powerful fortification, one of the last to fall to the Romans in A.D. 70. Josephus also says that Herod Antipas imprisoned the Baptist because he feared that this popular preacher might start a revolution. This perhaps was the official reason given. But Mark, followed by Matthew, relates the true reason. It was because John the Baptist had preached against the· unlawful marriage of Herod Antipas to Herodias, his brother's wife (Mark 6:14 ff.; Matt. 4:1 ff.; cf. Luke 9:7-9). It was at Machaerus that later the Baptist was beheaded at the insistence of Herodias.

The Departure for Galilee (4:1-4)

The arrest of the Baptist would have been sufficient reason for Jesus to leave Judea. For already His ministry was linked in people's minds with that of the Baptist. And even though Galilee was still in the area ruled over by Antipas, it was wise that Jesus should stay as far away from him as possible. His "hour" was in God's hands, not Herod's.

However, John gives an additional reason for Jesus' departure (vv. 1-2). The Pharisees had heard of Jesus' growing popularity beyond that of the Baptist. They did not accept the latter's ministry. And their attitude would be no different concerning Jesus. Indeed, their clash with Him when He cleansed the temple had served to focus the religious leaders upon Him. And they looked with disfavor upon the success of His ministry.

So leaving Judea, Jesus set forth for Galilee. There is a diversity of opinion as to whether John 4:1 should read "Jesus," or "Lord." There is strong manuscript evidence for both, with the weight of evidence calling for "Lord." Bernard uses "Lord" *(ho kurios)* but suggests that the text here has been altered to suit the terminology applied to Jesus after His resurrection. However, Godet, Dods, Robertson, and Barclay use the reading "Lord" without serious question. It would seem that this is the correct reading.

"And he must needs go through Samaria" (v. 3). Whereas Galilee and Perea were under the jurisdiction of Herod Antipas, Samaria, along with Judea, was under Pontius Pilate. Both ruled under the Romans, Antipas as a tetrarch, the ruler of a fourth part of a kingdom, and Pilate as the Roman procurator.

However, the "must" in verse 4 has nothing to do with the fact that Pilate was over Samaria. At first glance, one notes that Samaria was on the most direct route between Judea and Galilee. But in view of John's use of "must" *(edei,* imperfect of *dei)* as expressing a moral and spiritual necessity, the geographical element hardly explains the necessity. Bernard explains John's use of *dei* as "Divine necessity," but does not so read it here.

Obviously John had some reason for the statement in verse 4. The Bible records an enmity between the Jews and Samaritans. Even between the northern and southern tribes of Israel often there was strong rivalry. This was enhanced into enmity when all of the tribes except Judah and Benjamin joined with Jeroboam I to form the northern Kingdom of Israel, as opposed to Judah and Benjamin as the southern kingdom of Judah under Rehoboam. At the time of the fall of Israel in 722 B.C. the Assyrians sent foreigners into the land to replace those Israelites deported to Assyria. These aliens intermarried with the remaining Israelites to produce the Samaritan people. Following the Jews' return from the Babylonian captivity, the Samaritans opposed the rebuilding of Jerusalem and the temple. In time they built their own temple on Mt. Gerizim. Also they had their own version of the Pentateuch, the five books of Moses. By the time of Jesus their temple had been destroyed. But the Samaritans continued to oppose the temple in Jerusalem, saying that on Mt. Gerizim was the true place of worship.

It is easy, therefore, to understand the estrangement between Jews and Samaritans. Strict Jews never went through Samaria, instead, they used the longer route from Judea to Galilee which led through Jericho to east of the Jordan, northward through Perea, and then back across the river into Galilee. Generally speaking the Samaritans did not object to Jews traveling northward from Judea. But they resented them traveling southward

toward Jerusalem and the Jewish temple. Josephus notes that
Jews on their way south toward the feasts were accustomed to
going through Samaria. But Jesus' experience on such a journey
(Luke 9:51-53) is reminiscent of the Samaritan attitude toward
such.

Even so, Jesus was going north away from Judea. So, other than
the fact that He did not share the prejudice of the stricter Jews,
this does not explain "must" in John 4:4. Though some do not see
it, there is the strong suggestion by the mystical John that Jesus
went through Samaria because of a "Divine necessity." And that
necessity becomes evident as the story unfolds.

The Scene of Action (4:5-6)

Journeying through Samaria Jesus and His disciples came to the
little town of Sychar (v. 5). John often uses the word "city" to
refer to small places. Sychar is usually identified with the modern
village of Askar, located not far from Jacob's well. From early
times this area has been associated with the patriarch Jacob (cf.
Gen. 33:18-19; 48:22). Furthermore, it was here that Joseph's
bones had been buried after having been brought out of Egypt by
the Israelites (Gen. 50:25-26; Exod. 13:19). So this section of
Samaria was filled with memories sacred to every Jewish heart.

A reminder of all this was Jacob's Well. Though there is no
specific record of it, perhaps Jacob himself had dug it (cf. v. 12).
At any rate it was a central watering place for this area. Indeed, one
may still drink fresh water out of this well. It is today the one
certain spot related to Jesus' ministry. It is located at a fork in the
road, one branch going northeast to Scythopolis and the other
northwest to Nablus and beyond.

When Jesus arrived at this well He was weary. "It was about
the sixth hour" (v. 6). Depending on whether or not one follows
strictly Jewish or Roman time in John, the hour was either noon
or six o'clock in the evening. Robertson holds to Roman time as
6:00 P.M. But as noted previously (1:39) this would be official
Roman time. The sixth hour would correspond to VI on the
Roman sun dial, which was noon. This also agrees with the
Jewish method of reckoning time.

Marcus Dods notes two evidences that the time was noon and not
6:00 P.M. First, there seems to be no preparation for night lodging.
The disciples had left Jesus at the well while they went into
Sychar to purchase food, probably for the noon meal (v. 8).

Second, had it been 6:00 P.M. there would have been many women at the well for water. The one woman, because of her reputation, probably came at this noon hour in order to avoid the other women.

So Jesus most likely arrived at Jacob's well about high noon, the hottest time of the day. Josephus describes Moses as sitting at the well *at midday* wearied by his journey, when Jethro's daughters came to draw water (cf. Exod. 2:17, note "stood up"). Thus Jesus, the Prophet spoken of by Moses, sat at another well *at midday* waiting for another rendezvous which was in God's purpose.

The Point of Contact (4:7-8)

This Samaritan woman came to draw water (v. 7). This was a woman's job then as it is now in Palestine. Near sunset the well would attract many women. But like Nicodemus' night visit in order to avoid publicity, so this woman came at noon to avoid the scorn and jibes of her more righteous kind. The similarity between these two people ends at that point. Otherwise they were at opposite poles of the ladder of society. Nicodemus was a cultured, powerful, and righteous *Jew*. This woman was an unknown and immoral *Samaritan* peasant. And yet Jesus had something for both of them.

Nicodemus came seeking spiritual food, and Jesus abruptly went to the heart of the matter. This woman had one aim, to fill her water jar and hasten home. So Jesus used the indirect approach on her. Only one thing did they have in common. Both wanted water. So Jesus said to her, "Give me to drink" (v. 7). Since evidently He and the woman were the only two people present (v. 8), she could not mistake that she was the one to whom the request was made.

So with this simple question the greatest example of personal soul-winning on record began. A volume could be written on this interview alone. At least in this work we can sketch the battle of wits and hearts which ensued.

The Answer of Prejudice (4:9)

Instead of granting Jesus' request the woman responded with a statement of surprise and scorn. "How is it that thou, being a Jew, askest drink of me, which am a woman of Samaria?" For the benefit of his Gentile readers John adds, "For the Jews have no

dealings with the Samaritans." Some manuscripts omit this explan-
atory word. However, the strongest manuscripts do have it. This
explanation is thoroughly in keeping with John's style. By the
word rendered, "have no dealings," we are not to understand
that they had none at all. For at the moment the disciples were in
Sychar purchasing food from a Samaritan. Jews were permitted to
trade with Samaritans, even with pagans. The point of John's
remark is that Jews and Samaritans did not mix socially. Godet
quotes one rule in this regard. "He who eats bread with a
Samaritan is as he who eats swine's flesh." Hence the woman's
surprise and scorn.

One can hardly imagine a more scornful or prejudiced question
than that which this woman asked. Let us translate it literally.
"How thou, being a Jew, from me asks to drink, being a woman of
Samaria?" Note that "thou" (su) has the emphatic position. It
immediately sets Him off from her. Furthermore, she sets "Jew"
over against "Samaritan." And we may well imagine that she spoke
the word "Jew" with scorn. How did she know that He was a
Jew? Evidently by slight differences in facial features, dress, and
accent. Edersheim points out that "the fringes on the Tallith of the
Samaritans are blue, while those worn by Jews are white." Still
further, here was a strange man talking to a strange woman. And
He was a Rabbi. The strict Rabbis forbade a rabbi even to speak
to his own wife, daughter, or sister in public. And yet Jesus spoke
to this strange woman. His request to drink evidently meant for
His lips to touch the container where Samaritan lips had once
drunk. This a Jew would never do, so thought the woman.

Thus we may read her question as full of prejudice: a woman
against a man, a woman against a Rabbi, a Samaritan against a
Jew. Her prejudice involved sex, social position, race, nationality,
and religion.

John, therefore, has drawn this picture with consumate skill.
He reports the facts, undoubtedly related to him by Jesus Himself. But his artistry is no less evident. Barclay notes that this is a
story full of surprises. The divine Son of God tired and thirsty.
The holy Son of God conversing with a woman of low moral
character. Here was Jesus, a Jew, crashing through the barriers
which separated Him from the rest of the world. Yet He did it.
And in so doing He demonstrated the universal nature of the
gospel. He showed God's love for all men, even for a fallen woman.

The Arousing of Interest (4:10-15)

Jesus did not upbraid this poor woman for her attitude. Neither did He seek to deal directly with it. He would not be drawn into a dispute over the problem which she personified. Rather He sought to deal with the cause, not the symptoms. She could never find a right relationship with other people, even with herself until she found a right relationship with God. Only as she had *life* could she have a right attitude toward life.

He had asked her for a gift of a drink of water. So He said that if she knew the gift of God, and the One asking her for water, she would ask Him, and from Him receive living water (v. 10). But, like Nicodemus, she misunderstood the meaning of Jesus' words. As he thought of *anōthen* in terms of a second natural birth, she thought of the water in Jacob's well. Since He had no rope or water skin, how could He draw water from the well (v. 11)? Note that here she addressed Jesus as "sir." The Greek word is *kurios* which may mean owner, lord, Lord, or sir. At this point she was not prepared to call Him "Lord." But at least "sir" was a title of respect. In part, then, Jesus had broken through her wall of scorn.

What did the term "living water" connote in that day? It was used of water found in a flowing stream, or, in the sense of a well, water which came from an underground flowing spring or fountain. Actually Jacob's well did not have "living water." It came from the seepage of rain water down through the ground. So, in effect, Jesus was speaking of "water" in contrast to that found in this well. And, of course, He spoke of the water of life which God would give through Him. In the Old Testament Jehovah is called the Fountain of living water (Ps. 36:9).

But the woman thought only of the water in Jacob's well. If Jesus could not even draw water from this well, how did He propose to provide living water? Even "our father Jacob" provided water from this well. Did Jesus claim to be greater than Jacob (v. 12)? Here then was a note of local pride. For the Samaritans claimed to be descendents of Joseph through Ephraim and Manasseh. There is a hint that she tried to draw Jesus into a discussion of tribal differences.

But He would not be dissuaded from His purpose. He went right on with the contrast between the water in Jacob's well and the "living water" of God. "Whosoever drinketh of this water shall thirst again" (v. 13). Literally, "each one drinking," even Jacob himself. How well this woman knew this, of which her repeated trips to the well reminded her. But by contrast each one who "may drink" of the water which Jesus offers "shall never thirst" (v. 14). Here Jesus used the double negative *(ou mē)* which in Greek makes the strongest possible negative. He "shall not never thirst." This living water will be a perpetual quencher of thirst. For this water "shall be in him a well of water springing [leaping] up into everlasting life" (v. 14). It will be a living fountain inside him, one giving eternal life. Of course, Jesus was speaking of water for the soul.

What a flood of ideas Jesus' words contained, a flood flowing out of the Old Testament Scriptures (cf. Isa. 49:10; 55:1; Jer. 2:13; 17:13; Zech. 13:1)! Isaiah 35:1-7 pictures the Messianic age as one in which "the wilderness and the solitary place shall be glad for them; and the desert shall rejoice, and blossom as a rose . . . and the parched ground shall become a pool, and the thirsty land springs of water." So, in effect, Jesus is presenting Himself as the Messiah.

But this poor woman evidently was not up on her Bible. Or else she was so chained to her material existence that she could not see spiritual truth. Her spiritual density is evidenced by her reply. "Sir, give me this water, that I thirst not, neither come hither to draw" (v. 15; cf. 6:34). All that she saw in Jesus' glorious offer was freedom from natural thirst and from the daily chore of this long trip to the well. Barclay sees her reply as a jest. To her Jesus must have seemed a bit out of His mind. All this talk about "living water" and an eternal quenching of thirst. Surely the noon-day sun was too much for Him. Quoting Barclay, she merely sought to humor Him. "She was jesting with a kind of humoring contempt about eternal things."

So she was even thirstier than she realized. In every man there is a thirst after God. "As the hart panteth after the water brooks, so panteth my soul after thee, O God. My soul thirsteth for God, for the living God" (Ps. 42:1-2). And yet no one is thirstier than he who does not realize it. In the very presence of Him who said, "If any man thirst, let him come unto me, and drink" (John 7:37), she prattled about her little jar of seepage. But is she any worse than those today who fret and toil for both food and drink which perish with the using, all the while ignoring Him who is not only nourishment but Life itself?

The Moves and Counter-moves (4:16-26)

"Enough of this!" said Jesus, "Let us get to the heart of your trouble." So He said, "Go, call thy husband, and come hither" (v. 16). Her trouble was not water, water jars, and daily trips to the well. Neither was it basically her racial and religious prejudice. It was her immoral life, her sin. As indeed it is that which separates every man from "the living water." Perhaps she herself was not aware of this. We can become so accustomed to our sins that they do not shock us anymore. At least we can *brass* it through in a given situation if we think that those about us are unaware of them. It was for these reasons that Jesus plunged His scalpel into this pus-pocket in her life.

One may well imagine that she was set back by His words. She stiffened as if to ward off a blow. For Jesus had struck at her Achilles heel. Perhaps, like David before Nathan, she was suddenly brought to face her sinful life. Feelings of shame and remorse long dormant suddenly came to life again. Not only did she know herself again, but she felt that somehow Jesus knew.

But still she tried to *brass it through.* "I have no husband," said she (v. 17). Maybe Jesus did not really know but was just fishing. Perhaps her denial of being married would end the unpleasant subject. So she thought. However, like a surgeon who has found the diseased organ, like a fighter who has found his opponent's weakness, Jesus moved in on her problem. "Thou hast well said, I have no husband. For thou hast had five husbands; and he whom thou now hast is not thy husband" (vv. 17-18). Not only had she been married five times, but she was now living with a man outside of wedlock.

The revelation of this sordid truth should have brought her to her knees in tears of repentance. But not so. Oh, she recognized Jesus as a "prophet" (v. 19). For how else could this stranger have known so much about her? Note the progress that Jesus was making with her. Her scorn had given place to interest, and now to respect. A prophet indeed! But to what use did she put this acknowledgment? She used it for an evasive tactic to get away from her personal life into a religious argument.

"Our fathers worshipped in this mountain; and ye say, that in Jerusalem is the place where men ought to worship" (v. 20). This was a dispute of long standing. Evidently she pointed toward Mt. Gerizim which towered above Jacob's well. It was just opposite Mt. Ebal (cf. Deut. 27:4 ff.). In the words of Barclay, the Samaritans had rewritten history to substantiate their religious differences with the Jews. They claimed that it was on Mt. Gerizim that Abraham had almost sacrificed Isaac, an event which actually occurred on Mt. Moriah at Jerusalem. According to them it was here that Melchizedek had met Abraham (Gen. 14:18-20), and that Moses upon entering the promised land (!) had erected an altar on Mt. Gerizim. Actually the altar was erected on Mt. Ebal (Deut. 27:4). Sanballat had built a temple here to rival the one in Jerusalem. It was destroyed by John Hyrcanus in 129 B.C. Note the words "our fathers worshipped" (v. 20). The past tense evidently took note of this destruction. However, the Samaritans continued to worship there, even as they do today.

Barclay sees the woman's question as being sincere. According to him she was repentant and wanted to offer a sacrifice for forgiveness. And she wanted this "prophet" to tell her where she should make it. Where could she find God? However, it seems more natural to see it either as an honest inquiry after a solution to this dispute; or else it was simply an effort to avoid further discussion about her life. The latter seems to be the case.

And once again Jesus ignored her *move*. Instead of being trapped on either horn of this debate He made a *counter-move*. He brushed aside this matter of worship-localities in order to go to the heart of the matter.

"Woman, believe me, the hour cometh, when ye shall neither in this mountain, nor yet in Jerusalem, worship the Father" (v. 21).

Already the temple on Gerizim was destroyed. In a little over forty years the one in Jerusalem will lie in ruins. What then? But Jesus said even more. He said that the worship of God is not to be tied to a given place. The time is coming when men shall worship God everywhere. It will be a time when the true spiritual nature of worship will be known. This knowledge will cause the rivalry under discussion to disappear. Already the prophets had forseen such a day (Zeph. 2:11; Mal. 1:11). In truth that day is being ushered in by Jesus Himself.

Furthermore, the main point is not the locality but the Object of worship. Jesus said that the Samaritans did not really *know* (oidate) God (v. 22). They had a knowledge of Him. But since they accepted as Scripture ónly the five books of Moses, they did not know the exalted concept of Jehovah as presented in the prophets. The Jews do have this *knowledge (oidamen)*. And however wrong may have been their present practices in worship, "salvation is of [ek] the Jews...." Ek means out of. Of course, this does not mean that only Jews will be saved. It means that it is through the Jews, not the Samaritans, that God has given His redemptive will and purpose. Not only is "the salvation" (he sōtēria) or the Messianic deliverance out of the Jewish nation, ho sōtērios, "the One bringing salvation," is out of Judah. Amos 9:8 speaks of the northern kingdom of Israel as a "sinful [unlawful] kingdom." This kingdom was founded in rebellion. Its history was one of rebellion against God. But inherent in the term "unlawful" is the thought that God's redemptive purpose ran through Judah, not through Israel. The Samaritans were the outgrowth of this "unlawful" kingdom, and their rebellion against Jehovah's purpose continued.

Jesus continued by saying that the hour had come when true worship of the Father will not be determined by geography but by the spirit and the element of worship (v .23). For worship to be real it must be spiritual, and so, true. For, literally, "God is Spirit, and the ones worshipping in spirit and truth it is necessary to worship" (v. 24). Both Jews and Samaritans thought of God as Spirit. But never before had the idea been stated so succinctly. Pneuma ho Theos. "God is Spirit" even as "God is love" (I John 4:8). And no one can truly worship God except in a spiritual experience.

Commenting on this thought Bernard says, "The pneuma is the highest in man, for it associates him with God who is Spirit.... To worship en pneumati is, then, to worship in harmony with the Divine Spirit, and so to worship in truth" (in loco; cf. John 16:13).

The woman made one last vain attempt to digress. But even this shows a much subdued nature. "I know that Messias cometh, which is called Christ: when he is come, he will tell us all things" (v. 25). Both Jews and Samaritans held that the Messiah would reveal new things about God. Certainly Jesus had revealed to her new things about His nature and worship. One can see in her remarks possibly two things. She was beginning to suspect that Jesus was the Christ, but she, like so many lost people, hesitated to take the plunge into faith. So her words may be taken as a faint effort to delay such a confession. However, she was now ripe for the plucking. Therefore, Jesus, knowing this, said, "I that speak unto thee am he" (v. 26). "I am, the one speaking to you" (cf. John 9:35-37). Since the term "Messiah" carried a nationalistic connotation to His contemporaries, Jesus avoided it in public address. But here in the privacy of the well He made this declaration to her.

Note that "I am" renders *Egō eimi*. Here the pronoun is written out plus being present in the verb. So it is emphatic. "I, and no one else, am." *Eimi* expresses essential, eternal being (cf. John 1:1). It was used to express the very being of Jehovah. Therefore, in this statement of Jesus one may see, not only His claim to Messiahship, but also His claim to deity.

The interview was interrupted at this point by the return of the disciples (v. 27). They were surprised to find that Jesus "was talking with a woman." The absence of the definite article means that they were not surprised that He was talking with *this* woman but to *any* woman in public. Lightfoot quotes a rabbinical precept, "Let no one talk with a woman in the street, no, not with his own wife." Since the disciples regarded Jesus as a rabbi, they felt that He was acting beneath the dignity of His position. But even though they thought it, out of respect for Him they made no mention of it.

The Timid Confession (4:28-30)

The woman used this interruption as an opportunity to leave the well (v. 28). So excited was she that she even left her waterpot. Hastily "she went into the city." The aorist verb form shows the speed with which she went. She actually ran into the city. She left the waterpot behind also because it would have impeded her progress. The pot was not filled, and to have done so would have taken time. Furthermore, Barclay is right when he suggests that she not one time entertained the idea that she was not coming back to the well where Jesus was.

Arriving in the village she saw "the men," and said, "Come, see a man, which told me all things that ever I did: is not this the Christ?" (v. 29). In her excitement she may have exaggerated as to what Jesus had told her. Or did she simply mean that He had revealed the life she had been living? This latter may also have determined the manner in which she phrased her words, "Is not this the Christ?" She did not use *ouk*, not. She used *mēti*. Usually this participle is left untranslated. It is not as strong a negative as *ouk*. It was used in questions which expect a negative answer. Where the questioner is in doubt, or wishes to appear so, it carries the idea of "perhaps." "Is this, perhaps, the Christ?"

Apparently she is almost sure of it. But lest these men deride her, she timidly put her question.

However, she got the desired response. For "they went out [aorist] of the city, and came [imperfect, were coming] to him" (v. 30). She ran into the city, and they ran back with her. There was excitement in Sychar that day!

The Concern of Jesus (4:31-38)

In the meantime while they were coming, Jesus' disciples "prayed" (imperfect, kept begging) Him to eat (v. 31). But He replied that He had already had a sumptuous meal, which they could not understand (v. 32). They evidenced their ignorance by asking among themselves as to whether some other "man" had fed Him (v. 33). Not a *man* but a *woman!* And she herself was not even aware of it. She had fed His soul as in His efforts to win her He had been doing His Father's will, which to Him was meat indeed (v. 34). He was finishing, bringing to a desired end, His Father's work insofar as this one woman was concerned. And this experience whetted His appetite, not for the meat which the disciples had brought, but for that which this one experience suggested.

"Say not ye, There are yet four months, and then cometh the harvest?" Was Jesus speaking of the actual time interval before the grain harvest would begin? If so, this would mean that it was then late January or early February. However, this hardly fits the context. For that would mean that this event occurred during the cool, rainy season when water would be available everywhere, not simply at this well. In all likelihood Jesus was citing a rural proverb. "Say" is a present tense. "Are ye not in the habit of saying that there are yet four months, and then the harvest comes?"

This might be true in the natural order. But the spiritual harvest does not wait upon such. Rather Jesus said to the disciples, "Lift up your eyes, and look on the fields; for they are white already to harvest" (v. 35). And the one who reaps will receive his reward (v. 36). He is gathering fruit unto life eternal, not the reaper's life but that of those who are reaped. In this both the sower and the reaper will rejoice. Both the sower and the reaper are necessary for the harvest (v. 37). Then Jesus said, "I sent you to reap that whereon ye bestowed no labor: other men labored, and ye are entered into their labor" (v. 38). The "other men" refer to all who previously had proclaimed God's message: e.g., the prophets, John the Baptist, the Samaritan woman. In the specific sense this refers to the Samaritans. The fact that they held a Messianic hope is due to previous laborers among them. Now Jesus Himself has reaped one soul as the result of the sowing of others. Soon others will be forthcoming. But in a sense Jesus has sown seed here which will later be reaped by Philip and others. So the larger harvest in Samaria is yet to come. And these disciples will live to see it. Yea, Peter and John will be at least two reapers from among this present group (Acts 8:14-17, 25).

The Reaping of the Harvest (4:39-42)

In fact, there was an immediate harvest in Sychar because of the seed sown by the Samaritan woman (v. 39). For about that time the group arrived from the village. They asked insistently, or repeatedly (imperfect tense of "besought"), for Jesus to remain in their village (v. 40). So He interrupted His return journey to Galilee for two days. During that time many more believed on Him because of His own witness (v. 41). For they said to the woman, "Now we believe, not because of thy saying: for we have heard Him ourselves" (v. 42). The woman had sown seed in their curiosity. She had done what she could. And now on the basis of Jesus' teaching they too believed on Him. The most unlikely of persons, like this woman, can share with others their experience with Christ. And He will bless their efforts. We are not told to be successful but faithful. We can leave the results with Him.

Having heard Jesus for themselves the men said, We "know truly [*oidamen*] that this is indeed the Christ, the Saviour of the world" (v. 42). (We have noted repeatedly the use of the verb *oida*. *Ginōskō* usually means to know by experience, such as seeing, hearing, or any other experience. *Oida* means to perceive experiential knowledge until it becomes a conviction of the soul, so, soul-knowledge.) It was this which these men had. They had heard (experiential knowledge) both the woman and Jesus. Now this has become soul-knowledge. They are convinced beyond doubt that Jesus is the Christ.

Furthermore, they are convinced that He is the Saviour, not of Jews and Samaritans alone, but of the whole world. Here then is once again the universal note in John's Gospel. It is a fitting note upon which to end this experience of Jesus. It is little wonder that "he must needs go through Samaria."

The Second Sign (4:43-54)

After two days Jesus and the disciples departed for Galilee (v. 43). Here John inserts a note which connects his account with that of the Synoptic Gospels. "For Jesus himself testified, that a prophet hath no honor in his own country" (v. 44; cf. Luke 4:24; see also Matt. 13:57; Mark 6:4). In this way John also takes note of the entire Galilean ministry, although, with one exception, he does not record it (v. 45).

This exception is the healing of the son of "a certain nobleman" of Capernaum. This man is called a *basilikos,* one connected with the king. Probably he was an officer of Herod Antipas stationed in Capernaum.

When he heard that Jesus was in Cana (v. 46) he *went* and *besought* Him to come to Capernaum and heal his son who was at the point of death. The former italicized word is an aorist, the latter is an imperfect. He went immediately and kept on asking, or asked strongly. At first Jesus regrets that "except ye see signs [*sēmeia*] and wonders [*terata,* note this added word for Jesus' miracles, only time in John], ye will not believe" (v. 48). This suggests Jesus' regret that in Galilee He is thought of only as a miracle worker. Nevertheless, in response to the man's plea (v. 49), Jesus told him to return home, that his son lives (v. 50). The man believed Jesus' word. Without any further plea he returned home. On the way his servants met him to tell him that his son was alive (v. 51). Upon inquiry he learned that his son's fever had left him the day before at the very hour that Jesus had said "Thy son liveth" (vv. 52-53). It is understandable that this resulted in faith in Jesus by the nobleman and his entire household.

John notes that this was the second "sign" which Jesus had performed in Galilee (v. 54). There will be many more. But this one John points out as a further evidence of Jesus' deity.

III
The Basis of Controversy

John 5

The Battle Joined

Some scholars place Chapter 5 after Chapter 6*. The reason being that Chapter 4 ends with Jesus in Galilee, and Chapter 7 begins with Him in Galilee. They hold that Chapter 6 should follow Chapter 4. However, there seems to be no real basis for such a position. There is no reason why Jesus could not have gone to Jerusalem sometime during His Galilean ministry. In fact, the words "after this" (meta touto, 5:1) and "after these things" (meta tauta) suggest that at these points John is fitting his account into the Synoptic Gospels which were certainly known to him and apparently to his readers.

The "Year of Obscurity" is over. Jesus now plunged into a busy ministry in Galilee, one that is characterized by a growing popularity with the people and by an increasing opposition by the religious leaders from Jerusalem. Indeed, we can hardly understand the latter without taking note of John's report of a visit to Jerusalem during the Galilean ministry. For it was during this visit that matters really came to a head between Jesus and the Pharisees (cf. Matt. 12:22-37).

John 5-11 shows clearly how this antagonism of the Jews toward Jesus developed. It is seen especially in Chapters 5, 7-11 with the climax coming over His raising of Lazarus from the dead. So, in truth Chapter 5 may be titled "The Battle Joined."

The Second Visit to Jerusalem (5:1)

Without the familiar Johannine "after this" (meta touto) we would be at a loss to understand the continuity between 4:54 and 5:1. For in the former verse John reports Jesus' arrival from Judea into Galilee. And then in the latter verse he takes Him right back to Jerusalem. But following Robertson's *A Harmony of the Gospels* we see that a considerable portion, probably six

---

*E.g. Bernard. Barclay leans to this position. But he treats the chapters as they appear in this Gospel.

months, of the Galilean ministry transpired between these verses. Certainly it involved several months, depending upon the time of year that Jesus arrived back in Galilee. Allowing for time for Jesus' Judean ministry following John 3, this arrival could have been in late Summer or early Fall of A.D. 27. This period, except for the healing of the nobleman's son (John 4:46 ff.) is recorded only in the Synoptic Gospels.

With his phrase "after this" (5:1) John serves notice that he is about to insert an event not found in the other Gospels. Therefore, after several months in Galilee Jesus returned to Jerusalem. Note that He "went up to Jerusalem." Though He went south He went up. This is another topographical note which suggests that the author was from Galilee.

At Jerusalem "there was a feast of the Jews" (v. 1). What feast was this? Various ones have had their champions: Dedication, Tabernacles, Purim, Pentecost, and Passover.* Dedication was one of the lesser feasts. Jesus did attend one of these (John 10:22) since at the time He was near Jerusalem. But He probably would not have traveled from Galilee to do so. While Pentecost is possible, it would be difficult to fit it into Jesus' known schedule. Purim would seem to be out of the picture. It was never observed on the Sabbath (cf. 5:9). Tabernacles usually was observed at one's place of residence (cf. Matt. 17:4). That Jesus went to Jerusalem for one such feast may be explained by the fact that He had missed the previous Passover (cf. John 6:4; 7:2). So this leaves only the Passover. This was the principal Jewish festival. And it is understandable why Jesus would interrupt a busy Galilean ministry in order to go to Jerusalem for this feast. In all likelihood, therefore, this was a Passover. Such a feast would allow time for Jesus' activities after the first Passover in John 2 and before the one in John 6. This also accounts for the six months between Passover in John 6:4 and Tabernacles in John 7:2.

The determination of this feast is important to the length of Jesus' ministry. If it were some other feast it would mean that His public ministry lasted only about two and one-half years. If it is a Passover then an additional year is seen. To hold that this was a Passover fits the chronology better.

---

*For a discussion of this see Robertson's *A Harmony of the Gospels,* pp. 267 ff.

So we conclude that this feast was the second Passover in Jesus' ministry. It would come in the Spring of A.D. 28.

The Healing of a Lame Man (5:2-9)

"Now there was at Jerusalem by the sheep market a pool, which is called in the Hebrew tongue Bethesda having five porches" (v. 2). The meaning of "Bethesda" is "house of mercy."*

The identity of this pool has been the subject of differing opinions. Through the years various pools have been suggested (e.g., Siloam, Virgin's Fountain). Yet each presented difficulties when related to John's account. But in 1888 a pool was discovered in the area mentioned by John. It was found that the Crusaders had built a church over it, showing that they regarded it as a sacred site. It is located near the "sheep gate" mentioned in Nehemiah (3:1, 32; 12:39). Actually the Greek text of John reads "by the sheep" or, "by the pertaining to sheep." The word "gate" must be supplied. It was located near the "sheep gate" not the "sheep market." "Market" (KJV) is supplied by the translators.

Furthermore, John says that this pool had "five porches," a covered colonnaded area about the pool. Excavation of this area is now in progress. It reveals two parallel pools, maybe one each for men and women, with porches along each side and one between the pools. There can be little question but that this is the pool of John 5:2.

This is important not only for the interpretation of the text. It also furnishes powerful evidence that the writer was a Palestinian Jew familiar with Jerusalem prior to its destruction in A.D. 70. The author, though living in Ephesus, knew of this pool and its exact location during the ministry of Jesus. It is difficult to visualize the author other than as one who had been present when the event of this narrative took place.

The pool itself was fed by a spring which flowed intermittently, causing the water to be troubled. Jewish belief was that an angel disturbed the water, and the first sick person to get into the pool thereafter was healed. However, it should be noted that verse 4 is not found in the best manuscripts. It was probably added by some copyist to explain verse 7. At any rate this belief

---

*Some manuscripts read "Bethzatha" or "Bethsaida."

serves to explain the presence of many sick people about the pool (v. 3).

One such man was there who had been infirm, evidently a cripple, for thirty-eight years (v. 5). As Jesus passed by He saw him lying on a pallet. Either by His own supernatural knowledge or from hearsay He knew that the man had been there for a long time. Probably friends brought him there and left him. Seeing him Jesus asked, "Do you wish to be made whole?" The man replied by telling Him that when the water was troubled others beat him into the pool, since he had no one to help him (v. 7). Jesus responded by commanding him, "Rise, take up thy bed, and walk" (v. 8). He told him immediately to pick up (aorist) his pallet, and to go on walking (present). "And immediately the man was made whole, and took up his bed, and walked" (v. 9). The word "immediately" with the aorist tenses ("was made," *egeneto,* became; *ēre,* took up) adds double emphasis to the miraculous healing. The imperfect tense *(periepatei,* went on walking) adds to the vivid nature of the picture.

Why the man so responded to Jesus' words is not explained. He evidently did not know who Jesus was (vv. 11, 13). But something in Jesus' look or in the tone of His voice caused the man to respond. And as he did so he found strength in his limbs.

John adds the ominous note that "on the same day was the sabbath" (v. 9)

The Sabbath Issue (5:10-16)

John's note is not without meaning. For this was the first time in Jerusalem that Jesus had violated the Jewish law concerning the Sabbath.

In order fully to understand this note and that which follows it is necessary to consider the place of the Sabbath in the Jewish theological system. Four things were basic in Judaism: the Law, or Scriptures, the Temple, the traditions, and the Sabbath. Other religions had the first three. Only the Sabbath was peculiar to the Jewish religion. So this was an especially tender spot to the Jews. Already Jesus had claimed authority over the temple. Later He will do the same with regard to the Law (Matt. 5:21 ff.). He has disregarded their traditions (Matt. 9:14-17; 15:1-20; Mark 2:18-22; 7:1-23; Luke 5:33-39). He will also claim Lordship over the Sabbath (Matt. 12:8; Mark 2:28; Luke 6:5). This He will do on His return journey to Galilee (cf. Mark 2:23-28). Only in the light of John 5 can we comprehend these Synoptic passages about the Sabbath.

A further word needs to be said about Sabbath observance. The Fourth Commandment simply said that men should keep the Sabbath day holy, and should refrain from labor on that day. However, the Jews had devised literally hundreds of regulations designed to define labor. For instance, a Sabbath-day's journey was limited to a little less than three-fourths of a mile. Debates were held over whether one should eat an egg laid on the Sabbath. Dragging a stick on the ground on the Sabbath was forbidden. That was plowing. A woman was forbidden on that day to look in a mirror. She might see a gray hair and pull it out. That was shearing. Problems such as the following were posed. Just at sunset on Friday, the beginning of the Sabbath, a man gets off his donkey. Should he take off the saddle? If so, he was working. Should he leave it on the donkey? If so, the donkey worked. Plucking a head of grain on the Sabbath was forbidden (cf. Luke 6:1-2). Rubbing out the grain was threshing. Blowing away the chaff was winnowing. Learned (?) debates were held as to whether one with a sore throat could treat it with oil on the Sabbath. The conclusion was that he might drink oil for food. If in the process it helped his sore throat, that was purely incidental. One can understand why Jesus would ignore such foolish rules. Never did He violate the Fourth Commandment. But He had no patience with these man-made regulations.

Of course, the Jews held that it was illegal for one to carry a burden on the Sabbath. So when the Jewish leaders saw this man carrying his pallet they said, "It is not lawful for thee to carry thy bed" (v. 10). This probably happened in the temple area some distance away. They did not yet know about the miracle. In response the man said that He who healed him told him to do this (v. 11). But when they asked the identity of the healer he could not tell them. For Jesus had slipped away in the crowd (vv. 12-13). Later Jesus found the man in the temple area and said to him, "Behold, thou art made whole: sin no more, lest a worse thing come unto thee" (v. 14). Why Jesus said this is not clear. The man's lameness may have been the result of sin. Or in his healed condition he might be more prone to submit to temptation.

Even so, the man now knew the identity of his Benefactor. And, strange to say, he immediately *went* and *told* the Jews that it was Jesus who had healed him (v. 15, both italicized words are aorists). Why did he do this? Was it out of ignorance as to the consequences for Jesus? Apparently the man knew that the Jewish penalty for breaking the Sabbath was death by stoning. It would appear, therefore, that he deliberately told the Jewish leaders in order to escape this dire fate.

The Jews could not have cared less that this poor man had been healed. But they were enraged that Jesus had done it on the Sabbath. "Therefore did the Jews persecute Jesus, and sought to slay him, because he had done these things on the sabbath day" (v. 16).

The word "persecute" is an imperfect form. They "began and continued to persecute Jesus." Since His cleansing of the temple, they had had it in for Him. But they had no particular grounds upon which to oppose Him. Word probably had come to them that Jesus had healed on the Sabbath in Capernaum (Mark 1: 21-28). But that was hearsay evidence, and from the country-bumpkins of Galilee. However, now He had healed on the Sabbath right there in Jerusalem. They had the evidence. Thus they had an issue. And they played it to the hilt. Henceforth they will watch Him, and on this issue dog His footsteps (cf. Matt. 12:1-8; Mark 2:23-28; Luke 6:1-5). So the Sabbath controversy is on, and it will rage more and more.

The Answer of Jesus (5:17-30)

In reply to their charge Jesus said, "My Father worketh hitherto, and I work" (v. 17). Literally, "My Father keeps on working even until now, and I keep on working." The Sabbath marked God's rest from His creative work. But He continues to work in His providential and redemptive activity even on the Sabbath. And Jesus does the same.

This statement enraged the Jews all the more, so much so that they "sought" (imperfect, kept on seeking) to stone Him (v. 18). Not only had He broken the Sabbath, but by calling God His Father, He had made Himself "equal with God." In their sight not only was Jesus a Sabbath-breaker; He was also a blasphemer. It is no wonder that they kept on seeking all the more to kill Him.

However, Jesus stood His ground. He answered their charge forthwith. As "the Son" He does nothing of Himself, only that which He sees the Father doing (v. 19). The Son in healing this man was acting within the will and work of the Father. So intimate is the love of the Father for the Son that He shows to the Son all of His work (v. 20). But if these Jews have wondered about this act of healing, they will see through the Son even greater works of the Father. They will even see the Son raise the dead in the Father's power (v. 21; cf. John 11).

These Jews were sitting in judgment upon Jesus. But He told them that even the Father does not directly judge any man (v. 22). This judgment He has committed unto His Son (v. 22). They thought to judge Jesus, when all the while He was their judge. For this reason they and all others should honor the Son (v. 23). To dishonor the Son is to dishonor the Father. These Jews so honored Jehovah that they would not even pronounce His name. Yet they were holding the Son up to scorn, even trying to kill Him.

Obviously they were not heeding Jesus' words. Therefore, to them He spoke some of His greatest words concerning the plan of salvation. Note their solemnity. "Verily, verily, I say unto you, He that heareth my word, and believeth on him that sent me, hath everlasting life, and shall not come into condemnation; but is passed from death unto life" (v. 24). Note that every verb in this verse save the last is a present tense. Even "shall not come" is a present tense with a future effect. Those hearing and believing do not come to the "judgment." Already they have been judged in Christ. And such an one "has passed out of death into life." "Has passed" is a perfect indicative form. It expresses the certainty of a completed act. If these words are words of assurance to every believer, they were words of condemnation for these Jews who stood looking at Jesus with venom in their eyes.

Then He added other solemn words. "The hour is coming, and now is, when the dead shall hear the voice of the Son of God: and they that hear shall live" (v. 25). Note that here Jesus uses "the Son of God." Thus He adds emphasis to His relation as "the Son." Here He is not speaking of a future resurrection. "The hour ... now is." He is speaking of the present resurrection from the death of sin (cf. Eph. 2:1) to the new life which He gives. Those who hear His voice now — shall live. "For as the Father hath life in himself; so hath he given to the Son to have life in himself" (v. 26). This is not only the life which is resident in Deity, but that which Deity imparts to those who will receive it. Furthermore, the Father has given to the Son the authority to execute judgment upon all unbelievers (v. 27). This is "because He is the Son of man."

The Son of God, the Son of man.

In Jesus are mysteriously combined these two natures. It is in Him that God and man meet in reconciliation (cf. I Tim. 2:5). By the same token, since Jesus partakes of man's nature, apart from sin, He is competent to judge man because of his sin. Paul in Romans 3:26 says that in Jesus God is both "just, and the justifier of him which believeth in Jesus." By living a perfect life in the flesh, He justified God in His penalty upon man for sin. On the cross He made possible man's justification before God. But it is only for "him which believeth in Jesus." Thus the Son is qualified to execute judgment because He is the Son of man.

Jesus literally heaped a mountain of truth before His Jewish adversaries. And its peak is seen in verses 28-29. For He points to the time when at His voice the graves will be opened. And all who are in the graves will come forth. "They that have done good, unto the resurrection of life; and they that have done evil, unto the resurrection of damnation" or "judgment." And Jesus will be the Judge. In John *doing good* and *doing evil* are synonymous with believing on Jesus or not believing upon Him respectively. Note here that Jesus speaks of only one final resurrection, but with different results.

However, Jesus points out that He will execute judgment in the Father's name (v. 30). The judgment of these Jewish leaders is unjust. But that of Jesus will be just. Because it will be in perfect harmony with the Father's will.

The Fivefold Witness (5:31-38)

After using the third person with reference to the Son, Jesus now returns to the first person. This does not mean that He and the Son are not the same. Beginning with verse 17 the identity is evident. However, for the sake of His audience, the Jews, He returns to the first person. For whatever they may think of His foregoing words, He has something more to say to them.

"If I bear witness of myself, my witness is not true" (v. 31). He does not mean that He is bearing false witness. The meaning is clear in the Greek text. Emphatically He says, "If I alone, I witness of myself with no corroborating witnesses, then my witness is not true" or acceptable. In both Jewish, Greek, and Roman law one's witness by itself is not admissable evidence. Deuteronomy

19:15 says that one witness alone is insufficient evidence of wrong-doing. "At the mouth of two witnesses, or at the mouth of three witnesses, shall the matter be established." In His statement, there-fore, Jesus is simply bowing to the rabbinical demand for wit-nesses outside Himself as to His true nature. He anticipates this demand in the minds of His critics.

The law called for not more than three corroborating wit-nesses. But Jesus went the law two better, as He proceeded to call *five* witnesses to prove that His words were true.

First, there is the witness of the Father (v. 32). He did not mention the Father's name. But the word "another" points to Him. This means another of the same kind *(allos)*. Jesus had already spoken of the unity of the Father and Son. This can refer to none other than God. In verse 37 His name is mentioned as the One sending Jesus and also bearing witness concerning Him. This He did specifically at Jesus' baptism (Matt. 3:17). But the primary reference here is God's witness in the hearts of believers. Since these Jewish leaders did not believe in Jesus, they have neither heard God's voice nor seen His form (vv. 37-38). The verbs "heard" and "seen" are perfect forms. They speak of the permanent state of spiritual deafness and blindness in these people. They claimed to be the official interpreters of God and His Word. Yet they were in ignorance of both. Therefore, they did not receive the Father's witness about the Son.

Second, there is the witness of John the Baptist (vv. 33-35). He had borne witness concerning Jesus, even to the delegation sent from the Sanhedrin (1:26-27; cf. 1:29 ff.). However, He added that He is not relying solely on the witness of a man (v. 34). He includes John the Baptist for their benefit, not His. It is to the end that if they should believe upon Him on the basis of the Baptist's testimony they would be saved.

In verses 33-34 there is a sharp contrast of persons. This is seen in the pronouns "ye" and "I." In both instances the pro-noun is written out (plus being in the verb form) and is in the emphatic position. "Ye, on the one hand, sent to John; but I, on the other hand, do not depend upon his testimony about me." Even so, they did not believe John's witness, neither did they believe Jesus or the Father.

Third, there is the witness of Jesus' works (v. 36). Greater than the witness of John whom they had heard is the witness of Jesus' works which they had seen. His various "signs" up to this point were evidences of His deity. Even greater "signs" are yet to come.

Yet they have rejected and will continue to reject them. Jesus had never done anything except something good. But none is so blind as those who will not to see.

Fourth, there is the witness of the Scriptures (vv. 39-44). These Jewish leaders, probably Pharisees in this case, claimed to be experts in the Scriptures. To study them was their very life. Said Jesus, "Search the scriptures; for in them ye think that ye have eternal life" (v. 39). "Search" may be either a present imperative or a present indicative. Either makes sense here. But the context seems to favor the indicative mode. Jesus does not command them to search the Scriptures. They were already doing that. "Ye keep on searching [make it a habit of life] the scriptures because ye think in them to have eternal life." The word "think" [*dokeo*] in John, Bernard says, always indicates a mistaken opinion (cf. 5:45; 11:13, 31; 13:29; 20:15). The Jews had the mistaken opinion that they had eternal life simply because they made it a practice of studying the Scriptures. However, they were blind to their message. They were familiar with the Messianic Scriptures. But while they testified of Jesus as the Christ, these would not come to Him for life (v. 40).

The fact that they did not give glory (*doxan,* honor) to Him does not bother Jesus except for what they are doing to themselves (v. 41). He "fully knows" (perfect tense) them. They do not truly love God, and therefore do not love Him (v. 42). Even though He has come in His Father's name they reject Him (v. 43). The irony is that when false messiahs appear they always find a following. But these will not follow the true Messiah. They are so intent upon personal glory that they are oblivious to the glory of God (v. 44). This is a sad picture of the sterile condition of Judaism and its teachers.

Fifth, there is the witness of Moses (vv. 45-47). Jesus has repeatedly spoken of judgment. In the judgment He will not be the one who "will accuse" them before the Father (v. 45). The word for "accuse" is *kategoreō*. It means to bring a public accusation as in a court. Jesus will not bring such an accusation against them. "The one bringing an accusation against you is Moses, in whom you have set your hope." The Jews' hope of salvation centered in Moses. Yet he is the very one who will condemn them. The Mosaic writings are often cited as speaking of Christ (cf. Deut. 18:18 f.; Acts 3:22; 6:14, 7:37; see also John 3:14; 8:56). Others found Him in the Mosaic books. But the Jewish rulers did not. Therefore, Jesus accuses them of not even

believing Moses. Else they would have believed in Him (v. 46).
So if they do not even believe Moses' writings, how shall they
believe the words of Jesus (v. 47)?

Thus Jesus assembled a formidable corps of witnesses. These
men might deny Jesus' words and His relation to the Father.
They did not accept John the Baptist as a prophet. They were
zealous after the Scriptures, but only in a rote, mechanical way.
And they set their hope in Moses. But their spiritual blindness
made it impossible to understand his writings properly. The overall
meaning of the citing of these witnesses was not only to substantiate Jesus' claims, but to show that their rejection of Him was
a compounded sin against knowledge.

John does not record any answer which they gave to Jesus'
words. In all probability they had none. But they refused to be
convinced. They had an issue against Jesus in the Sabbath question. And they will pursue it to the end. It will be a battle unto
death, Jesus' death intermediately but theirs eternally.

IV

The Climax and Collapse
of the Galilean Ministry

John 6

The Nature of the Christ

John makes no mention of Jesus' return to Galilee. By comparing his Gospel with the Synoptics we know of this return. On the way back and shortly after His arrival in Capernaum they note two additional controversies about the Sabbath (Matt. 12:1-14; Mark 2:23—3:6; Luke 6:1-11). It would appear that a group of Pharisees went along from Jerusalem for the express purpose of checking on Jesus' further Sabbath-breaking.

Assuming that the feast in John 5:1 was a Passover, a year transpires between John 5 and 6. This was the latter half of the Galilean ministry, a ministry which involved in all about eighteen months. This latter half was characterized by Jesus' growing popularity among the Galilean people and an increasing hostility on the part of the Jewish religious leaders. During this time John the Baptist was beheaded, and Herod Antipas had come to think of Jesus as the Baptist come to life again.

It was at the end of this period that Jesus began a series of four withdrawals from Galilee. This series lasted for about six months from Passover to Tabernacles in A.D. 29. During this time He and the Twelve apostles* went respectively eastward across the sea of Galilee, northwestward to the Mediterranean coast, eastward to an area east of the sea of Galilee, and thence northward to the area about Caesarea-Philippi. Five reasons account for these withdrawals. Jesus wished to stay out of the area ruled by Herod Antipas, to escape the hostility of the Jewish rulers, to get away from the fanatical crowds, to have privacy in which to teach the Twelve, and to rest away from the hot summer about the sea of Galilee.

Only one year remained before the arrival of Jesus' "hour." So the major burden of His teaching in this time was to instruct the Twelve as to the true nature of the Christ.

---

*About the middle of the Galilean ministry Jesus chose twelve men as apostles, including the original six (Mark 3:13-19; Luke 6:12-15).

The Feeding of the Multitudes (6:1-13)

John begins Chapter 6 with the familiar phrase *meta tauta,* "after these things." We have seen the interval of time between Chapters 5 and 6. Therefore, we are not to understand "after these things" as referring to the previous events. in Jerusalem. John is simply saying that once more he is making contact with the Synoptic record. In so doing he joins with them in relating the feeding of the five thousand. While John has made such contacts before, this is the one and only time that he parallels them in a story prior to the last week in Jerusalem (Matt. 14: 13-21; Mark 6:30-44; Luke 9:10-17; John 6:1-13). Two reasons prompted John to do this. This feeding of the multitude marked the turning point of Jesus' popularity with the people of Galilee. And John relates the miracle in order to record additional material which clearly shows His rejection by the Galileans.

On His first withdrawal Jesus crossed the sea of Galilee (v. 1). John adds that it was the sea "of Tiberias." This he did evidently for the benefit of His Gentile readers. In A.D. 22 Herod Antipas had built his capital city of Tiberias on the western shore of the lake. Actually the sea of Galilee is a large inland lake. It is shaped like a pear, and is thirteen miles long, and seven miles wide at its broadest point. It lies 780 feet below sea level. East of the lake was the Decapolis, a region which took its name from ten Greek cities in the area.

Even though it was the time of the Passover (v. 4) Jesus did not go to Jerusalem. He was not yet ready again to challenge His opponents in their stronghold. So for the reasons stated above He took His little band and crossed the sea to the area near Bethsaida Julias (Luke 9:10). This city was in the tetrarchy of Herod Philip. He had added "Julias" to distinguish it from Bethsaida near Capernaum (Mark 6:45). Matthew and Mark note that they went to a deserted area. Though the place was thickly populated, Jesus led His apostles to an area where they might be alone.

But such was not to be. For a great multitude from Galilee followed them (v. 2). From the level of the lake Jesus and the Twelve had gone up into the high hills beyond (v. 3). But when He saw the crowd of people approaching, He said to Philip, "Whence shall we buy bread, that these may eat?" (v. 5). It probably was now past the middle of the afternoon, and the people, failing to bring provisions, had not eaten since breakfast. The Synoptics relate that this condition was first mentioned to Jesus by the Twelve. They suggested that Jesus should send them away to the farms and villages that they might purchase food. Instead, Jesus told them to feed them. They protested that they could not provide so much food. It is at this point that John takes up the story.

Perhaps in reply to the Twelve's suggestion Jesus asked Philip, "Whence shall we buy bread, that these may eat?" (v. 5). But John notes that He asked this to test Philip, knowing all the while what would be necessary to feed this crowd (v. 6). Philip replied that "two hundred pennyworth" *(denarii)* would not buy enough food for each to have even a little (v. 7). A *denarion* was worth about seventeen cents. So Philip was talking about thirty-four dollars, a sum hardly available from the meager treasury of Jesus and the Twelve. (Of course, this money had a much greater purchasing power than it would have today.)

Evidently Jesus told His band to look around to see what food they could find. So Andrew came with the report, "There is a lad here, which hath five barley loaves, and two small fishes: but what are they among so many?" (vv. 8-9). Barley cakes and dried or pickled fish about the size of sardines were the food of the poor. Perhaps this lad's mother had prepared them for his lunch. Someone remarked that there were two miracles that day: Jesus' and the fact that this late in the day the boy had not eaten his lunch.

Even so, Andrew, true to his nature, brought someone to Jesus. This time it was a small boy with a meager lunch. Obviously this would not last long with these hungry people.

But Andrew did not reckon with the power of Jesus. For He told them to have "the men" sit down (v. 10). John says nothing about "women and children" (Matt. 14:21), though we may think of "men" generically. But John makes an on-the-spot mention that there was much green grass there (cf. Mark 6:39). This would be true at this season. Luke notes that Jesus caused the people to sit in groups of about fifty each. Note Jesus' use of organization. Mark is more picturesque. For literally he says that they sat down "garden beds" (6:40). In their multicolored robes the groups looked like blooming garden beds among the grass. John, like the others, notes that there were five thousand men in the group.

Jesus then took the food, and having given thanks He gave it to the Twelve, who, in turn, distributed it among the people

(v. 11). After all had eaten their fill, Jesus told the Twelve to gather that which remained (v. 12). This was uneaten food, not scraps. And they gathered twelve baskets full (v. 13). The Jews had a custom of saving some food for those who served. So apparently each of these had observed this custom, each one not eating quite all that was given to him.

The type basket used was called a *cophinos*. This would be one for each of the Twelve. They had served, and so got the leftovers. Roberston comments with wry wit, "What about the lad?" Or, Jesus, for that matter? These baskets are of interest. Wherever a Jew went he carried his basket. Juvenal, a Roman writer, speaks of "the Jew with his basket and his truss of hay." When a Jew traveled, the hay was for his bed and the basket was for food so that he would not need to buy from a Gentile. So whether or not the Twelve had their hay, they had their baskets. And they came in for good use.

The Abortive Attempt at Revolution (6:14-15)

When the people saw this "sign" of Jesus they said, "This is of a truth that prophet which should come into the world" (v. 14). This obviously is a reference to Deuteronomy 18:15. There Moses had spoken of a prophet who should come after him. "The Lord thy God will raise up unto thee a Prophet from the midst of thee, of thy brethren, like unto me; unto him ye shall hearken." The Jews had come to relate this Prophet to the Messiah.

Therefore, these people reasoned. Jesus was certainly a prophet, as was evidenced by His "signs" and teachings. He was a Galilean, so He was "in the midst of thee." And He was a Jew, "of thy brethren." Furthermore, this "sign" showed that He was "like unto me," like Moses who had fed the Israelites with manna and quail. And that did it! Here was the prophet promised by Moses. Here was the Messiah!

Since they thought of the Messiah as a political-military leader who would lead them in the overthrow of the Romans, they tried to take Jesus by force and make Him their king (v. 15). With Him as their military leader they would need no commissary. He could feed an army with a few cakes and fish. There would be no need for a medical corps. He could heal their wounds. Neither would they need a recruiting force. If one soldier were killed, He would restore him to life and to battle.

Of course, had they succeeded in their purpose, it would have brought the wrath of Rome down upon them. And Jesus, instead of dying for the sin of the world, would have died in a futile fight or as a criminal on a cross. Or else He would have become a hunted man as so many messianic pretenders had done. The whole thing was contrary to God's purpose and to Jesus' Messianic nature as the Suffering Servant of Jehovah. So He put an end to it.

John records only that Jesus "departed again into a mountain himself alone" (v. 15). From the Synoptics we know that He first sent the Twelve away and then dismissed the crowd (Matt. 14:22-23; Mark 6:45-46). The fact that He first sent the disciples away allows two possible interpretations. Some see in this Jesus' desire to get them out of this revolutionary atmosphere lest they be affected by it. The other and more plausible position is that they themselves were the cause of this abortive attempt at revolution. Jesus' veiled reference to Judas the next day (vv. 70-71) suggests that he may have been at the bottom of the entire thing. If this be a correct surmise then Jesus had to send the Twelve away before He could control the crowd. Afterward, He slipped away to pray.

And well He might pray. For the whole affair showed how far the apostles and the people were from understanding His nature and mission. There remained much teaching to be done, a task to which He set Himself in the coming months.

The Miracle at Sea (6:16-21)

By the time that the Twelve embarked it was late evening (v. 16). They started across toward Capernaum without Jesus (v. 17). The sea "was rising" (imperfect) because of a strong wind (v. 18). The perfect tense of "rowed" indicates that it was hard rowing in the wind and waves (v. 19). About halfway across the lake they saw Jesus walking toward them on the water. Naturally they became afraid. John has abbreviated the account since it was more fully related by Matthew and Mark. But his story fits well into theirs. Seeing their fear Jesus said, "It is I; be not afraid" (v. 20) or "stop being afraid." Hearing His voice they willingly received Him into the boat. "And immediately the ship was at the land whither they went" (v. 21). This does not mean that magically they were suddenly at land. This wording takes account of the Synoptic report of Jesus' miraculous stilling of the storm (cf. Matt. 14:32). With the quiet sea the rowing was easier. And shortly they reached the port.

The Carnal Crowd (6:22-34)

The next morning the crowd, seeing that Jesus had departed, returned to Capernaum seeking Him (vv. 22-24). They found Him in the synagogue (vv. 25, 59). In response to their inquiry as to when He returned, Jesus said, "Ye seek me, not because ye saw the miracles [signs], but because ye did eat of the loaves, and were filled" (v. 26). The words "were filled" render a verb *(chortazō)* used to express the idea of feeding cattle. One reference uses it in the sense of a cow eating her food, filling her stomach, yet never saying "thanks" or asking whence the food came or for what purpose it was given. It is used in the sense of being gorged (cf. Rev. 19:21). The crowd had gorged itself and nothing more. They sought Jesus on this morning simply because it was feeding time again. Like so many today they thought more of their stomachs than they did of their souls.

Seeing this, Jesus said, "Labor not [stop laboring] for the meat which perisheth" (v. 27). In so short a time they had gone from being gorged to being hungry again. Truly that *meat* perished. Rather they should work for that meat which abides unto eternal life. The Father had set His seal on the Son as the one to give such food.

Hearing the word "labor" the people immediately thought of works for salvation (v. 28). This was in keeping with current Jewish theology. To their question as to what "works of God" they should do, Jesus said, "This is the work of God, that ye believe on him whom he hath sent." Westcott says, "This simple formula contains the complete solution of the relation of faith and works." "Works?" the people asked. Jesus replied, "Not works, but faith." This should forever settle the question. But, alas, it has not!

One can hardly believe his ears as he hears the people ask Jesus for a "sign" in order that they may believe (v. 30). They had seen many of His signs (cf. Matt. 14:14). Apparently the impression of the sign of the cakes and fishes perished with the food they ate. They were ready yesterday to acclaim Him a greater than Moses. But now they threw Moses in His face. "Our fathers did eat manna in the desert; as it is written, He gave them bread from heaven to eat" (v. 31). Whence did they think the food of yesterday came? Is not this a subtle suggestion that Moses had fed their fathers each morning? So now Jesus should do the same.

Jesus agreed to the miracle through Moses. But it was a miracle of physical food which perished with the using, as did the food the day before. Now the Lord seeks to lead them to see the truth of the true, living bread from heaven which gives spiritual life (zōē) to the world (vv. 32-33). Chrysostom long ago noted that the manna gave nourishment (trophē) but not life (zōē). This entire discussion turns on the Jewish expectation of a greater Moses. But so wedded were they to Moses that they could not see Him of whom Moses wrote.

If one thinks that Jesus has gotten through to them he is in for disappointment. For like the Samaritan woman's desire for water, they said, "Lord [or did they merely mean "Sir?"], evermore give us this bread" (v. 34). They would welcome a perpetual supply of bread such as their fathers had enjoyed under Moses. But their carnal natures prevented them from comprehending the true sense of Jesus' words.

The Bread of Life (6:35-40)

So Jesus plainly said, "I am the bread of life: he that cometh to me shall never hunger; and he that believeth on me shall never thirst" (v. 35). Here He used two strong double negatives. "Shall not never hunger . . . shall not never thirst." He could not have made it any stronger. Hunger and thirst are the two most demanding of physical needs. Jesus transfers them to the spiritual sphere, and promises the complete, abiding satisfaction of both. Unhappily, however, they, having seen Him, do not believe in Him (v. 36).

Still Jesus made another effort. "All that the Father giveth me shall come to me; and him that cometh to me I will in no wise cast out" (v. 37). Here again He used the strong double negative. "I not never cast out." He came from heaven to do only the Father's will (v. 38). And the Father's will is "that of all which he hath given me I should lose nothing, but should raise it up again at the last day" (v. 39).

Does the idea of "all which he hath given me" teach that some are elected to salvation to the exclusion of all others? If so, it contradicts the vast body of teachings throughout the New Testament and ignores the Biblical teaching of the free will of man. In Ephesians 1 we find Paul's great teaching on election. The sum and substance of it is that God in His sovereignty has *elected* a plan of salvation "in Christ." All who are in Him shall be saved. All others will be lost. In eleven verses Paul uses the equivalent of "in Christ" ten times. Man is still free to accept or reject God's sovereign offer. But he is responsible for his choice.

It would seem, therefore, what Jesus said is that in His sovereign will God has taken the initiative in salvation. But still the ultimate choice lies in the free will of man. And all who receive the Son "may have everlasting life" (v. 40). Though they may die physically, they will live on spiritually. For the Son will raise them up at the last day.

Physical bread may sustain life. But it cannot give life. Jesus, the living Bread, both gives and sustains life.

The Flesh and the Spirit (6:41-65)

Regardless of whether or not these people would ever accept Jesus other than as a doer of signs, it is quite evident that they caught the import of His words. He definitely claimed to be the Son of God and the "Son of man" (v. 27), both of which involved Messianic claims. As living bread He also claimed that He came down from heaven.

So, "the Jews murmured at him" (v. 41). The word "murmured" renders *egogguzon,* the very sound of which was like the buzzing of angry bees. Note that John calls them "Jews." Of course, the Galileans were Jews. But there seems to be in this use something more than that. Habitually John uses this term to refer to the Jewish rulers in Jerusalem who were in opposition to Jesus. Does he mean there that some of them were present? This is possible. However, verse 42 suggests that they were Galileans. Heretofore they have been enthusiastic for Jesus. But here they show a different attitude. It would seem, therefore, that John simply means that these Galileans are now speaking and acting like the Jews in Jerusalem. They clearly are doubting His claims concerning Himself.

For they said, "Is not this Jesus, the son of Joseph, whose father and mother we know? how is it then that he saith, I came down from heaven" (v. 42)?

He was calling God His Father. Yet insofar as they knew, mistakenly, of course, Joseph, the carpenter of Nazareth, was His father. Some of them may have been from Nazareth, knew His mother, and had known Joseph before his death. They spoke so wisely after the flesh. But how little they knew after the spirit.

Hearing their buzzing Jesus said, "Stop murmuring among yourselves" (v. 43). And then He resumed His line of teaching. Repeating the thoughts just spoken (vv. 44-47; cf. vv. 37-40) He reiterated His claim, "I am the bread of life" (v. 48). "I am" expresses essential, eternal being. And the "I" is written out, so it is emphatic. "I and no one else am always essentially the bread of life." The Israelites ate physical manna in the wilderness. But ultimately they died physically (v. 49). On the other hand if one eats this bread from heaven, he will never die (v. 50). Jesus summarized by repeating His claim to being that bread which, if one eats it, shall live forever (v. 51). Then He adds a new note. "The bread that I will give is my flesh, which I will give for the life of the world."

Still speaking like "Jews" the people "strove among themselves," saying, "How can this man give us flesh to eat" (v. 52)? "Strove" means to fight a civil war with either weapons or words. "This man" actually is "this one." In contempt they did not refer to Him by name as they did in verse 42. Note also that "his" is not in the best manuscripts. While it may be understood here, this could also have another meaning. They had been talking about manna and bread. Now Jesus likens this bread to His flesh. Remembering the quail which the Israelites ate in the wilderness, this may be the point of their question. How can this fellow do as Moses did in giving our fathers flesh to eat?

To remove any doubt in their minds as to what He meant, Jesus said, "Except ye eat the flesh of the Son of man, and drink his blood, ye have no life in you," or "in yourselves" (v. 53). But the one eating and drinking His flesh and blood has eternal life. For these are "meat" and "drink" indeed (vv. 54-55). The one so eating and drinking knows intimate communion with Christ (v. 56). The Son lives in the Father who sent Him; those who are in this communion with the Son shall live "by" (*dia*, through) Him (v. 57). For in contrast to the manna which sustained only physical life, He is the true heavenly Bread who both gives and sustains spiritual life eternally (v. 58).

Since John does not record the actual institution of the Lord's Supper, some see this passage as his reference to it. They, therefore, see the elements of the Supper in a purely physical sense as having saving grace. This is to make the same error as these Galileans made, to see Jesus' reference as pertaining to actual flesh and blood. However, that was in neither Jesus' mind nor in the thinking of John. Jesus is simply using physical terms to express the spiritual truth of the intimate relationship between Him and those who believe in Him.

That this is their true meaning is seen in that which follows. "Many therefore of his disciples [pupils, not true believers], when they heard this, said, 'This is an hard saying, who can hear it?' " (v. 60). To them this sounded like cannibalism. In reply Jesus adding the thought of His ascension back into heaven, said that the flesh profiteth nothing; it is the spirit which makes one alive (vv. 61-62). "The words that I [emphatic, I as opposed to others] speak unto you, are spirit and life" (v. 63). Seeing that His hearers are offended by His words, Jesus tells them to look behind the physical symbols to the spiritual meaning which He is teaching. However, He knows that some present will not believe in Him, and, therefore, will never know the true meaning of His words (v. 64). At this point John anticipates a further word by noting that Jesus knew who would betray Him.

The Lord closed this session by repeating that God takes the initiative in offering salvation. But only those who respond favorably will ever know it by experience (v. 65).

The Great Defection (6:66)

"From that time many of his disciples went back, and walked no more with him." Literally, "Out of this," or "out of this circumstance" the Galilean crowds forsook Jesus. They were never true believers. They saw Jesus only as a worker of signs. So recently they were ready to make Him their Messiah, but in a role far removed from His true nature. Jesus had refused the role. Furthermore, they would have accepted Him as a *Bread Messiah*. When He showed them that He would have none of that either, they left Him. He would not be the kind of Christ that they wanted. They would not receive Him as the Christ He was. So the result was inevitable. "They turned back, and walked no more with him."

Never again will the Galilean crowds flock to Him. Luke 9:51 — 18:14 shows that afterward for a time the people of Judea did flock about Him. But in the end all will forsake Him. In truth this event in Capernaum was the beginning of the end. That is why John recorded it. But not until the time of the end will he join bodily with the Synoptic record. Even then he includes in his account vital material not found in the other Gospels.

The Loyal Nucleus (6:67-69)

As Jesus saw the crowds stalk out of the synagogue (vv. 59, 66) He turned to the Twelve. Apparently they also were restless. Like all others they gauged success by numbers. Later they will caution Jesus not to offend (cf. Matt. 15:12). So now, perhaps with dismay, they looked upon the backs of the departing congregation.

Suddenly they were brought back to reality by a question from Jesus. "Will ye also go away?" (v. 67). How this question must have probed them! Only Jesus and the Twelve remain. So little out of so much work! Indeed, it would have been so easy to have joined the crowd, to have returned to their nets, to their accustomed place, or to whatever had been their calling prior to Jesus' call.

And yet, would it have been easy? If they went away from Jesus, where and to whom would they go? Having turned their backs on the past, He was all that they had. And despite their present misgivings, they still felt strangely drawn to Him as the source of their very beings.

So Peter, always ready with an answer, spoke for his fellow-disciples. "Lord, to whom shall we go? thou hast the words of eternal life. And we believe and are sure that thou art the Christ, the Son of the living God" (vv. 68-69; cf. Matt. 16:16). Actually the best manuscripts read "thou art the Holy One of God." But it carries the same idea. Some would make this John's report of Peter's words in Matthew 16:16. However, there is no reason to think so. The conditions are entirely different. There is no reason why Peter could not have made both confessions. Certainly the situation here makes it altogether appropriate, even as is true of Matthew 16:16.

Peter put his answer in the strongest possible words. For "believe" and "are sure" are both perfect indicative forms. "Of a certainty we have come to believe and still believe, we have come to know and still know that thou art the Holy One of God." They did not understand all that was happening. But they had had an experience with Jesus. And that experience anchored them in the storm.

The Incipient Infamy (6:70-71)

But there was one who was not anchored, and for whom Peter did not speak. Jesus knew this. So He asked, "Have not I chosen you twelve, and one of you is a devil? (v. 70). Note that he *is* one *now*. He *was* *not* one when he was chosen. John notes in retrospect that He spoke of Judas Iscariot who "should betray him" (v. 71).

This brings up the knotty question as to why Jesus, after a night of prayer, chose Judas as one of the Twelve. More consideration will be given to this at a later point (cf. 12:1-8). Suffice to say presently that in Judas, as in the other eleven, Jesus saw qualities which if dedicated to Him would make him a valuable member of the group. But Judas, unlike the others, did not give himself to Jesus. The only one from Judea, he evidently was even more possessed by the concept of a political-military Messiah. He had been severely shaken by the events of these two days. If he was the instigator of the abortive revolutionary effort, Jesus' subsequent actions had been a rebuke to him. His words in the synagogue that day had further disturbed Judas. He now saw clearly that he was mistaken in his initial idea about Jesus (cf. v. 64). Therefore, he was beginning to have second thoughts. He must reappraise the situation, and plan a new course of action. It will be a year before he will make his fatal decision. But the devil has found a likely tool in him.

Jesus also had been reassessing Judas. Probably observing his actions during these two days, He saw the seeds of betrayal beginning to work. So without calling his name, He sought to warn him against such. It is not too late for Judas to change. But Jesus cannot alter His own course as a spiritual Messiah. This is His true nature. Men will either have to accept or reject Him as such. The eleven, while still confused as to His Messianic nature (cf. Matt. 16:21-23), will go on fully to know. But Judas, never. If this was the beginning of the end for Jesus, it was also true of Judas.

V
The Rising Controversy
in Jerusalem

The Continuing Conflict (I)

With his familiar phrase "after these things" *(meta tauta)* John takes note of the fact that he is about to relate further material not found in the Synoptic Gospels (v. 1). However, here he adds an additional word about the intervening period. "Jesus walked in Galilee: for he would not walk in Jewry ["Judea" in best manuscripts], because the Jews sought to kill him." The imperfect tenses of "walked," "would," and "sought" speak of continuing action. He "kept on walking in Galilee: for he kept on not willing to walk in Judea, because the Jews kept on seeking to kill him." The period covered in this sentence is about six months from Passover to Tabernacles in A.D. 29. This was the time during which Jesus continued His series of withdrawals.

At the close of this period Luke says that Jesus left Galilee for Jerusalem (9:51). Thereafter through 18:14 he records a Judean and Perean ministry not related elsewhere. He does not, however, tell of Jesus actually being in Jerusalem until His arrival for the last week which ended in the crucifixion.

It is to John that we are indebted for this ministry. It covers a period from Tabernacles to Dedication. The period between these feasts evidently includes a Judean ministry of which we have no record. Unless, of course, a portion of Luke's Judean ministry belongs here. In his *Harmony* Robertson places this after the feast of Dedication, and so after John's account of the Jerusalem ministry.

John's extended record of this Jerusalem ministry is marked by the continuing conflict between Jesus and the Jewish rulers. The Pharisees had stayed close on His heels throughout the Galilean ministry. And their opposition grew in hatred and violence. At one time they were joined by the Herodians, a political party bent upon restoring the House of Herod to rule in Judea (Mark 3:6). Ordinarily they were in the opposite camp from the highly nationalistic Pharisees. At another time they were even joined by the Sadducees, who were both theological and political opposites from the Pharisees (Matt. 16:1). Since the Sadducees were in cahoots with the Romans they were opposed to both the Pharisees and the Herodians. Their common cause against Jesus made them strange bedfellows indeed.

So after about eighteen months absence from Jerusalem, Jesus returned to make a personal challenge to the city and to these religious leaders. He finally will throw down the gauntlet to the central power, the Sadducees, as He raises Lazarus from the dead.

The Unbelieving Brethren (7:1-9)

At the end of the period of withdrawals "the Jews' feast of tabernacles was at hand," or "was near" (vv. 1-2; cf. Matt. 17:4). John identifies this as a Jewish feast for the benefit of his Gentile readers.

The Feast of Tabernacles was one of the chief feasts of the Jews. It began on the 15th of Tisri (near the end of September or the first of October) and lasted for seven days. Since the time of Nehemiah it had included an eighth day (Neh. 8:18). It was called the Feast of Booths, commemorating the Israelites' dwelling in booths during their wilderness wanderings. It therefore reminded the Jews of God's care for His people during that period of their history. In Exodus 23:16 and 34:22 it is called the Feast of Ingathering, marking the end of the harvest of fruits, oil and wine. Thus it took on the character of an American Thanksgiving. It was a time of great rejoicing. And while it might be observed at one's home, great throngs always celebrated it in Jerusalem.

So it happened that shortly after Jesus' return from the region around Caesarea-Philippi, His half-brothers, (Matt. 13:55) were preparing to depart for Jerusalem for this feast. They told Him that He should go with them (v. 3). After all it had been eighteen months since He had been there. If He expected to get ahead with His work He should go to the heart of things instead of spending His time in the comparatively unimportant area of Galilee. Why spin His wheels "in secret?" "If thou do these things, show thyself to the world" (v. 4). The "if" clause assumes that He has been doing them. But on the sidelines, not in the center of the arena. It is so easy to tell another how to do his work. Even if they knew they ignored Jesus' two previous visits to Jerusalem with their negative results.

Of course, this advice was given in irony more than in good faith. "For neither did his brethren believe on him" (v. 5). The imperfect tense of "believe" means a continued, obstinate refusal to believe. It was not until after His resurrection that they accepted Jesus as the Christ (cf. I Cor. 15:7).

Knowing their sarcastic attitude Jesus said, "My time is not yet come: but your time is alway ready" (v. 6). The word for "time" here and in verse 8 is *kairos,* and appears only here in this Gospel. The usual word in this regard is *hōra* (2:4) which Bernard renders as "the predestined hour." But *kairos* means the fitting or proper time for Jesus to present Himself in Jerusalem. Any time was fitting for them but not for Him. Jerusalem posed no threat to them as it did to Him (v. 7). No one would hardly know that they were there. But His coming would be quite different. For this reason He would go at a time and in a manner which would be fitting for His arrival. So He told them, "Ye [emphatic] go up unto the feast; for mine fitting time is not yet fully fulfilled" (v. 8). The word "yet" in verse 8b is not in the best manuscripts; but it is genuine in 8c. The former "yet" was probably added to make verse 8 agree with verse 10. For subsequently Jesus did *go up* to the feast. Note the words "go up" in verse 8. This is another evidence of the author's knowledge of the topography.

Did Jesus change His mind about going to Jerusalem? Not if one figures the entire picture. Apparently His half-brothers were traveling in a caravan. Its entrance into Jerusalem would be more like a parade. They were suggesting that Jesus should make such an entrance into the city. He will reserve such an entrance until later. This is what He means in "my time is not yet fully come." His procession into Jerusalem would be in fulfilment of Scripture, not merely at the suggestion of unbelievers. Therefore, even though He did plan to go to the feast, He rejected the manner and time in which He should go. In fact, rather than a public procession, He literally *slipped* into the city at this time. The "not go" refers to the time and manner of going, not that He would not go at all. So while the brothers went ahead in a caravan, Jesus remained behind in Galilee (v. 9).

The Confused City (7:10-36)

Since Jesus did not reach Jerusalem until about the middle (10-18) of the week (v. 14), He evidently delayed several days before

(10 - 18)

departing. But He went "not openly, but as it were in secret" (v. 10). Note the contrast. His half-brothers had told Him to go up "openly" (note *phanerōson,* v. 4, and *phanerōs,* v. 10). But Jesus went up "in secret" *(en kruptōi).* Rather than to travel in a caravan through Perea, He went through Samaria accompanied only by His disciples (cf. Luke 9:51-56).

In the meantime the Jewish rulers "were seeking" (imperfect) Him in Jerusalem. They "kept on saying" (imperfect), "Where is he?" (v. 11). It had been so long since Jesus had visited Jerusalem they figured that He would surely come to this feast. The imperfect tenses draw a vivid picture of these hostile rulers going about seeking and asking. We may be sure that they watched for Him in every caravan which arrived from Galilee.

The entire city was buzzing like a hive of bees (murmured, *goggusmos,* (v. 12). Knowing their leaders' attitude toward and interest in Jesus, they were disputing among themselves. "He is a good man," said some. These probably were from outside Jerusalem, maybe from Galilee (cf. v. 20). But others, perhaps Jerusalemites accepting the verdict of their leaders (cf. v. 25), said, "Nay; but he deceiveth the people." But they kept their arguments to themselves. "No man spake openly of him for fear of the Jews" (v. 13).

About the middle of the feast Jesus "went up" (aorist) into the temple area, and "was teaching" (imperfect). The aorist tense suggests that He did this immediately upon His arrival in the city. The Jewish rulers had been looking for Him. Now He was here. And as they heard Him teach they wondered, "How knoweth this fellow [*houtos,* they showed their contempt for Him by ignoring His name] letters, having never learned?" (v. 15). Dods suggests that they did not wonder about Jesus' wisdom but His learning. And "knoweth" *(oiden)* shows that He not only knew facts but had perceived their meaning. Their wonder was that this Galilean peasant who had attended neither of their Rabbinical schools (Hillel, Shammai), and thus was not an accredited Rabbi, should teach not only great truths but do it so skilfully.

Hearing their question Jesus replied, "My teaching is not mine, but the one sending me. If anyone may will to do his will, he shall know concerning the teaching, whether it is out of God, or I am speaking from myself" (v. 17). In other words, Jesus had attended a seminary of which they were not aware. He had been taught, not by their Rabbis, but by God. And if they would put

His teachings into practice they would know this. Furthermore, was Jesus advancing His own selfish cause or the cause of God? "The one speaking from himself is seeking his own glory. But the one seeking the glory of the one sending him, that one is true, and unrighteousness is not in him" (v. 18). Jesus was teaching to glorify His Teacher and no one else. (19-24)

On the other hand, these Jewish leaders claimed to be teaching in the name of Moses. Yet, said Jesus, they are not doing the law. They are a shame to Moses, not a glory. In His previous visit to Jerusalem He had made the same accusation (5:39, 45-47). During that visit they had sought to stone Him (5:16), not for breaking Moses' law but theirs. So now Jesus brings this event into focus with a startling question. "Why are you seeking to kill me?" (v. 19). This suggests that they still have murderous designs toward Him. They sought to kill Him eighteen months ago, and they are seeking to do so now.

In the listening group were those who apparently were pilgrims from outside Jerusalem. Therefore, they were unaware of the earlier attempt on Jesus' life, neither did they know of this present venomous intent of the Jewish leaders. So they said, "You have a demon [you are crazy]: who is seeking to kill you?" (v. 20).

But Jesus continued to press His point. "I have done one work, and ye all marvel" (v. 21). He had done many wondrous works in Jerusalem, but He singled out the one healing of a lame man on the Sabbath (5:1 ff.). For this was the "one work" which caused the Jews to seek His life. Now He reminded them that Moses, whom they followed, had given them the rite of circumcision (v. 22). He did not originate it, but passed it on from his forefathers. Yet they circumcised a child on the Sabbath if the time for the rite fell on that day. So Jesus pointed out that in reality they broke one Mosaic law (Sabbath) in order to observe another (circumcision). Why, then, when they broke the Sabbath law (according to their own interpretation) in performing the rite of circumcision, were they mad at Him for healing a man on the Sabbath (v. 23)? If they *cut* a baby on the Sabbath, why could He not *heal* a man on that day? Said He, "Stop judging according to outward appearance, rather judge a righteous judgment" (v. 24). Circumstances alter cases. Instead of judging superficially, they should consider all factors. He did not condemn them for their practice in circumcision. Neither should they condemn His act of healing. Under the circumstances each act was justified. Hence, a righteous judgment.

(25-30)

Then there came a question by "some of them of Jerusalem" (v. 25). These were some living in Jerusalem or Jerusalemites. Contrary to the ignorance of the pilgrims these residents knew of the incident eighteen months before. So they "kept saying, Is not this he, whom they are seeking to kill?" The form of their question invites an affirmative answer. "But, lo, he keeps on speaking openly, and they are saying nothing to him. Do the rulers truly know that this one is the Christ?" (v. 26). This question invites a negative answer. Robertson raises the question as to whether their inquiry is with respect to the rulers' examination of Jesus (cf. 5:19 ff.). If so "Did they come to know or find out" (and so hold now) that this is the Christ? Are the rulers holding out on them? No, that could not be true. Hence their form of question which anticipates a negative answer.

To satisfy their own minds they recalled a bit of current popular theology. The Sanhedrin had said, "Three things come wholly unexpected — Messiah, a godsend, and a scorpion." So "this fellow" cannot be the Messiah (v. 27). "We know ... whence he is: but when Christ cometh, no man knoweth whence he is." They "know" (oidamen), or else they thought they did. From Nazareth of Galilee, so people said. But they knew nothing of Bethlehem and what lay behind it. So they did not know after all. Had they really known, what a difference it might have made. But they were the prisoners of a false theology and a popular conception of the Christ.

All the while Jesus had been teaching in the temple area (v. 28). Knowing what these Jerusalemites had said, He cried, "Ye both know me, and ye know whence I am." He repeats their own words. This does not mean that they really know Him. They know something about Him. But His words were simply taking note of their false theology. "So you know me, do you?" "Well, you do not know Him who has sent me." In contrast to their ignorance He says, "But I know [oida, really know] him, for I am from him, and he hath sent me" (v. 29). Note Jesus' three claims. "I know him ... I am from him ... he sent me." Bernard says that the three words, "I know him," contain the "unique claim of Jesus which runs through all of these controversies in John. He knows the Father, and has come from His bosom to reveal Him to men. But these Jerusalemites did not receive Him or His witness. Instead they "were seeking," or "began to seek" to arrest Him (a citizens' arrest?). But still no one laid a hand on Him. His "hour" was not in their hands but in God's hand.

(31-36)

By contrast to the reaction of the Jerusalemites, many of the people, probably pilgrims, believed on Him (v. 31). They were not intimidated by the Jewish leaders in Jerusalem. So they believed as they asked, "When Christ cometh, will he do more miracles [signs] than these which this man hath done?"

But what was the reaction of the Pharisees to all this? They saw that the situation could get out of hand. So they enlisted the aid of the "chief priests" or Sadducees, and together they sent some temple police to arrest Jesus (v. 32).

It was apparently when Jesus saw these officers that He spoke verses 33-34. For they were but a foretoken of the time six months later when a similar detail would be sent to arrest Him. And they would succeed then, because His "hour" would be come. So in anticipation of that time Jesus said that He would be with them for a little while. Then He would return to the Father. They would seek Him then, but not find Him. Where He will be they cannot come. Now He is available to them. But they reject Him. Now they are seeking to kill Him. Then they will be seeking Him for help. But it will be too late. He will be in the bosom of the Father. They will still be in their sins. Because they will not believe in Him.

This word of Jesus was lost upon them. They simply thought that His going away meant that He would leave Palestine in order to preach to the Jews of the Dispersion or, perhaps, even to Gentiles (v. 35). So Jesus' words left them puzzled (v. 36).

The Water of Life (7:37-44)

Throughout the week Jesus doubtless continued to teach in the temple. On the last day of the feast, the eighth day, the day of the Holy Convocation, He was there. Daily during the first seven days of the Feast of Tabernacles at the time of Jesus, a priest went to the pool of Siloam. In a golden pitcher he bore water back to the temple. As he did so the singers chanted Isaiah 12:3: "With joy shall ye draw water out of the wells of salvation." The water was then poured out upon the altar as an offering to God. As this was being done the choir accompanied by flutes sang "The Hallel," Psalm 113-118. This ceremony was designed to express thanks to God for water, as a prayer for rain for their next crops, and in commemoration of the water from the rock given to the Israelites in their wilderness wanderings.

This was not a part of the original celebration of this feast.

It was added later. And for this reason its meaning is not entirely clear. Some hold that this ceremony ceased with the seventh day. Others have varying understandings as to the procedure on the eighth day. Barclay holds that on the eighth day the ceremony was held, with the people marching seven times about the altar as Israel had done about Jericho before the city fell. Another view relates this ceremony ultimately to God's promise to give life through His Spirit. But that on the eighth day the pitcher was empty, depicting that the promise had not yet been fulfilled. Certainly there were those who throughout these ceremonies felt acutely that they did not quench the thirst of their souls. And they longed for the fulfilment of God's promise through Ezekiel that a river would flow out of God's temple.

Whatever the various meanings that may have been involved, it was against their background that we may understand Jesus' cry in verses 37-38. For suddenly above it all came His words. "If any man thirst, let him come unto me, and drink. He that believeth in me, as the scripture hath said, out of his belly shall flow rivers of living water." No one specific Old Testament passage can be cited for this. But there are many which teach the idea (cf. Isa. 55:1; 58:11; Ezek. 47:1). Jesus was simply summing up the teaching of Scripture.

However one may interpret the ceremony in detail, Jesus' words carry tremendous significance. For all of the water involved merely symbolized the water of life that is in Him. Westcott notes, "It is uncertain whether the libations were made upon the eighth day. If they were not made, the significant cessation of the striking rites on this one day of the feast would give a still more fitting occasion for the words." The same thing is true if an empty pitcher were used on this day. It may also be insisted that the endless annual repetition of the rite left many hearts empty and thirsty for spiritual reality. So that in any event Jesus' words carry tremendous meaning.

John himself relates this saying to the coming of the Holy Spirit at Pentecost (v. 39). But in the overall it is Jesus' call to every man to come to Him for complete quenching of spiritual thirst, and His promise that those coming to Him will also become sources of blessing to other thirsty souls. All of this is made possible through the work of the Holy Spirit.

The people who heard Jesus' cry had varied reactions. Some (pilgrims?) said, "Of a truth this is the Prophet" (v. 40; cf. Deut. 18:15). Others said, "This is the Christ" (v. 41). But still others

(Jerusalemites?) raised the question, "Shall Christ come out of Galilee?" The Scriptures taught that He would come from the seed of David and out of Bethlehem (v. 42). These were so sure in their own minds. They were up on the Messianic teachings. But they knew little about Jesus' lineage and origin. It is no wonder that "there was a division among the people because of him" (v. 43). There always is where faith and unbelief clash. For no one can be neutral about Him. Still some wished to arrest Jesus. But no one dared to lay hands upon Him (v. 44).

The Frustrated Foe (7:45-52)

If there was confusion among the people they were not alone. For it was found among the members of the Sanhedrin also. The temple police returned without having arrested Jesus (v. 45). When asked why they had not brought Him, they said, "Never man spake like this man" (v. 46). They too had come under the power of Jesus' words. Scornfully the Pharisees asked them, "Are ye also led astray?" (v. 48). Have any of the Sanhedrin, even of the Pharisees, the most orthodox of all, believed on Him (v. 48)? It was understandable how this had happened to the common people. Since they do not know the law they are accursed anyway (v. 49). But surely none of this intelligentsia!

But had they? For at that point Nicodemus spoke up (v. 59). He apparently had remained silent all this while. But this was too much. Still he did not avow a faith in Jesus as the Christ. But he did raise a point of law in His behalf. "Doth our law judge any man before it hear him, and know what he doeth?" (v. 51). His question invited a negative answer. In their confusion they were violating their own law (cf. Exod. 23:1; Deut. 1:16).

Nicodemus reaped only scorn for his effort. "Art thou also of Galilee?" they asked (v. 52). For the most part the Sanhedrin had the Jerusalemites under control. But the Galileans were another matter. To the Judeans they were accursed indeed. Bernard notes that "these aristocrats of Jerusalem had a scornful contempt for the rural Galileans." So they taunted their colleague by saying that he was talking like a Galilean. And then they added, "Search, and look: for out of Galilee ariseth no prophet." As a matter of fact many prophets had come from that area (cf. Elijah, Elisha, Jonah, and others). But they asked this question both out of prejudice and in a senseless rage. Bernard suggests this meaning of their words. "If you will take the trouble to look, you will see that out of Galilee no prophet is arising."

The closing verse (53) of this chapter is not found in the best manuscripts of John. (See next chapter for a discussion of this matter, John 7:53—8:11.) But it most likely belongs to a true incident in the life of Jesus. And it certainly makes a fitting ending to the chapter.

"And every man went to his own house." The meeting broke up in confusion. The Sanhedrin had made a mess of things so far. Therefore, they went home. But there will be another day. And they will be back. The conflict with Jesus will continue to the bitter end.

The Continuing Conflict (II)

The problem relative to John 7:53—8:11 has been noted previously. It certainly does not appear here in the oldest and strongest manuscripts of this Gospel. The early Greek commentators make no mention of it. However, it is found in many lesser manuscripts beginning about the sixth century A.D. Some place it at the end of John's Gospel. Others include it in Luke. Westcott and Hort place it at the end of John. Nestle places it at this point within the Gospel, but it is in brackets. Dods takes note of the problem, but includes it in his treatment. On the other hand Bernard omits it from the body of his text, but treats it at the end of Volume II. Nevertheless, it most likely is a true story out of the life of Jesus. And it is so treated here.

Whereas the members of the Sanhedrin went to their homes for the night (7:53), Jesus went unto the Mount of Olives (8:1). He either slept out in the open, or, as is more likely, He was staying in the home of His friends, Mary, Martha, and Lazarus (cf. Luke 10:38 ff.; John 11). This seems to be in keeping with His custom when in the Jerusalem area. In fact, the first night that He is reported as spending in Jerusalem and its immediate vicinity He was arrested. About daybreak the next morning He returned to the city and to the temple area. "And all the people were coming to him, and taking his seat, he was teaching them" (v. 2). His conflict with the rulers had not dimmed His popularity among the masses.

The Woman Taken in Adultery (8:3-11)

While Jesus was teaching He was interrupted by the scribes and Pharisees. They had seized an adulterous woman whom they brought and placed before Him in the crowd (v. 3). They had found a choice case with which to challenge Jesus.

"Teacher [*didaskale*, note that they did not call Him "Rabbi"], this woman has been taken in adultery, in the very act" (v. 4).

There was no question about her guilt. She was a married woman seized while in the act of adultery.

Reminding Jesus that the Mosaic law required that she should be stoned to death, they asked what He had to say about it (v. 5). It was obvious that they had an ulterior motive in asking this. Else they would have let the law follow its course. But they were more concerned with *baiting* Jesus than with punishing the woman (v. 6a). Knowing His disposition they expected and hoped that He would prescribe mercy. If so, then they could accuse Him before the people of breaking the law of Moses. Furthermore, they could imply that He was in sympathy with the woman's sinful act. On the other hand, knowing them, we may surmise that had He counseled stoning they probably would have accused Him of being without mercy. For it was allowed that if the wronged husband wished, he might divorce his wife privately (cf. Matt. 1:19). So in any case they thought that they had Jesus in a trap.

However, instead of answering them, for the moment He ignored them. Rather, He bent forward and down, and *wrote* on the ground. The imperfect tense of "wrote" graphically portrays His act of writing (v. 6b). This is the only mention of Jesus writing. It is mere speculation as to what He wrote. He may simply have been making marks, though, of course, He could have written a sentence. All the while Jesus' critics kept on asking for His reply. Suddenly He "lifted up" (aorist) Himself, and said, "He that is without sin among you, let him first cast a stone at her" (v. 7).

According to Deuteronomy 17:7 in such a case the accusing witness was to cast the first stone, being followed by others who also should cast stones. However, in this case Jesus went even farther. Let the one among them who was sinless cast the first stone or be the executioner. This could mean one who is free from any sin. Or in this case it could mean the one who was free from this particular sin. Assuming that none of them was guilty of the overt act, it could even include the lustful look or desire (cf. Matt. 5:27-28).

Having given them that thought to ponder, Jesus repeated His act of writing on the ground (v. 8). It was evident that they had been caught in their own trap. Their embarrassment must have been equaled only by the admiration which the people had for Jesus because of His clever strategy. So while Jesus *was writing* they *were leaving* one by one (v. 9). The imperfect tenses bring this scene to life. From judging the woman they were caused to judge themselves. The first to leave were the older ones. Having lived longer they had had more impure thoughts of which they were guilty. But the last one of the accusers departed, each with his own knowledge of guilt. Only Jesus who had never had such an impure thought was left. One might suppose that the crowd also left with the same sense of guilt. But this is not necessarily true. The idea seems to include only the scribes and Pharisees. The fact that the woman was still "standing in the midst" (v. 9) suggests the presence of the people and the Twelve.

At any rate seeing the woman alone without her accusers, Jesus asked, "Woman, where are those thine accusers? hath no man condemned thee?" (v. 10). The word "condemned" here and in verse 11 means to find guilty and pronounce sentence. It is the strong verb *krinō*, to judge, with the preposition *kata*, down; so *katakrinō*, to judge down. It is used in the papyri in this sense.

No one remained to accuse or condemn. The witnesses had all disappeared. So legally there was no case. Therefore, since Jesus had been asked to serve as judge, He threw the case out of court. Neither did He find her guilty and pronounce sentence upon her. This does not mean that she was not guilty. Neither does it mean that Jesus condoned her sin. But with no witness there was no case for Him to judge. This is not to take away from Jesus' merciful attitude. Had they remained and proved their charges, we may still hold that Jesus, upon her repentance and faith, would have forgiven her regardless of any untoward circumstances for Himself. Finally He went to the cross to make possible such forgiveness. However, the fact remains that Jesus never had to face that question in this particular case. He simply caused the accusers to drop the case lest they incriminate themselves with the same guilt and sentence. Talk about a clever lawyer! The Judge beat them at their own game. He turned the charges around so that the accusers simply faded out of the picture. No accusers, no witnesses, no case. So the wise Judge threw the case out of court.

But that Jesus was concerned about the woman is seen in His parting admonition. "Go, and sin no more" (v. 11). She was free to leave the court. But the kind Judge ordered her "henceforth no longer go on sinning." He felt that such as she could be saved. In her reply, "No one, Lord" (*kurios*), she at the moment probably meant only "No man, Sir." We can only hope that she obeyed

Jesus' admonition; furthermore, that she came to know Him as *Lord* in the truest spiritual sense of the word.

The Light of the World (8:12)

If we lift the above passage out of the text of John, then this verse follows immediately after 7:52. Some hold that it was spoken on the same occasion, at least on the last day of the Feast of Tabernacles. However, the fact that 7:52 comes in the private meeting of the Jewish leaders, it is unlikely that 8:12 is simply a continuation of the events of that day. It seems more likely that it came later, probably the next day in the temple area.

We know that Jesus was in the Court of the Women (v. 20). It was here that the treasury boxes were located (Mark 12:41 ff.; Luke 21:1 ff.). During the Feast of Tabernacles the candelabra in this Court were lighted. This was to commemorate the pillar of cloud by day and the pillar of fire by night which guided Israel in the wilderness and gave her the realization of God's abiding presence. But at the end of the eighth day the candelabra were extinguished. Apparently on the next day Jesus seized upon this fact to teach another lesson as He had done the previous day with reference to water.

So He said, "I always am [*eimi*] the light of the world [both Jews and Gentiles]: the one following me shall not never [double negative, *ou mē*] walk [present subjunctive, but with the force of certainty] in the darkness, but shall have the light of the life."

This is tantamount to a claim to deity. In the Christ "always was life: and the life was the light of men" (1:4). In Jesus the Light came into the world as flesh (1:8, 14). Now Jesus claims that He always is the Light of the world. So He always has been and always will be; eternally He is the Light of the world! This is but one of many such claims. Already Jesus has identified Himself as the Christ (4:26), the Son of God (5:19), the Bread from heaven (6:35), the Water of life (7:37), and now, the Light of the world. Such claims are without meaning if Jesus be only a man. One cannot call Jesus a good man, and at the same time deny His deity. For either He is deity or else He is an imposter and suffered from megalomania. History affirms the former and denies the latter.

The Witness Concerning Jesus (8:13-20)

In response to Jesus' claim the Pharisees challenged His witness.

"You are bearing witness concerning yourself; your witness is not
true" (v. 13). Here they technically challenged His testimony as
not being supported by other witnesses (cf. 5:31 ff.). In 5:31 Jesus
had acknowledged this legal technicality, and proceeded to cite
five such witnesses. Here, however, He avows the truth of His
unsupported testimony. His knowledge of Himself, a knowledge
unknown to them, is true (v. 14). His very shining in the world
as evidenced by His power to change men from darkness to light
declares this truth. One might as well deny the shining of the
sun. Its shining is self-evidence of its nature. The same is true
of Jesus. The Pharisees render judgment by fleshly standards.
Jesus of Himself does not judge any man (v. 15). His first coming
was not to judge men but to save them (3:17). Men are judged
by their unbelief in Him (3:18). But even if He passes judgment,
it is a true judgment (v. 16). For His judgment ultimately is
that of the Father. Even so, Jesus still satisfied the Pharisees' legal
demand for supported testimony. Because both He and His Father
testify concerning Him (vv. 17-18).

Evidently the Pharisees were getting tired of hearing Jesus claim
God as His Father. For they raised the question as to His par-
entage. "Where is thy Father?" they asked (v. 19). Dods cites
Augustine's understanding of their question as referring to Jesus'
human father. So where is he that we may ask him? Cyril saw
in this an aspersion upon Jesus' birth, which may or may not
be true here (but see v. 41). Bernard touches on the vital point
that they asked not "who" but "where" is His Father. So their
question probably was intended to cite the Rabbinical doctrine
of evidence to the effect that since God is not visible no such
testimony is acceptable. But Jesus responded by accusing them
of ignorance concerning both Him and the Father. "If ye had
known me, ye should have known my Father also" (v. 19; cf.
14:9). Of course, God cannot be discerned by the natural senses.
But they are incapable of making a spiritual judgment (cf. v. 15).
This sounds very much like a judgment upon the Russian cos-
monaut who proudly and arrogantly said that he did not see
God in space. And a commendation of John Glenn who on the
same space journey said that God is everywhere.

John notes that this encounter with the Pharisees took place
in "the treasury," the Court of the Women (v. 20). And though
the conflict was sharp, yet no man arrested Jesus, "for his hour
was not yet come."

The Earthly and the Heavenly (8:21-30)

"Then said Jesus again unto them" (v. 21). Note the word "again" *(palin)* as in verse 12. So here it probably means on another day, maybe the next. As was His custom while in Jerusalem He was once more teaching in the temple area.

Here Jesus repeats the warning given in 7:34. He is going away. They then will seek Him whom they are now rejecting. But it will be too late. They will die in their sins. Because where He is going they cannot come (but cf. 14:3 spoken to believers). Of course, He spoke of His ascension into heaven. But, as two days before, His hearers were earthbound. The Jewish leaders asked, "Will he kill himself?" (v. 22). Is He going to commit suicide? The irony is that they will play a major role in killing Him.

Their response to Jesus' words showed the broad chasm between Him and them. He spoke of heavenly things; they spoke of earthly things (v. 23). They were of the earth earthy. He was of heaven heavenly. So no matter what He said about spiritual reality, they thought only of material things. Therefore with emphasis Jesus repeated that they will die in their sins (v. 24). For said He, "If ye believe not that I am ... ye shall die in your sins" (v. 24). Note that "he" is not in the Greek text. "I am" *(egō eimi)* is a claim to deity, to eternal being (cf. 1:1). These words are used of Jehovah (cf. Exod. 3:13-14; Deut. 32:39). The "I am's" of Jesus make a fruitful study. "I am" bread, water, light, etc. But they boil down to a claim far greater than that of a mere man, even the greatest of men. To see them as less than a claim to deity is to ignore the significance of these words as found in the Scripture with respect to Jehovah and Jesus. If one does not see in Jesus the great *I AM,* he will die in his sins.

The Jews recognized the import of Jesus' words. So they asked, "Who art thou?" (v. 25). Jesus had told them repeatedly, but because of their earthbound unbelief they would not accept His claims. So instead of repeating these claims, Jesus spoke of judgment upon them (v. 26). Even if they do not believe Him, God is true. And since He is speaking God's truth they will be judged thereby. Still denying any other than earthly being to Jesus, they did not perceive that He spoke of the Father (v. 27). So Jesus went a step farther (v. 28). When they have "lifted up [crucified] the Son of man, then they will know that I am" *(egō eimi)*. This seems to be a veiled reference to His resurrection, a "sign" which He had given to them but which they later will deny. But if they had had spiritual discernment they would have accepted it. Even so, when through the Holy Spirit He is loosed upon the world they will know, whether or not they admit it.

He is never absent from the Father (v. 29) because He is a bodily expression of the Father's will. With this "many believed on him" (v. 30). They "began to believe" (ingressive aorist). But again Jesus did not commit Himself to them (cf. 2:24 f.). Knowing the nature of man He proceeded to test the genuineness of their faith.

The Question of Freedom (8:31-36)

Since John says that those who believed in Jesus were "Jews," we may assume that they were some of the Pharisees (v. 31). The word "believed" in this verse is a perfect participle. It expresses a complete belief. However, in this context it can hardly include commitment to Him. Rather it means that they fully believed that He was the Christ, but a political-military Christ in keeping with their Messianic concept. Therefore, Jesus sought to test the genuineness of their faith. "If ye continue [abide] in my word [not their concept of the Christ], then ye are my disciples indeed," or "are truly my disciples." Many make professions of faith in Christ, but the subsequent life proves or disproves the true nature of their faith.

One of the basic passions of the heart of a Pharisee was freedom. A free nation ruled by Jews alone with no foreign domination was his dream. So Jesus said, "And ye shall know the truth, and the truth shall make you free," or "shall liberate you" (v. 32). "Truth" in this sense was one of the qualities of Christ's nature as deity (cf. 14:6). In John 1:14 "grace and truth" are linked together. While "grace" is not mentioned after 1:17, "truth" is used repeatedly. One is justified, therefore, to see in "truth" a combination of these two ideas. We come to know Christ who is truth through God's grace.

This word of Jesus about freedom drew sparks from the Pharisees. "We be Abraham's seed, and were never in bondage to any man" (v. 33). The perfect tense says, "We never have been, are not now, and never will be in bondage to any man." They could mean that they remained free in that they refused to recognize political bondage. But as a matter of fact the Jews as a people had been in bondage numerous times (Egyptian, Babylonian, Persian, Greek, Roman). Even as they spoke they were a vassal nation of Rome. Even if they refused to recognize it, they were not free politically. However, they challenged Jesus' words about freedom.

The bondage of which Jesus spoke was the bondage of sin. "Whosoever is doing sin is a slave of sin" (v. 34). Even if they refused to recognize this bondage, it was nevertheless true. "The slave does not abide in the house forever; the Son does abide forever." A slave could be thrown out at any moment. But the Son of the house has permanent residence. The only way that a slave can remain in the house is to become a son through faith in the Son. "If the Son therefore shall make you free, ye shall be free indeed" (v. 36).

There is a false and a true freedom. The false is freedom from outward restraint. The true is freedom from inward bondages. The false is freedom to do as one wishes. The true is freedom to do as one should. And even though one is politically free from outward restraint so that he can do as he wishes, he may be a slave to inward bondage which prevents him from doing as he should. Even true freedom is governed by the restraint of relationships. But it enables one to live properly within those relationships. False freedom produces anarchy. True freedom assumes the responsibilities which are inherent in it. And in this acceptance one knows freedom indeed. Only Christ can give such freedom.

The Seed of Abraham (8:37-59)

Jesus accepted the Pharisees at their word. They are indeed Abraham's seed after the flesh (v. 37). Yet "ye are seeking to kill me." The reason being that His teaching does not have free course within them. Some of them have come to believe that He is the Messiah, but a Messiah of their own ideas. However, they refuse to accept Him as the spiritual Messiah which He has shown Himself to be.

Then Jesus introduced a contrast of fatherhood (v. 38). They insist that Abraham is their father; He insists that God is His Father. On the word "father" Jesus changes the course of the conversation. He is speaking that which He has seen with His Father. In seeking to kill Him they are doing that which they have seen with their *father*. Upon their insistence that Abraham is their father, Jesus makes a telling point (vv. 39-40). If they were Abraham's children they would do his works. Because He has told them the truth from God they are seeking to kill Him. This Abraham did not do. He was the father of the faithful, not of murderous unbelievers. And even though they claim Abraham as their father, their deeds prove that they have another father. So while Jesus admitted that they are physical descendants of Abraham, He also insisted that they are not his spiritual descendants.

Implied in this is that they claim one man as their father, when actually another is. So they snapped back, "We be not born of fornication; we have one Father, even God" (v. 41). While this seems to be the primary sense of these words, they could also carry a veiled reference to Jesus' birth. The Jewish Talmud refers to Jesus as the illegitimate son of Mary. Even then being ignorant of the true nature of Jesus' birth, this slanderous idea could have been held by His foes. One can see how the conflict grows in intensity.

The Pharisees claimed only one Father, God, though they claimed to be children of Abraham also. But Jesus said that their attitude toward Him proved that God is not their Father (vv. 42-43).

Then like a bolt of lightning Jesus struck home. "Ye are of your father the devil, and the lusts of your father ye will do," or "ye will to go on doing" (v. 44). "He always was a mankiller from the beginning, and in the truth he has never stood, because truth is not in him. When he speaks a lie, he speaks out of his own nature; because he is a liar, and the father of it." So when the Pharisees reject truth for lies and try to kill Him for speaking the truth, they are merely acting like their father (v. 45). Then He challenged them to convict Him of any sin (v. 46). Since they cannot do so, then why do they refuse to believe Him? God's own hear His words (v. 47). Their very refusal to hear and heed His words prove that they are not God's own. And since they must ultimately be children of God or of the devil, their refusal proves that the devil is their father. These are strong words coming from Jesus, words which must have been spoken with strong feeling.

Probably responding not only to Jesus' words but to the manner in which He spoke them, the Pharisees said, "Say we not well that thou art a Samaritan, and hast a demon?" (v. 48). In short, "You are a crazy Samaritan." In their rage they could think of no worse thing to say to Jesus. But Jesus denied this, saying, rather that He spoke honoring His Father (v. 49). But they certainly were dishonoring Jesus. However, since He was not seeking self-glory but God's glory, or that which God gives, what they said about Him was inconsequential (v. 50). After all, the glory which comes from God is all that matters. And God's glory on Him would be God's judgment on them. So Jesus repeated, "If a man keep my saying, he shall never see death" (v. 51). Implied, of course, is the fact that they are already abiding in spiritual death.

This last word brought a rejoinder from the Pharisees (v. 52): "Now we know fully [perfect tense] that you are crazy." Abraham and the prophets surely kept God's word. Yet they are dead. (They had missed the point of Jesus' meaning of death.) Yet, said they, you say that if a man keeps your word, he will never see death. Are you greater than "our father Abraham," or the prophets? Just whom are you claiming to be anyway?

This implied that Jesus was seeking a greater honor than that of Moses and the prophets. So He said, "If I honor myself, my honor is nothing: it is my Father that honoreth me; of whom ye say, that he is your Father" (v. 54). Even though they claimed God as their Father, they did not even know Him, not even partially so (v. 55). "But I really know [oida] him," said Jesus. If He disclaimed this intimate knowledge of God He would be as great a liar as they were when they claimed God as their Father.

In verse 53 the Pharisees again had claimed Abraham as their father. So Jesus said, "Your father Abraham rejoiced to see my day: and he saw it, and was glad" (v. 56; cf. Heb. 11:16). Abraham looked forward with hope and joy to the promised Messianic age. Yet the Messiah was there among those who claimed him as father, and they were rejecting Him.

But Jesus' words were lost on them. They could only speak of comparative ages. "Thou art not yet fifty years old, and hast thou seen Abraham?" (v. 57). They must have asked this with a derisive laugh. This does not mean that Jesus was about this age. Actually He was about thirty-three years old at the time. They just picked a number out of their hats.

However, their derision furnished the occasion for one of Jesus' greatest claims as to His being. They jested about the whole matter. But Jesus solemnly avowed, "Verily, verily, I say unto you, Before Abraham was, I am" (v. 58). "Before Abraham came into existence [was born], I always am (egō eimi)." Abraham had being only in time. But Jesus claimed eternal being. Here is another of Jesus' clear claims to deity.

Some today may deny this. But the Pharisees caught the point. To them this claim to deity was blasphemy. So "then they took up stones to cast at him" (v. 59). The penalty for blasphemy was death by stoning. They were not even going to wait for a trial. They would execute Him in mob violence.

However, "Jesus hid himself" (v. 59). He did not simply vanish into thin air. He simply turned His back on them and left the temple area. He did not turn His heels and run. He simply walked away. When the debate reached the point that they could answer only with violence, He broke it off. He was walking by God's timetable. And His hour had not arrived.

The Continuing Conflict (III)

The time of the event recorded in John 9:1—10:39 is in dispute. Westcott holds that it was at the Feast of Dedication (10:22). However, the weight of evidence seems to favor the position held by many that it is related to the account which ends with 8:59. Dods thinks that it may have occurred immediately thereafter. Bernard suggests that Chapters 9 and 10 must be considered together, but seems to end this particular event with 10:21. The tone of this section differs from that of Chapter 8. However, on the whole it appears that the controversy in that chapter is continued in Chapter 9 but with a different emphasis. Robertson is probably right in seeing 9:1 ff. as an event which took place the next day after 8:59. The only specific time element is that it occurred on a Sabbath (v. 14).

The Healing of a Blind Man (9:1-12)

Beggars usually congregated near the entrances to the temple area (cf. Acts 3:2). So probably Jesus was about to enter the temple when He saw a man who was blind from birth (v. 1). This is the only case reported in the Gospels where someone healed had been so afflicted from birth. Seeing him Jesus' disciples asked, "Rabbi, who sinned, this man or his parents, that he was born blind?" (v. 2). Their question reflects the idea commonly held then, as now, that illness is connected with sin. The book of Job should already have answered this false idea. But, alas, it persists even today. Sickness may be caused by some specific sin, but not necessarily so. Of course, all sickness generally is related to the evil principle at work in the universe. But specifics have to be decided on the merits of each case.

But the disciples, thinking that either this man's sin or that of his parents was responsible for his blindness, wanted to know which. It could have been due to the sin of the parents. But a prenatal sin is ridiculous.

In reply Jesus brushed aside both alternatives. "Neither hath this man sinned, nor his parents" (v. 3). So much for that. But what else did Jesus say? According to the English translation He said, "But that the works of God should be made manifest in him." This says that the man was born blind in order that God's work of healing might be worked upon him. However, this poses another problem. Did God permit this man to be born blind solely for the purpose that on this occasion He might get glory out of his healing? This seems to be the general thought among most interpreters. Bernard even says, "The doctrine of predestination is apparent at every point in the Fourth Gospel." Perhaps so, but what about man's free will? It is also everywhere apparent in it. This position seems to place an undue emphasis upon the former and too little upon the latter. We need not speculate as to how the man's blindness occurred. But are we shut up to the idea that God predestined this? Did He will that this man should walk in physical darkness all these years for the purpose of healing him at this time? Such a position is contrary to the very nature of God.

But what may we say otherwise? Let us note Jesus' further reply. "I must work the works of him that sent me, while it is day: the night cometh when no man can work. As long as I am in the world, I am the light of the world" (vv. 4-5).

However, we would note that we are not hopelessly confined to this translation. It is a matter of punctuation. Originally the Greek text had no punctuation except question marks (;). So otherwise the punctuation as we have it is not inspired. This was added later. And the one adding it did so according to his own interpretation of the meaning. We are justified, therefore, in using our own where it does not contradict the overall teaching of the Bible. So let us try our hand at it.

"Neither hath this man sinned, nor his parents." Note the period instead of a colon. Jesus emphatically denied that his blindness was caused by either. As in so many other cases, Jesus abruptly brushed aside false teachings. And then He continued. "But that the works of God should be made manifest in him, we must [dei] work the works of him that sent me while it is day: the night cometh when no man can work. As long as I am in the world, I am the light of the world." G. Campbell Morgan makes the same translation.

Thus Jesus did not say that God permitted this blindness in order that He might get glory from it. Jesus simply recognized the fact of his condition. It was useless to debate as to the cause.

The fact was that he was blind. The concern of Jesus and the Twelve should be to do something about it. And so Jesus proceeded to do so. The work of God was not to make the man blind, but to give him sight.

Having said this Jesus "spat on the ground, and made clay of the spittle, and he anointed the eyes of the blind man with clay" (v. 6). Of passing interest is the fact that the Greek verb for "spit" is *ptuō*. It carries the sound of the act of spitting. The Jews thought that spittle was beneficial in curing blindness (cf. Mark 8:23). Did Jesus also believe this? He also healed blindness without resorting to spittle (cf. Matt. 20:30 ff.), which shows that He did not hold to such a view. Why then did He use it here? He probably did so as an aid to the man's faith, something that was unnecessary in Matthew 20.

Having placed the clay on the man's eyes, Jesus told him to go to the pool of Siloam and wash them (v. 7). This pool is located on the southeastern edge of the city just outside and below the temple area. For the benefit of his Gentile readers John translated the Hebrew word into Greek ("Sent"). There was no healing power in the water as there was none in the spittle. But Jesus' instruction was intended as a test of the man's faith. He did as Jesus said, "and came seeing."

When the "neighbors" saw him they began to ask questions (v. 8). The word "neighbors" implies that he had returned to his home. "Is not this he that sat and begged?" asked they. Some said that was he, while others said that he was like him. His opened eyes probably had changed his appearance somewhat. But the man himself said, "I am he" (v. 9). In reply as to how his eyes had been opened, he related that "a man that is called Jesus" had done it (v. 10). Explaining what had happened, he said, "And I received my sight" (v. 11). Usually the Greek verb means to see again. But since this man had never had sight, it simply means that he received sight. The aorist tense means that he did so immediately upon washing his eyes. It was definitely a miracle. "Where is he?" they asked (v. 12). But he did not know.

The Sabbath Question Again (9:13-16)

The neighbors brought "the once blind man" to the Pharisees (v. 13). Apparently they did so, not because he was healed, but because it had been done on the Sabbath (v. 14). These Jerusalemites recognized this as a breach of their Sabbath laws. So

under the domination of their religious rulers they soon forgot
the miracle in favor of their zeal for their rote rules.

When the Pharisees learned of this (v. 15) the reaction of
some was automatic. "This man is not from God, because he does
not keep the sabbath day" (v. 16). To them a Sabbath-breaker
could not be from God. But others, probably in wonder, asked,
"How is a man a sinner able to do such signs?" And there "was"
(imperfect, began to be) a schism among them. In an effort
to solve their own problem they asked the healed man for his
own opinion of Jesus. "He is a prophet," said the man (v. 17).
In view of the facts, he certainly could not have said less. But
the segment of the rulers who called Jesus a sinner simply refused
to believe the man (v. 18). Thus they make efforts to disprove
the whole thing.

First, they sought to deny that the man was ever blind. Evidently his parents were in the group. So they "called" (a loud call) them
to step forward (v. 18). Then they asked them a three-pronged
question, probably in an effort to confuse them (v. 19). "Is this
your son?" "Who ye say was born blind?" "How then doth he now
see?" And they answered all three questions (vv. 20-21). "We surely
know [*oidamen*] that this is our son." We *surely* know "that he
was born blind." This cut the ground from under the Pharisees'
denial as to his blindness. "But by what means he now seeth, we
know not [*oidamen*], or who hath opened his eyes, we know not
[*oidamen*]." Just as emphatically as they knew that their son had
been born blind, they also denied any knowledge of how or by
whom he now saw. They ignored their son's explanation and the
identity of the one who had done this (cf. v. 11). It was a clear
case of attempted evasion. They sought to get out of this tight
spot by reminding the Pharisees that their son was of age and was
capable of speaking for himself. So why not ask him?

The reason for their effort to evade the matter was that the
rulers had already said that anyone who confessed Jesus as the
Christ would be put out of the synagogue (v. 22). This implies
that they suspected that Jesus was the Christ. And lest under
questioning they be forced to admit their private belief, they said,
"He is of age; ask him" (v. 23).

To put one out of the synagogue was *excommunication*. It
might be for thirty days, for a longer period, or for life. Permanent
excommunication called for one to be cursed publicly. Thereafter,
he was shut off from social or business relations. But what was
even worse, he was shut off from God. It is easy to understand the

parents' fear. Even so, it shows them in a very bad light. For to protect themselves they placed their son in the same jeopardy.

But following their suggestion the Pharisees again called the son before them. They put him under oath as they said, "Give God the praise: we know that this man is a sinner" (v. 24). They wanted him to say the same thing under oath. Instead he said that he did not know [*oida*] about their fine points of theology. But of one thing he was certain (*oida* again) "Whereas I was blind, now I see" (v. 25). They could argue their theology all day. But they could not debate away his experience.

Having failed in this attempt, the Pharisees tried another approach (v. 26). They wanted to know how Jesus had opened his eyes. At this point the man began to toy with them. He had told them once already, but they did not heed him. "Wherefore do ye wish to hear it again? do ye also wish to become his disciples?" (v. 27). Even though his question invited a negative answer, it definitely was ironic. They answered by reviling him. "Thou art his disciple; but we are Moses' disciples. We know that God spoke unto Moses: as for this fellow, we know not from whence he is" (vv. 28-29). The Jerusalemites knew, or thought they did (cf. 7:27). Apparently the Pharisees also knew of Jesus' Galilean residence. But truly they did not know His true origin (cf. 8:14) ; what is more, they did not care.

However, their admission of ignorance left them open to a further jibe from the man. "Why herein is a marvelous thing, that ye know not from whence he is, and yet he hath opened mine eyes" (v. 30). As the religious leaders they were supposed to be up on such matters.

And then this former beggar turned teacher. "We know [note that he includes himself as one of the scholars] that God does not hear sinners; but if anyone is a worshipper of God and does his will, he hears that one" (v. 31). Since this was in accord with the theology of the Pharisees, they would have to agree with him. So they must have nodded their heads in agreement. Continuing the man reminded them that in all history no one had ever heard of anyone else opening the eyes of one born blind (v. 32). Again they would have to agree. But as they nodded their heads in assent he delivered his knockout punch. "If this man were not of God [as you say] he could do nothing" (v. 33). With his one-two punch of both Scripture and logic he had them down for the count.

Unable to answer him in like kind they could resort only to ridicule and violence. "Thou wast altogether born in sins, and dost thou teach us?" (v. 34). It was unthinkable that one so totally depraved would pose as a teacher of teachers. So "they cast him out" (v. 34). Does this mean that they excommunicated him? Dods thinks so on the basis of 9:22. Bernard, Robertson, and Barclay hold that they merely cast him out of their presence. This position is based on the requirement of a formal meeting of the Sanhedrin in order to excommunicate him. No such meeting is implied. They are probably correct. Whatever may be the meaning, they were through with him. After all, their only interest in him was to make him a tool against Jesus. When his obstinate loyalty to Jesus could not be shaken, they flung him aside as useless to their purpose.

The Converted and the Condemned (9:35-41)

Hearing what had happened to the man, Jesus sought him out. "Dost thou believe on the Son of God?" asked Jesus (v. 35). The man did not know of whom He spoke, "Who is he, Sir [kurie], that I might believe on him?" (v. 36). When Jesus identified himself as He, the man said, "Lord [kurie, note change in meaning, the same word but a different attitude], I believe. And he began to worship [ingressive aorist] him" (vv. 37-38). It is no wonder that he did so, after what Jesus had done for him.

Jesus then spoke of "judgment" (v. 39, krima). This word, found only here in John, means the result of the act of judging (krisis, 3:19). The Father did not send Jesus into the world primarily for judgment but for salvation (3:17). Nevertheless, men are judged in regard to their reaction toward Him (3:18-21). So in this sense, for "judgment" (krima) He has come into the world. He came that those who are blind might see both physically and spiritually. Conversely that those who see physically shall by rejecting him become blind spiritually. The Pharisees fall in this latter group, even as the blind man falls in the former one. And the Pharisees caught the point. For they asked, "Are we blind also?" (v. 40). Not physically, to be sure, but they were spiritually blind.

Jesus took note of this fact. "If ye were blind, ye should have no sin" (v. 41). Here He spoke not of physical blindness. Robertson sees it as "moral blindness," such as an idiot, and so without responsibility. But this was not true of the Pharisees. They were the moral teachers of their people. "But now ye say, We see; therefore your sin remaineth." They claim moral sight. But they are spiritually blind. So they have no excuse. Their sin "continues to abide" (present tense). Jesus could heal physical blindness. But none are so blind as those who will not to see. They are hopelessly bound to their sin of wilful unbelief, an unbelief which persisted in the light of full knowledge.

The Allegory of the Sheep and the Shepherd (10:1-6)

Even though there is a chapter break, there is a continuity of thought. This is seen in Jesus' words "verily, verily." These words in John never introduce a new topic of conversation (cf. 8:34, 51, 58; 10:7). Thus we may assume that after pronouncing judgment upon the Pharisees, Jesus continued to condemn them in Chapter 10.

They had assumed the role of spiritual shepherds over the Jews (cf. 9:24, 29). It is evident, however, that they are not true shepherds. Indeed, the Jewish people are shepherdless sheep. This is the point of the opening verses of this chapter.

Those who do not enter into the sheepfold through the door, but who climb over the wall, are not shepherds. They are thieves and robbers (v. 1). The real shepherd enters through the door, being given entrance by the doorkeeper (vv. 2-3). Furthermore, a true shepherd knows his sheep by name, the sheep know his voice and follow him out of the fold into pasture (vv. 3-4).

This picture was true to life then, as it is now. At night many flocks would use the same fold. In the morning when a given shepherd was ready to lead his flock out, he would give a certain sound. He might even call his sheep by their names. And only his sheep would follow him. They would not follow a strange shepherd with a strange voice (v. 5).

This "parable" Jesus spoke to and of the Pharisees (v. 6). But they were so dense that they did not catch its meaning. Actually this word for "parable" means "proverb" (paroimian), a wayside saying. Because of its length it may just as well be called an allegory. But call it what you will, the Pharisees did not know what Jesus "was saying."

The Shepherd and the Hirelings (10:7-18)

So Jesus proceeded to explain His meaning. But in so doing He changed his metaphors in order to reflect different facets of truth.

First, He said, "I am the door of the sheep" v. 7). He is the only entrance into the fold. And all who ever come before Him are "thieves and robbers." This reference applies to false messiahs and false prophets who sought to mislead the sheep (v. 8). "All that ever came before me," of course, does not refer to true prophets. For they pointed toward Him. Fortunately for the true sheep, they did not follow the thieves and robbers. But anyone who follows Jesus, "the door," will be saved. He will be safe from those who falsely claim to be their shepherds. In Jesus they not only are saved and safe, but are also nourished (v. 9).

On the other hand, "the thief does not come, except in order that he may steal, and may kill, and may destroy" (v. 10). Note the order of the verbs. The thief comes to steal. And if necessary he will kill and destroy in order to accomplish his purpose. He thinks only of himself and cares for no one, or nothing else. But by contrast Jesus said, "I came in order that they may have life, and may have it abundantly" (v. 10). "I" is written out, and so is emphatic. Jesus in contrast to the thieves and robbers. They come to *steal;* He comes to *give.* They come to *kill;* He comes to *give life.* They come to *destroy;* He comes to *build up.* And the life which He gives is the overflowing life (*perisson,* abundantly).

Second, Jesus calls Himself "the good shepherd" (v. 11). Instead of destroying the sheep, He "gives his life for the sheep." The word "for" renders *huper.* This means for, on behalf of, as a substitute for. It basically means upper, or over. As a blow is about to fall upon its victim, another throws his body over him and takes the blow intended for him. Though innocent, he receives the other's punishment. Jesus does this for the sheep. He dies as their substitute that they may live. The good shepherd places his body between the sheep and vicious animals. He will die protecting the sheep. So Jesus did for lost men. Before spiritual death can seize them it must first destroy Him. Death did its worst to Jesus. But He overcame it in life.

On the other hand, the hireling, one who works for wages and so is not the true shepherd, forsakes the sheep when wolves approach (v. 12). And thus the sheep are left helpless. The wolf "snatches" some and kills them. Those who are spared this fate are scattered. This is a vivid picture of wolves wreaking havoc on a shepherdless flock. The hireling flees because he is a hireling. He cares only for his own skin (v. 13). The hireling most likely epitomizes the Pharisees. They pose as shepherds. But they are merely wage earners. So as they selfishly use their position, the sheep are being destroyed by the enemy of souls. By contrast Jesus is the good, the true shepherd. He knows His sheep and they know

Him (v. 14). The intimate knowledge enjoyed between Father and Son He shares with His own. For He lays down His life for the sheep (v. 15).

Then Jesus spoke of "other sheep ... which are not of this fold" (v. 16). The word for "other" means "other of a different kind." This does not mean *goats* but true sheep. Thus He referred to Gentiles who will believe in Him. He is the Saviour not only of Jews but of Gentiles also. The two will be combined into one fold with one Shepherd (cf. Eph. 2:11-19). This is not the first reference to the universal nature of Jesus' mission (cf. 3:16; 4:42). All who hear His voice, both Jews and Gentiles, will become His sheep.

This inclusive concept must have sounded rather strange to both the Pharisees and to His disciples. It was in direct contrast to their narrow concept of salvation for Jews only. One of the greatest struggles for the gospel in early Christianity was to break out of this crusted mold. But it was/is in God's plan that all men should be saved. God's love for the Son is definitely related to His willingness to lay down His life for all men (v. 17). He will not die as a martyr, or unwillingly as a criminal (v. 18). Rather, of Himself He will lay down His life, and He will take it up again through the Father's power. It is God's command that He shall do these things. And He ever does the Father's will.

The Enemy Divided (10:19-21)

These various sayings of Jesus produced another division of opinion among the Jewish leaders (v. 19). Many said, "He has a demon, and is mad; why hear ye him?" (v. 20). They simply said that He raved wildly like a demoniac. So why waste time listening to Him? Theirs was the easy way of disposing of one whom they could not answer.

But "others" *(alloi)* had a different view (v. 21). This word means that they also were Pharisees. But they were of a different mind from those mentioned above. To them Jesus was not so easily brushed aside. Said they, "These are not the words of him that hath a demon, and is mad." His teachings were far from being the wild ravings of one possessed of a demon. And besides, "Can a demon open the eyes of the blind?" (v. 21). Despite agnostic denials they were still faced with the evident results of a benevolent act. Demons might blind one, but no demon would cause one to see. Yes, the arch-demon had blinded the eyes of many Pharisees to the nature of Jesus' person and mission. But despite all that the devil could do, some still kept an open mind about Him. They were not ready to receive Him. Neither were they ready to reject Him. We can only hope that they persisted until in faith the eyes of their souls were opened.

The Answer of Desperation (10:22-39)

Almost three months intervened between verses 21 and 22. It was the period from shortly after the Feast of Tabernacles until the Feast of Dedication (v. 22). During this interval Jesus probably ministered somewhere in Judea. It is at this point that Robertson's *Harmony* inserts Luke's account of a Judean ministry (10:1 — 13:21).

The Feast of Dedication began on the 25th of Chisleu and lasted for eight days. It came somewhere about the middle of December. The temple in Jerusalem had been desecrated by Antiochus Epiphanes. Judas Maccabeus led in a successful revolt against him. And in 164 B.C. he cleansed and rededicated the temple. This feast commemorated that event. It was not one of the major feasts of the Jews. Therefore, it might be celebrated at home. But since Jesus was already in Judea, He observed it in Jerusalem.

John notes that "it was winter" (v. 22). This explains why Jesus was walking on Solomon's Porch (v. 23). This was a covered portico on the east side of the temple area, and so would be suited to all types of weather. This would be the rainy season in Palestine.

As Jesus was walking along He *was suddenly encircled* (aorist) by Jewish leaders (v. 24). They were still chafing from the verbal beating of several weeks ago. Seeing Him once again they asked, "How long do you hold us in suspense?" (v. 24). Literally, "Until when do you lift up our souls?" "If thou be the Christ, tell us plainly."

They were becoming desperate. They had toyed with Jesus indirectly. Now they came straight to the point. Of course, their purpose was to ensnare Him. If He would just say in plain words, "I am the Christ," they could use that claim to accuse Him before the Roman governor. Because to them "Christ" meant a revolutionary leader. Revolutionary claims Rome would not tolerate.

Jesus reminded them that He had already told them, and they did not believe Him (v. 25). He had called Himself "Son of God" and "Son of man." He had claimed pre-existence, and power to raise the dead. His oft-used phrase "I am" was a definite claim to deity. Furthermore, His works done in the Father's name bore testimony to the truth of His claims. But they did not believe them either. The reason being that they are not His sheep (v. 26). This caused Him to take up where He had left off on His recent visit to Jerusalem. This subject especially rubbed the Jewish rulers the wrong way.

Repeating His previous claim as the good Shepherd of the sheep (v. 27), Jesus said, "I give unto them eternal life; and they shall never perish" (v. 28). Again He used the strong double negative. "They shall not never be destroyed," or "go to hell." The word "perish" *(apolōntai)* is the verb form whence comes the name Apollyon, one name of Satan. "Neither shall any man pluck [snatch] them out of my hand." The word "man" is not in the Greek text. So the meaning is *anyone,* or *anything.* And then to make the promise even stronger, He added, "My Father . . . is greater than all; and no one [or no thing, neither man, thing, nor devil] is able to pluck [snatch] them out of my Father's hand" (v. 29). Jesus and His Father control every force in the universe.

This is one of the great passages on the security of the believer. Note that we do not hold on to Jesus or the Father. We are held by them. And before either man, thing, or devil can recapture to destroy us, such must overcome both the Son and the Father. And, of course, that is impossible. Our challenge is not to hold on to them, but to be sure that by faith and through divine grace we are in their hands. For God our Saviour not only saves, but safeguards!

The rulers had challenged Jesus to declare plainly His identity. So here it is. "I and my Father are one" (v. 30). Literally, "I and the Father are one." Note that "I" comes first. It is emphatic. This does not mean that Jesus placed Himself before the Father. The rulers had asked as to His identity. So He answered by saying, "I alone and the Father are one." Repeating, He did not place Himself *before* the Father. He identified Himself as *one with the Father.* One in nature, but two in outward revelation (cf. 17:11, 21-22). *Here Jesus clearly claimed deity.* Robertson calls this "the climax of Christ's claims concerning the relation between the Father and himself (the Son)."

But despite this clear claim to deity, there are those who deny that Jesus ever made such a claim. They may miss the point of His words. But the Jewish rulers did not. "Then the Jews took up stones again to stone him" (v. 31). Note the word "again." They had done so previously (8:59; cf. 5:16, 18). However, there is one difference. In John 8:59 they merely took up stones. But here the word rendered "took up" means to take up, to carry. It seems that they had to go elsewhere for stones. Robertson says that this perhaps means "they fetched stones from a distance." This was no spur-of-the-moment act. It speaks of a deep-seated purpose. It was not an act of sudden rage which would soon subside. It was one committed with a venomous resolve.

Jesus, seeing their resolve, asked for which of His good works did they propose to stone Him (v. 32)? Was it for His Sabbath healing of the lame man (5:9) or of the blind man (9:14)? They replied, "For a good work we stone thee not; but for blasphemy; and because thou, being a man, makest thyself God" (v. 33). Note the emphatic position of "thou," and the contrast: "man ... God."

Here, then, is the reason why they were so deeply enraged that "they fetched stones from a distance." In John 8:58 Jesus had claimed to be eternal and before Abraham. So in a moment of anger they picked up stones to stone Him. In John 5:18 they sought to kill Him not only because He had broken their Sabbath laws, but because He had claimed God as His Father, thus *making Himself equal with God*. But in John 10:33 it was "because that thou, *being a man, makest thyself God*" (author's italics). There can be no mistaking this. Jesus did make Himself God. If the claim is true then it is His most exalted claim. If it be not true, then it is blasphemy of the worst sort. History affirms the former. The Jewish rulers contended for the latter. In this passage only in John does the word "blasphemy" *(blasphēmia)* occur. Thus it seems that John himself records this statement to show the clarity of Jesus' claim and its rejection by these leaders.

There hardly can be any question but at the moment Jesus was in dire peril. The conflict between Him and the Jewish leaders had come to this critical point. For with murder in their eyes they probably stood with the stones poised. However, Jesus was equal to the occasion.

The most vulnerable spot about the Pharisees was the Scriptures. So Jesus quoted Psalm 82:6 where unjust judges were called "gods" (v. 34, *elohim*). If this be true, He asked, why then did they accuse Him of blasphemy when He claimed to be God (vv. 35-36)? These judges were but servants of God. He is the one whom the Father set apart and sent into the world for redemption. And, said Jesus, "the scripture cannot be broken." The Pharisees would have to agree to this. Thus with their own Scriptures He had answered their charge of blasphemy. We may well imagine that with this the poised stones were lowered.

He then challenged them to judge His works. If they were not the works of the Father, they should not believe Him (v. 37). But if they were then they should at least believe them, that they *might come to know* (ingressive aorist) and to *keep on knowing* (present tense) that the Father is in Him and He in the Father (v. 38).

They did not throw the stones. But they *kept on seeking* (imperfect) to seize Him. But He escaped out of their hand. Dropping the stones they grabbed for Him, but He walked away leaving them empty-handed and empty of soul.

The Peaceful Interlude (10:40-42)

The Conflict had reached the point where Jesus deemed it wise to leave Jerusalem and Judea, the center of Pharisaic power. So He went "beyond Jordan into the place where John at first baptized" (v. 40). This would be Perea. So this would be the beginning of His Perean ministry, the greater part of which is recorded in the Synoptic Gospels. "There he abode" (v. 40) suggests that He spent some time there. This would mean about three and one-half months, from Dedication until shortly before Passover (A.D. 29 — A.D. 30). Only one time during this period did He return to the vicinity of Jerusalem (Chapter 11). But even then He did not enter the city.

The immediate success of the Perean ministry John attributes to the faithful ministry of John the Baptist (v. 41). He worked no signs. But so faithfully did he speak of Jesus, that when Jesus arrived in that area the people recognized Him. "And many believed on him there" (v. 42).

This is the last mention of John the Baptist in this Gospel. It is a fitting epitaph to a great life. And it clearly showed that the Baptist did not seek to perpetuate himself. In fidelity he pointed to "the Lamb of God, which taketh away the sin of the world" (1:29).

VI
The Challenge to
the Sadducees

John 11

The Gauntlet Thrown Down

It was only a matter of weeks before the Passover in A.D. 30. Jesus was in the midst of His Perean ministry. After showing that Jesus went to this area (10:40-42) John makes no further mention of this ministry. It had already been related up to this point by Luke. But shortly before Jesus began His final journey from Galilee to Jerusalem through Perea, John inserts into the Gospel record a visit to Bethany near Jerusalem. Perhaps he had two purposes in doing so. Secondarily, he wished to relate another side to Martha's nature, and Mary's, from the ones found in Luke (10:38-42). Primarily, he proposed to present the event which brought the wrath of the Sadducees down upon Jesus, thus precipitating His death. Heretofore, with rare exceptions, the Sadducees had remained in the background, letting the Pharisees bear the brunt of opposing Jesus. But during the last week of Jesus' life they suddenly emerged as the leaders in destroying Him. Without John's account we would be at a loss fully to understand this. For in his Gospel John shows that Jesus clearly challenged them at their most sensitive spot, the matter of the resurrection of the dead. He threw down the gauntlet to them as though He dared them to pick it up. And pick it up they did.

The Distress in Bethany (11:1-4)

The event took place in Bethany, a small village about two miles east of Jerusalem. It was located just over the brow of the Mount of Olives eastward from the city. It is identified with the modern village of El 'Azariyeh. Although Luke records a previous visit to Bethany, he does not in that account give its name. We are indebted to John for identifying it as the home of Mary and Martha (v. 1). Furthermore, Luke does not mention their brother Lazarus. He does mention a Lazarus (16:20). But he does not relate him to the Lazarus in John. One can hardly read Luke's account, however, without wondering whether or not Jesus chose this name at that time looking forward to the event related by John. Certainly the name of the modern village El 'Azariyeh reflects this event in John 11. For Lazarus is but another form for Eleazar.

It is clear that John assumes that his readers know about Mary and Martha, probably from Luke. He simply mentions them as being of Bethany, the name omitted by Luke. And as mentioned above, he tells of their brother. It is assumed from various Gospel accounts that Jesus was accustomed to visiting in their home. It could well have been His headquarters while in the vicinity of Jerusalem. Thus we may assume that this family was unusually close to Jesus' heart (cf. vv. 3, 36).

Note that in identifying the two sisters John mentions Mary first. Luke reverses the order, even as John does in verse 19. His purpose in placing Mary first in verse 1 is explained in verse 2. Mary was better known to his Gentile readers for her act of anointing Jesus for burial. Her memoral was truly being spread abroad (cf. Mark 14:9). John assumes this widespread knowledge of Mary, even though he does not identify her until 12:13. But other than this one event it is evident that Martha is regarded as the one who bore the major responsibility for the home.

Lazarus "was sick" (v. 1). The form of the Greek verb shows that he had been ill for some time, and evidently had grown progressively worse. Apparently after the sisters had done all that they could for him to no avail, they sent a messenger to tell Jesus of his condition (v. 3). "Lord, behold, he whom thou lovest is sick." The verb "lovest" renders the Greek verb *phileō,* which means to love as a friend. It suggests a warm friendship between him and Jesus. And while it is not stated it is implied that the sisters expected Jesus to come to their aid immediately. In their dire need they turned to Jesus in faith.

Depending upon where Jesus was when the messengers found Him, He was at least two, probably three days from Bethany. But when He heard the news He said, "This sickness is not unto death, but for the glory of God, that the Son of God might be glorified thereby" (v. 4). As a matter of fact Lazarus did die. But it was only for a time. Its final issue was not permanent death. But it did furnish the occasion for the greatest evidence of the glory of God and of His Son prior to His own resurrection from the dead. However, the term "glorified" suggests something else. In keeping with John's use of that word it suggests Jesus' crucifixion. So the occasion of Lazarus' sickness will be definitely connected with the forthcoming crucifixion of the Son of God. It was this event which brought the greatest glory to the Father and the Son as Redeemer. Thus we see evolving the primary purpose of the author in relating this incident.

The Delay of Jesus (11:5-6)

If the sisters expected an immediate response from Jesus, they were in for a disappointment. In a sense they had prayed to Jesus. But they did not receive the expected answer. Oftentimes when we do not receive that for which we pray, we say that our prayer was not answered. What we mean is that we did not receive the answer that we wanted. "No" can be an answer. In fact, God has one of three answers for every prayer offered in faith: "No," "Yes," and "Wait." God in His merciful wisdom may say, "No," immediately. Or He may say, "Yes," immediately. Or He may say, "Wait"; wait until you are prepared to receive it. For He designs some far better thing than you desire. It was this last answer that Jesus gave to this prayer.

Strange indeed sound the words of John's record. "Now Jesus loved Martha, and her sister, and Lazarus" (v. 5). Here "loved" is different from the word in verse 3. It is *agapaō*, expressing the highest kind of love. In this sense it means *divine love*. From it comes the word *agapē* (cf. I John 4:8). At times this verb is used interchangeably with *phileō*. But there is a distinction between them (cf. John 21). So while Jesus loved Lazarus as a friend *(phileō)*, He also loved him and his sisters with divine love *(agapaō)*. That which follows shows this to be true.

But what a strange reaction even for divine love. "When he had heard therefore that he was sick, he abode two days still in the same place where he was" (v. 6). Even as one reads the account he gets a shock. The natural impulse is to expect Jesus to rush off to Bethany. Had John been inventing the story, that is most likely what he would have said. But while man gets in a hurry, God never does. He works according to His knowledge and benevolent purpose.

Why did Jesus delay? It certainly was not out of indifference for His friends' need. Such would be completely out of character for Jesus. Was it to test the faith of the sisters? Did He delay in order to give Lazarus time to die? Robertson suggests that this may have been the case. Dods follows Godet and others in suggesting that Jesus waited for a prompting from the Father. Bernard notes the distance from Bethany, suggesting that probably Jesus knew that

Lazarus was already dead. However, he raises a question based upon Martha's statement in verse 21 to the effect that she means that Jesus had had time to arrive before Lazarus' death. However, as will be seen at that point her words may carry an entirely different meaning.

The writer is in agreement with Bernard's former position. Assuming that Jesus was only a two days' journey from Bethany, when He arrived Lazarus had been dead four days. Even without His delay of two days, He would have arrived two days after his death. It would appear, therefore, that he had died at about the time the messenger reached Jesus (cf. v. 14). And knowing this with a knowledge beyond man's understanding, He knew that there was no reason for haste. Some even see a strangeness in the fact that Jesus permitted the sisters to be in agony for an additional two days. But even this additional time probably figured in Jesus' purpose, as will be pointed out when we discuss verse 17. For Jesus planned for the sisters an even greater joy than they could have known had He simply healed their brother. In reply to their prayer, therefore, He said, "Wait, and you shall see the glory of the Lord beyond anything that you dare to ask or to expect."

The Danger in Judea (11:7-16)

At the end of the two days of waiting Jesus said, "Let us go into Judea again" (v. 7). It had not been long since He had left that area because of the growing hatred of the Jewish leaders. Even though Perea was in the territory of Herod Antipas it was less perilous than Judea.

Knowing this the Twelve sought to dissuade Jesus from His purpose. "Master [Rabbi], the Jews of late sought to stone thee; and goest thou thither again?" (v. 8). "Sought" is an imperfect form. So recently they "were seeking" to stone Him to death. To them it seemed to be suicidal madness to leave this safe retreat. However, Jesus persisted. In effect He said that there are twelve hours of daylight·in which to work (v. 9). One cannot stumble in broad daylight. So that is the time to work. He was in the daylight of God's will in going to Bethany. He had faith to believe that God would watch over Him until His "hour" should come. While He did not foolishly expose Himself to the murderous intent of the Jews, He would not act the coward in shirking His duty. Only the man who walks in spiritual darkness outside the will of God needs to fear (v. 10).

And then He gave His purpose for going to Bethany. "Our friend Lazarus sleepeth; but I go, that I may awake him out of sleep" (v. 11). Mistaking the import of His words the disciples said, "Lord, if he sleeps, he doeth well" (v. 12). Thinking entirely of Lazarus' illness they thought of physical sleep. To them sleep was a sign of abating fever. So they said, "He will recover." The words "will recover" render the verb *sōzō,* the word for being saved. But it also means to be rescued from danger or to be healed. This last meaning applies here. Since Lazarus was getting better there was no need for Jesus to take the risk involved in His proposed journey.

It was then that Jesus explained the meaning of His word "sleepeth" (v. 13). Plainly He said, "Lazarus is dead" (v. 14). And for their sakes He was glad that He was not in Bethany during His illness. For He proposed a greater "sign" than merely healing the sick (v. 15). They had seen Him do this many times. On two previous occasions they had even seen Him raise the dead (cf. Mark 5:35-42; Luke 7:11-17). But there were circumstances in Lazarus' case that made Jesus' forthcoming act different. Therefore, the disciples' faith in Him would be strengthened immeasurably by what was to be His greatest "sign."

Jesus' use of the term *sleep* in connection with death has led some to believe in *soul sleeping,* or that after death the soul remains in an unconscious state until the resurrection. However, this view is contrary to the abundant teaching of the New Testament. *Sleep* in this sense simply means rest from the cares and labors of life.

So despite the danger and the fact that Lazarus was dead, Jesus said, "Nevertheless let us go unto him" (v. 15). Seeing, therefore, that Jesus intended to go, Thomas (Didymus, a twin,) said, "Let us also go, that we may die with him" (v. 16). Actually, both "Thomas" and "Didymus" mean "twin." The former is Aramaic; the latter is Greek. Robertson notes that in Greek circles he probably was called Didymus. Clearly, then, he had either a twin brother or sister (cf. 20:24; 21:2).

This is the first mention of Thomas in this Gospel (cf. 14:5; 20:24, 26-29; 21:2). And it presents quite a different picture than the one usually associated with him (cf. John 20). Here he stands out as a man of great loyalty and courage. Lazarus is dead, the Jews will kill Jesus if He goes to Bethany, but he is ready to die with Him. Even if, as Robertson says, it was a "pessimistic courage," it was courage nevertheless. Dods notes that "if Thomas is

stiff and obstinate in his incredulity, he is also stiff and obstinate
in his affection and allegiance." So he might well be called
"Thomas the Heroic." And his example inspired the same quality
in the other disciples. For they all went with Jesus to what they
thought might well be His death and theirs. It is a noble picture of
this little band. One hesitates to ascribe such loyalty and courage
to Judas. Perhaps he lacked the moral courage to break with the
band. But, even so, he had not yet fully surrendered to Satan's
wiles. The fact is that he also went along on this perilous mission.

The Arrival in Bethany (11:17-22)

When Jesus arrived in Bethany He found that Lazarus had
been buried four days (v. 17). Due to the lack of means by which
to preserve bodies he probably was buried on the day of his death
(cf. Acts 6:6, 10). But allowing two days travel time for Jesus
this would still mean that Lazarus had died about the time that
the messenger had reached Him with the news of his sickness.

Since Bethany was only about two miles from Jerusalem (v. 18),
many Jews had come from there and from elsewhere to comfort
the bereaved sisters (v. 19). Mourning for the dead lasted for
seven days (I Sam. 31:13). Robertson notes that the large number of mourners speaks for the prominence of this family. Evidence
shows that most of these probably were not unfriendly to Jesus,
but even in so tender a scene unbelief raised its ugly head (cf.
vv. 36-37).

Martha heard that Jesus was coming. So even before He reached
the village, she went out and met Him (v. 20). All the while Mary
"was sitting" in the house. Thus both sisters appear in character.
Martha ever busy, Mary ever sitting (cf. Luke 10:38-42). The
suggestion is that Mary had given in to her grief. But Martha in
her grief remained busy, which within itself is good therapy. One
can easily imagine that Martha was looking after the needs of her
guests, the mourners.

When Martha met Jesus she said, "Lord, if thou hadst been
here, my brother had not died" (v. 21). One might see in this a
gentle note of rebuke. But, on the other hand, in view of the time
element noted above (v. 17), it is probably more an expression of
faith. Had Jesus been there He could have healed Lazarus. Of
course, we know that had Jesus chosen He could have healed from
a distance (cf. 4:50-53). But it was not within His purpose to do so.

Nevertheless, even in her grief Martha clung to her faith. "But

I know [*oida,* a thorough knowledge], that even now, whatsoever thou wilt ask of God, God will give it thee" (v. 22). The subjunctive form of "ask" suggests that she was not certain as to what Jesus will ask. But there is also the subtle suggestion that He may ask that her brother shall be restored to her. In despair she still holds on to her hope as well as her faith.

The Assurance of Jesus (11:23-27)

And she was not disappointed. For Jesus assured her that her brother shall rise again (v. 23). How often friends say this as consolation to those in bereavement. It may even appear to be trite from its much using. But trite or not, it is nevertheless true. If it consoles when spoken by a friend, how much more so when spoken by the Friend. However, at the moment it did not seem to satisfy Martha. "I know that he shall rise again in the resurrection at the last day" (v. 24). She shared with most other righteous Jews in the hope of a final resurrection of the righteous. But that seemed so far away in time. Even without that hope how could one endure the loss of a loved one in death. Such may ease the present hurt, but it does not fully remove the loneliness of heart.

She thought of the future. But Jesus spoke of the present. "I am the resurrection, and the life: he that believeth in me, though he were dead, yet shall he live" (v. 25). "I am" *(egō eimi).* "I and no one else am the resurrection, and the life." Not "I will be," "I am." Such words coming from anyone who could not use the words "I am" in the sense of deity would be a mockery. But they fall naturally from Jesus' lips.

However, there is more. "And whosoever liveth and believeth in me shall never die" (v. 26). Here Jesus used the strong double negative. "Shall not never die." Of course, Lazarus was dead. Yet he had believed in Jesus. So He was not speaking of physical death, but of spiritual death. The Christian already has eternal life. It is not some future hope but a present reality. The mere accident of physical death does not change that. Even though Lazarus had died physically, he continued to live. Westcott notes that "The Resurrection is one manifestation of the Life: it is involved in the Life."

Jesus, therefore, put Martha's faith to the test. "Believest thou this?" (v. 26). It was one thing to speak of eternal life in an academic way. But in the presence of physical death, did she still believe this? Did she believe that her brother was alive even though his body lay in a nearby tomb? This is a test of our faith also. All of the mortician's art cannot remove the ugly presence of death. Only a firm faith in Him who is Life can do that. The blessed assurance of the Christian is not based *only* upon the hope of a final resurrection, but upon the conviction of a continuing life for the true self of those whom we have loved and lost for awhile.

And Martha came through the test with her colors flying. "Yea, Lord: I believe that thou art the Christ, the Son of God, which should come into the world" (v. 27). The perfect form of "believe *(pepisteuka)* following the emphatic use of "I" *(egō)* speaks of her firmly fixed faith. She had believed it, still believes it, and will continue to believe it — regardless of what was happening to her at the moment. Outward circumstances did not change her abiding faith.

What Jesus had just said was too much for her to digest in a moment. But where she could not fully comprehend, she could fully trust. Her faith went farther than her understanding. And her faith never wavered.

It is this writer's conviction that hers was the greatest confession of Jesus' Messiahship recorded in the Gospels. Yes, even greater than Peter's (cf. Matt. 16:16). For he made his from the mountain top of many glorious experiences with Jesus. While Martha made hers from the pit of despondency. She could not explain all that had happened to her. But in spite of it all she did not falter in her faith concerning Jesus.

Here we see John's secondary purpose in recording this event. It shows that while Martha was a practical woman in every respect, as shown in Luke, she was also a woman of tremendous faith. These two elements are not necessarily antagonistic to each other. One can have both. One can be a "Martha," and at the same time be a person of strong spiritual qualities. It is not either/or. It can be both/and. Martha is a shining example of this combination.

The Dual Reaction of Jesus (11:28-38)

Strengthened by her faith in Jesus, Martha went to tell Mary that He had arrived. "The Master is here, and is calling you" (v. 28). Quickly Mary went out to where He was waiting (vv. 29-30). Since Martha had told her of Jesus' arrival secretly, the friends assumed that her quick departure meant that she was going to the tomb of her brother to weep (v. 31).

Mary acted as we would expect her to do. She ran and fell at

Jesus' feet. As she did so she repeated exactly what Martha had said (v. 32; cf. v. 21). Evidently they had said many times to one another in their ordeal, "If Jesus were only here He could do something." But, alas, He came too late! Note that while Mary expressed faith that had Jesus been there her brother would not have died, she did not express the faith uttered by Martha as to future assurance. Hers was a grief of despair.

Indeed, some interpreters see a note of displeasure in Jesus' reaction before Mary's hopeless weeping or wailing coupled with that of her friends (v. 33). "He groaned in his spirit, and was troubled." Was this a reaction of sympathy alone? The word "groaned" renders the verb *embrimaomai*. Robertson notes that it means to snort with anger like a horse. He further points out its use in Daniel 11:30 (Septuagint) for "violent displeasure" (cf. Lam. 2:6; Mark 14:5 where "murmured" means "were indignant"). This word is used of Jesus in Matthew 9:30 and Mark 1:43 where it is rendered "straitly charged," or as a stern admonition. So certainly in John 11:33 this word connotes a strong emotion within Jesus.

But what kind of emotion was it? Some see it as an effort to refrain from giving in to grief Himself. But He did do this in verse 35. Bernard suggests that it could refer to spiritual agitation due to the spiritual energy required to work the forthcoming miracle. However, he concludes that it "may well express the physical effect of powerful emotion upon his voice. It represents the inarticulate sounds which escape men when they are physically overwhelmed by a great wave of emotion." Dods, after taking note of the basic meaning of the verb *embrimaomai*, rejects the idea of indignation and relates it to a sympathetic reaction. Barclay notes that the verb ordinarily carries the idea of sternness, or of rebuke. But he rejects this idea here. Instead, he sees it as expressing the idea that unlike the apathetic nature of Greek pagan gods, Jesus shows that God identifies Himself with our sorrow. Even Arndt and Gingrich give the meanings of censure, stern charging, and of being indignant. These are based upon both Biblical and extra-Biblical usages. Yet in John 11:33 and 38 they give the meaning of being deeply moved. However, they do not specify the nature of this emotion. But Robertson sees indignation in these uses. The writer is inclined to agree with him. One wonders if various scholars have not read into this usage a meaning which at first sight seems to fit the context, but which is not in keeping with other uses of the word.

But let us look at it in this context. Note first of all that Jesus was moved "in spirit and troubled himself" (v. 33). In verse 38 He was moved "in himself." These uses suggest a deep-seated spiritual agitation, not merely a human emotion. Now what would cause such an agitation? In the case of Mary and her friends they had given themselves to a hopeless wailing, for that is the meaning of the words "weeping" in verse 33 *(klaiō)*. Mary's own words carry no element of a future faith and hope. Certainly here she, unlike Martha, had not chosen the better part (Luke 10:42). Seeing this, Jesus was indignant in His spirit that she who had so often sat at His feet should, in this crisis, give way to despair. In verse 38 Jesus' "groaning" followed immediately upon the expression of unbelief in verse 37. It is natural, therefore, that He would be indignant "in himself," or in His deeper self, that such criticism should be made. So we conclude that in each of these uses the verb *embrimaomai* carries its usual meaning of one who is indignant.

Now this does not in any sense remove Jesus from the intense suffering of His friends. As God He was indignant in the presence of unbelief. But as the God-Man He did enter into their sorrow. For as He asked to be taken to the tomb, He "wept" (vv. 34-35). "Jesus wept," is the shortest verse in the Bible. But in it is bound up all of Jesus' sympathetic response to human suffering. Literally, "Jesus burst into tears." The verb here is *dakruō* coming from the word for "tear." This word never means to wail, as *klaiō* sometimes does. It simply means to shed tears. In the light of Jesus' words to Martha about the resurrection and the life, these could hardly be tears of personal bereavement. For more than anyone else He knew that Lazarus was still living, indeed was more alive at the moment to spiritual realities than he had ever been before. It has even been suggested that Jesus wept because He knew that He was about to call His friend back into the cares of this world. However, there is no real evidence to support such a position. We can best explain Jesus' tears as His response to the sorrows of those about Him. He entered into their suffering in a way more eloquent than words.

There were two reactions to Jesus' tears. Some of the Jews said, "Behold how he loved him!" (v. 36). Yes. And them also. But others said, "Could not this man, which opened the eyes of the blind, have caused that even this man should not have died?" (v. 37). They remembered the miracle performed three months previously (cf. 9:1 ff.). It is of interest that they made no mention of the two occasions when Jesus had raised the dead in Galilee. Did they not know about them? It is difficult to believe that these tremendous acts were unknown in Jerusalem. Perhaps the Jewish leaders had denied the authenticity of such reports, attributing them to the naiveté of the rural Galileans, and the Jerusalemites had accepted their denial. Actually the absence of any reference to these deeds speaks for the historical value of the Fourth Gospel. Anyone inventing this story would certainly have made reference to the previous raisings of the dead. Godet points to this as an evidence of a first-century authorship of the Gospel. By the second century the stories of the Galilean miracles would have been well known around Ephesus. If the Gospel had been written then it most likely would have made reference to them.

It would appear, therefore, that the author, who most likely was an eyewitness, reported what actually happened. One thing is certain. The healing of the blind man had made a lasting impression upon the inhabitants of Jerusalem.

What was the attitude in which these Jews raised this question? Did they ask it in good faith? To say the least, they were skeptical as to Jesus' previous actions. There are two possible meanings in the question. Either they doubted that Jesus could have healed Lazarus, or else they admitted that He could have but did not. On the one hand, it would be a question as to Jesus' power to heal. On the other hand, it would be a question as to His willingness to do so. In either case, it would reflect unfavorably upon Him.

This explains Jesus' indignant groaning following their inquiry. As He was indignant at the lack of a future faith (v. 32), so here He was indignant because of a lack of a present faith (v. 38). Godet notes that Jesus' disturbance was less pronounced here ("groaned in himself") than in verse 33 ("groaned in the spirit, and was troubled"). This may be explained in that His agitation over Mary's lack of a future faith was greater than the lack of a present faith on the part of unbelieving Jews. At any rate it was in such a disturbed spirit that Jesus arrived at the tomb.

The Raising of Lazarus (11:39-46)

The tomb of Lazarus was a cave, a commonly used method of burial among the Jews. It could be either a natural or an artificial cave such as the one in which Jesus was buried. After the body was placed in the cave a stone was placed over the entrance.

When Jesus arrived at this cave He said, "Take ye away the stone" (v. 39)). He would do what only God could do, but He employed man's power to the limit of its ability. However, Martha protested that "by this time he stinketh: for he hath been dead four days." She assumed this to be the case as well she might.

It is at this point that the purpose of Jesus' delay of two days in Perea comes into focus. Lightfoot cites a Jewish tradition to the effect that upon death the soul hovers around the tomb for three days hoping to re-enter the body. But on the fourth day it departs. Now we are not required to suppose that Martha believed this. Certainly Jesus did not. But evidently this was believed among the Jews generally.

Had Jesus raised Lazarus prior to the fourth day, this most likely would have been used to explain away His "sign." But on the fourth day even the Jews would admit that Lazarus was truly dead, and that his soul had departed. Therefore, in Perea, knowing that Lazarus was dead, Jesus deliberately waited two days. He timed His arrival in Bethany for the fourth day after death. He knew what He would do. But it must be done in a way and at a time when everyone, including the Jewish leaders, would have to admit that Lazarus was really dead and that Jesus had raised him from the dead. Incidentally, this fact also answers the claim that Lazarus was simply in a coma. So for the present and for all time to come, Jesus provided an answer for all adverse critics.

In reply to Martha's protest Jesus reminded her of His promise recorded in verses 25-26 (v. 40). He wills to raise Lazarus, and to do it for God's glory (cf. v. 4). After the stone had been removed Jesus prayed (v. 41). He thanked the Father for answering His prayer even before He prayed it. He was aware of God's willingness to hear Him. But He prayed audibly in order that those about Him might come to believe that the Father had sent Him. (v. 42).

"And when he thus had spoken, he cried with a loud voice, Lazarus, come forth" (v. 43). Literally, "Lazarus, hither out." Jesus' loud voice was not for the dead man's benefit. It was for the benefit of those about Him. He wanted them to see that Lazarus came forth in response to His call. Immediately Lazarus "came forth" (aorist, v. 44). As he did so the people saw that he had been properly prepared for burial, He was bound "as to the feet and hands." Evidently his legs were bound separately, thus allowing him to walk. He also had a napkin about his face (cf. 20:6-7). One can imagine the astonishment of the people, including Martha and Mary. But Jesus broke in upon their amazement with a command. "Loose him [from the grave clothes], and let him go." Again Jesus permitted men to do what they were capable of doing.

Was the raising of Lazarus a resurrection? Hardly so, since Jesus Himself was the "first-fruits" from the dead (I Cor. 15:20). *Resurrection* means that one is raised from the dead to die no more. This was not true of Lazarus, the widow's son at Nain, or the daughter of Jairus. They were brought back to earthly life to die again physically. So theirs was a resusitation, not a resurrection. This does not mean that they were any less dead. It simply means that they did not experience a resurrection in the sense that Jesus did or that will occur when He comes again.

One can hardly imagine but one reaction to so tremendous a "sign." However, that was not the case. Many of the Jews "seeing what he did, believed on him" (v. 45). They not only believed what they saw, they also believed in Him who had done this. But some had quite a different reaction. They believed what they saw, for there was no denying it. But they did not believe on Jesus. Rather they "went immediately" (aorist) to Jerusalem, and reported the incident to the Pharisees (v. 46). Instead of falling at Jesus' feet in faith, they *hot-footed* it to tell His enemies. Strange indeed are the ways of some who stand in the presence of the power of God, and yet turn away from it to walk in the power of Satan!

The Fateful Decision (11:47-53)

Jesus had thrown down the gauntlet to His enemies. And they were not long in taking it up.

To be sure this report created a crisis among the "chief priests [Sadducees] and the Pharisees" (v. 47). So they called the Sanhedrin into session. One would think that the Pharisees would have rejoiced over such news. But they were dominated by their hatred for Jesus, and apparently by the Sadducees. It is an open question as to whether or not the Pharisees ever would have killed Jesus. They might have argued Him to death. At times their venomous hatred had driven them to the brink of stoning Him. But they had never taken the fateful plunge.

However, the realistic Sadducees were another matter. Spas-modically they had joined with the Pharisees in opposing Jesus. But so long as He merely spoke words or even performed certain "signs" they were content to leave the matter largely in the hands of their arch-rivals. However, when Jesus raised Lazarus from the dead His doom was sealed. Oh, there had been reports of similar events in Galilee. But these were far away and among a simple, rural people. The Galileans would believe anything. But when within two miles of the temple and in the presence of Jerusalem-ites He raised the dead, that was too much. The chief priests could neither ignore it nor deny it. Therefore, they asked the Sanhedrin, "What are we doing? for this man is doing many signs" (v. 47). This question evidently was hurled at the Pharisees. The chief priests had been letting them handle the matter. And it had come to this. The Pharisees had failed, so now they must take charge. Note that they no longer contemptuously called Jesus "this fellow." They could ignore Him no longer. He was a serious threat and must be dealt with.

"If we let him thus alone, all men will believe on him [they feared a revolution]: and the Romans will come and take away both our place and nation" (v. 48). Note that they put "place" before "nation." They were more concerned about their position of power and privilege than about their nation. They were poli-ticians in the worst sense of the word. Rome would not counte-nance rebellion. Two things they required above all others: to keep peace and to collect taxes. Actually, in about forty years they did come and take away both *place* and *nation*. But the Sadducees could not foresee that. They were concerned with the expediency of the moment.

Evidently the meeting was turning into a squabble between the contending groups, and they were getting nowhere. So Caiaphas, the high priest, broke into the discussion. "Ye know nothing at all" (v. 49). Since they had no solution to the problem, he of-fered one. "Nor consider that it is expedient for us, that one man should die for [*huper*] the people, and that the whole nation perish not" (v. 50). Note the words "expedient *for us* (author's italics). He played one of the oldest tricks in the game of power politics. In the name of patriotism (nation perish not) he sought to save his own position of power.

John comments that there was more in Caiaphas' words than he knew (vv. 51-52). Though his words were only cunning and selfish, unconsciously he had prophesied the manner of Jesus' death: "for [huper, as a substitute for] that nation and not for that nation [Jews] only, but that he should gather together in one the children of God that were scattered abroad." This last phrase does not refer merely to the Jews of the Dispersion outside of Palestine, but to God's children who might believe on Jesus wherever and whoever they might be. Here again is seen the universal nature of the Saviourhood of Jesus.

At this point the Sanhedrin made its fateful decision. They had a choice. Either Jesus must die or they must lose their *place* and *nation*. So they all voted in favor of Jesus being the *substitute*. They neither knew nor cared that they were voting for the *substitutionary atonement*. It was either Jesus or themselves. And they cast their lots for Jesus, not in faith but in faithless expediency.

Having decided, it was only a matter of time. Actually it was only a few weeks. "Then from that day forth they took counsel together for to put him to death" (v. 53). They became companions in crime, the crime of the ages.

The Caution of Jesus (11:54)

Evidently Jesus heard about their decision. At any rate He knew what their reaction to His *gauntlet* would be. Therefore, He "walked no more openly among the Jews." The imperfect tense means that He ceased His habit of walking about where they could seize Him. He had no fear. But neither did He tempt God by unnecessary exposure.

Therefore, Jesus left the vicinity of Jerusalem. He went into the wilderness, or a thinly populated area called Ephraim. The exact location of this village is not known. Josephus mentions a small fort near Bethel. II Chronicles 13:19 mentions such a town near Bethel. It was probably in the northeastern part of Judea. Here Jesus was comparatively safe, and could spend some precious time teaching His disciples.

Luke 17:11 says, "And it came to pass, as he went to Jerusalem, that he passed through the midst of Samaria and Galilee." This was the beginning of Jesus' final journey to Jerusalem. Were Luke simply describing a journey from Galilee he would have said "through the midst of Galilee and Samaria." Since he reversed the order, it means that from somewhere in Judea Jesus went north through Samaria into Galilee. There He joined a caravan traveling the usual route through Perea.

This account blends naturally with John's record. From Ephraim Jesus and the Twelve journeyed through Samaria to Galilee, and thence toward Jerusalem.

The Last Passover (11:55-57)

The fourth Passover in Jesus' ministry was near at hand (v. 55). Many Jews "went out of the country up to Jerusalem." Note the topographical note "up to Jerusalem." "Out of the country" means all of Palestine, and could even include Jews from other parts of the world. These went to Jerusalem prior to Passover week in order to purify themselves that they might be ready to participate in the festal ceremonies.

The whole country was buzzing about Jesus. Evidently word of the raising of Lazarus was getting around. So these early arrivers "were seeking" (imperfect) Jesus (v. 56). They stood as "knots of people in the Temple precincts" (Bernard). And they "were saying among themselves" (imperfect), "What think ye, that he will not come to the feast?" (v. 56). Using the strong double negative (ou mē) with the aorist subjunctive, they strongly suggest that under the circumstances surely Jesus would not dare come to this feast.

And why? Because the Sanhedrin had given strict orders that should anyone know of Jesus' whereabouts, he should report it to them (v. 57). They were determined to seize Him and put an end to His work. Poor wretches, indeed, for despite their evil designs, God was moving toward the climactic events whereby neither He nor His work would ever end.

And the doubts of the people were wrong also. For Jesus' "hour" was hastening on. He will make one last challenge to the city which has rejected Him repeatedly. Even then His footsteps were leading Him toward Jerusalem and His rendezvous with God's eternal purpose of redemption.

VII
The Approaching Climax

John 12

The Gathering Storm

Jerusalem and its environs were alive with activity. From every direction pilgrims were arriving for the Passover. Every male Jew living within twenty miles of Jerusalem was required to attend the feast. Since it was the principal Jewish feast multitudes of people came from afar to celebrate it. No matter where a Jew lived in the world, he hoped to be able to attend at least one such feast in his lifetime.

This season was always one of excitement. Since it commemorated Israel's deliverance from Egyptian bondage, it was hoped that at some Passover God would again deliver His people from their oppressors. This hope centered in the Messiah whom the Jews had come to think of in political-military terms. It was widely reported that Jesus was the Christ. And due to His growing conflict with the Jewish leaders, it was expected that this also would come to a head at this Passover. Such could well mean that He was about to declare Himself and through revolt against Rome establish His kingdom. Therefore, the excitement ran unusually high this year of A.D. 30. So much so that the Jewish leaders had given orders for Jesus to be arrested should He appear in the area. Thus they hoped to avoid the crisis at this time. They had vowed to put Jesus to death. But it must be accomplished at a time when it could be done without incurring a rebellion among the people. It was in such an atmosphere that Jesus arrived in the vicinity of Jerusalem.

In order to establish a true sequence of events it is necessary to rearrange the material in this chapter. From the Synoptic Gospels (Matthew and Mark) we know that the supper in Bethany took place on Tuesday evening of Passion Week. John places it immediately upon Jesus' arrival in Bethany, probably on Friday night, before that week. He does not definitely name the night. But he certainly relates the event at a time different from the others. This is understandable, however, in that John is not trying to establish a sequence. He simply tells the story in con-

(12: 2-8) is on page 201.

nection with his last mention of Bethany. But following the Synoptics we shall place it at the end of Chapter 12.

The Arrival at Bethany (12:1, 9-11)

Six days before the Passover Jesus and His disciples arrived in Bethany (v. 1). In all likelihood this was late on Friday afternoon. While it is not stated, they probably stayed at the home of Martha, Mary, and Lazarus. It must have been a time of rejoicing, since it was Jesus' first visit with them after He had raised Lazarus from the dead.

Word soon spread abroad that Jesus was there (v. 9). So the next day (Saturday) "much people," or "the common people" came to Bethany, not only to see Jesus, but to see the one whom He had raised from the dead. This group would certainly include many pilgrims who wanted to see such a man. The word of Jesus' "sign" was racing through the gathering throng.

So much so that the chief priests decided to add Lazarus to their list of *most wanted men* (v. 10). So long as he was around they could not hope to put an end to the story. As it was he only added to the revolutionary excitement. Because of him many of the Jews, even Jerusalemites, "were going away and were believing on Jesus" (v. 11). These two imperfect tenses suggest a growing defection from the Sanhedrin's leadership to that of Jesus. This very resolve of the chief priests may explain why the Synoptic Gospels did not include the story of the raising of Lazarus, and that in the story of the feats in Bethany they omit the names of Lazarus and his sisters. If they were still living these accounts could have endangered them. Most likely they had died before John wrote, so that these matters were no longer a threat to their safety.

The Royal Entry (12:12-19)

At this point John begins his second parallel to the Synoptic account, although he also continues to relate events not found in it. This parallel is understandable since it involves the crux of Jesus' ministry.

It was Sunday (Palm Sunday). And in spite of the threat of the Jewish leaders Jesus proposed to go into Jerusalem. Heretofore, He had entered the city unobserved. But now He did so amid a public demonstration. Since this event was already fully recorded by the Synoptics, John gives only an abbreviated account of it. But he does include it because of its vital implications.

The tone of the story shows signs of deliberate preparation. Jesus had arranged for a donkey on which to ride into the city (cf. Mark 11:1 ff. and Synoptic parallels). And this was not done without a purpose. This event is called Jesus' "Triumphal Entry" into Jerusalem. But the facts indicate otherwise. In ancient times when a king or general returned to his capital city from a victorious military campaign, he had a triumphal entry. Usually he rode in his chariot or on a white horse, symbolizing victory, and was followed by defeated kings or other captives as evidence of victory. Riding through the shouting multitudes, he threw gifts of money into the crowd. In this sense it is more in keeping with custom to see Jesus' triumphal entry into His capital city (heaven) as recorded in Ephesians 4:8 ff.

But His entry into Jerusalem was quite different. He came to Jerusalem *before* the final battle, not *after* the victory. Furthermore, He came riding upon a donkey, signifying that He came as a king of peace. Zechariah 9:9 reads, "Rejoice greatly, O daughter of Zion; shout, O daughter of Jerusalem: behold, thy King cometh unto thee: he is just, and having salvation; lowly, and riding upon an ass, and upon a colt the foal of an ass."

Jesus, therefore, came into Jerusalem, not as a conquering king but as the King of peace. Instead of this being His *Triumphal Entry* it was His *Royal Entry*. It was the King coming in peace to His own city. Thus far Jerusalem, the capital city of Judaism, had rejected Him. Now in a final effort He rode into the city, not as a political-military Messiah but as one just, lowly, and bringing salvation. Jerusalem must receive Him or else finally and fatally reject Him.

Why did He choose this particular occasion for such a challenge? To begin with, the season was ripe for it. A head-on collision between Jesus and the Jewish leaders was inevitable. And as always Jesus chose the time and place for it. Either He or they must prevail. The people must decide with whom their loyalty lay. Again, at no other place or season could Jesus find a larger convocation of Jews. Furthermore, it included Jews from all over the world, at least the Roman world. So in a sense Jesus presented Himself not to Palestinian Jews alone but to the Jews of the world.

Thirty years later at the Passover a Roman governor took a census of the number of lambs slain. The number was 250,000.

Since one lamb was required for ten people, this meant that 2,500,000 Jews were present for that one Passover. We may assume that there were at least that many present when Jesus made His *Royal Entry* into Jerusalem.

Therefore, "on the next day a great multitude, the one coming unto the feast, hearing that Jesus is coming into Jerusalem, took the branches of the palm trees, and began to cry out, Hosanna: blessed is the one coming in the name of the Lord, even the king of Israel" (vv. 12-13). These were Messianic cries. Seeing Jesus riding on a donkey they caught the significance of His act. It was a fulfilment of Zechariah 9:9 (vv. 14-15). Therefore, in hilarious spirit they acclaimed Jesus as Christ and King. So confused were they by current Messianic expectations that they lost the full significance of it all. But according to their understanding world Jewry did herald Him as the long looked-for Messiah. However, when He failed to fulfil their erroneous idea they later turned on Him. Even the Twelve did not fully comprehend the meaning of Jesus' *Royal Entry* until after the resurrection (v. 16). And from subsequent events we know that Judas suffered bitter disappointment when Jesus failed to use this occasion to declare His kingdom. The Twelve and others who were present at the raising of Lazarus related the two events, and were convinced (all but Judas) all the more that Jesus was the Christ (v. 17).

Because of this demonstration people in Jerusalem who knew about the "sign" in Bethany also met Jesus (v. 18). Thus the people with Jesus were met by those coming out of the city. Converging, they accompanied Him into the city to the tune of their Messianic cries.

Meanwhile the Pharisees stood by helpless. "Perceive ye how ye prevail nothing? behold, the world is gone after him" (v. 19). These words probably were directed at the Sadducees. They had accused the Pharisees of failure. Now it was their turn to look into the grim jaws of defeat. Their well-laid plans to arrest Jesus had gone awry. Instead of leading Jesus into the city in chains, they could only stand by in mutual condemnation as He was ushered into Jerusalem by this shouting throng.

The Synoptic Gospels tell how Jesus entered the temple area, looked around, and that evening returned to Bethany (cf. Matt. 21:10-11, 14-17; Mark 11:11). Contrary to popular expectation He did not proclaim a revolution. What that morning had been a shouting multitude was now a disorganized, disgruntled group.

They were prime material out of which to form a mob. And the Sanhedrin was not unaware of this fact. Even so, they deemed it wise to postpone seizing Jesus until after these pilgrims had departed (cf. Matt. 26:3-5). The Jerusalemites they could handle. But they were not so sure about these outsiders.

The Visit of the Greeks (12:20-32)

The next day (Monday) Jesus cleansed the temple a second time (cf. Matt. 21:12-13; Mark 11:15-18; Luke 19:45-48). Sometime later that day, probably in the temple area, a group of Greeks approached those gathered around Jesus (v. 20). These were not Greek-speaking Jews but true Greeks. Since they had come to the feast they probably were either Jewish proselytes or else God-fearers. The latter were Gentiles who were studying the Jewish religion but who had not accepted it as their own (cf. Acts 10:2). The former were Gentiles who had become Jews in religion through circumcision, certain sacrifices, and by accepting the law of Moses (cf. Matt. 23:18; Acts 2:10; 6:5; 13:53).

These Greeks approached Philip (v. 21). His name was Greek which indicates that he would be sympathetic toward these men. It is possible that they knew him, perhaps were from his hometown of Bethsaida, an area where many Greeks lived. At any rate they expressed their desire to him. "Sir, we wish to see Jesus." This request posed a problem to Philip. Would Jesus grant an audience to Greeks? For the moment he forgot His words about "other sheep" (10:16). So he brought the problem to Andrew, another man with a Greek name. Together they decided to tell Jesus (v. 22). Once again we see Andrew as the means of bringing someone to Jesus.

This news disturbed Jesus, but not because of racial prejudice as Philip feared. It was for the very opposite reason. For in this little group of Gentiles He saw the foretaste of innumerable Gentiles who should believe on Him. This brought Jesus face to face with His "hour" by which both Jews and Gentiles would be saved.

Therefore, in response to the word of His two disciples Jesus said, "The hour is come, that the Son of man should be glorified" (v. 23). The perfect tense of "come" means that the hour of which He had spoken so often finally had arrived. He would soon be "glorified," or crucified. And this was as it should be. For even the law of nature said that if a grain of wheat was to reproduce itself it must "fall into the ground and die" (v. 24), otherwise, it would remain as just one grain of wheat. Only in dying could it multiply itself. And the same law applied to Jesus in the spiritual realm. Only by way of the cross could He draw a lost world to Himself (cf. 3:14-15).

The same principle applies to these who propose to follow Jesus (vv. 25-26). "The one loving his life shall lose it, and the one hating his life in this world unto life eternal shall guard it" (cf. Matt. 16:24-27). *Loving* and *hating* refer to choice. The one who chooses this present life only shall lose it. But the one who chooses the life that Jesus offers shall guard it unto eternity. This contrast in life applies not only to soul salvation, but also to the use made of one's life. The quality of one's earthly life is at best temporal. But a life lived for Jesus is eternal both as to its present nature and to its extent. So as Jesus must die in order to bear fruit, so must we die to self and live for Him if we are to multiply ourselves and Him in the lives of others.

If one proposes to serve Jesus he must be prepared to follow Him, even to the point of dying. In such case he will be with His lord, and will be a joint-heir with Christ in glory (cf. Rom. 8:17).

With this fresh reminder of the cross Jesus became troubled. "Now is my soul troubled; and what shall I say? Father, save me from this hour: but for this cause came I unto this hour. Father, glorify thy name" (vv. 27-28).

What did Jesus mean by these words? Did He pray to be delivered from the cross? This is how it must be interpreted as it reads in the English text (KJV). But is this a true reading? If so, it means that after facing this hour from the beginning, Jesus suddenly seeks to avoid it. Robertson and Bernard hold to this reading as showing a momentary human weakness which was instantly overcome (cf. Williams' translation). But as in John 9:3-4 must we accept this punctuation here? There is manuscript evidence to the contrary. For in one manuscript (W) "Father, save me from this hour" ends with a question mark (;), the only punctuation mark used in the original Greek text. Granted that there is strong manuscript evidence to the contrary, the writer is inclined to accept the question mark as the true reading. And he is not alone (cf. Dods, Godet, Moffatt, Phillips, Revised Standard Version; Robertson in his *Harmony* and *Chronological New Testament* gives this as a marginal reading).

The question hinges on whether this sentence is a part of

Jesus' prayer or a soliloquy within His mind. The tone of this passage seems to favor the latter. Within Himself, and possibly audibly, Jesus says, "Now is my soul troubled; and what shall I say?" Obviously He had two alternatives: surrender to the cross or ask to be saved from it. From the outset He had been surrendered to it. Now that it looms before Him, shall He suddenly change His attitude? He could have. For no one, not even the Father, would nail Him to the cross against His will. He must lay down His life Himself, or it would not be a substitutionary, atoning death. Therefore, in this decisive moment "What shall I say? Shall I say, Father, save me from this hour? But for this cause came I unto this hour." This was the very purpose of the Incarnation, His reason for being in the flesh. No, He will not pray that.

And then from a soliloquy He turned to prayer. "Father, glorify thy name." That was His prayer after facing the alternative. He will not return to heaven defeated and a shame to His Father. He will return, having first revealed His Father in His greatest glory as Redeemer.

His prayer received an immediate answer. From heaven once again came the audible voice of the Father (cf. Matt. 3:17; 17:5). "I have both glorified it, and will glorify it again" (v. 28). The Son is still well-pleasing to the Father. They are together in this matter to the end.

The people standing about Jesus heard the sound, but did not comprehend the meaning. Some thought that it was a loud clap of thunder ("thundered" a perfect tense). But others said that surely an angel had spoken (perfect) to Him (v. 29). The two words "said" in this verse are an imperfect and an aorist respectively. Some *began to say* that it thundered; others *immediately said* that it was the voice of an angel.

But Jesus said that this "voice" (*phonē,* sound to them, voice to Jesus) came not because He needed to hear it, but because they did (v. 30). In response to Jesus' prayer it was an evidence to those who would understand that they still were to hear Him as He spoke of the cross (cf. Matt. 17:5).

With this Jesus pointed ahead to the cross and the resurrection as "a judgment [crisis] of this world" (v. 31, no definite article with "judgment"). The world had faced many crises. But this will be its greatest. What the world did to Jesus and what God subsequently did to Him will be a judgment of the world indeed (cf. Acts 3:14 f.; 4:10). Furthermore, "the prince of this world will be cast out." The "prince," or "ruler" in this case is Satan (cf. 14:30; 16:11). In the wilderness temptation Satan had claimed sovereignty in the cosmos (cf. Matt. 4:9) which he promised to give Jesus in exchange for His obeisance to him. Satan's first temptation was for Jesus to avoid the cross. But He chose to walk in God's will. Now that the cross is just ahead Jesus said literally, *"Now* [author's italics, not as Satan had proposed but as God wills] the prince of this world shall be fully cast out" (future passive of *ekballō,* to cast out). This is made even stronger by Jesus' addition of *exō* which Robertson renders as "clean out." So Jesus said that Satan will be *cast out, clean out.* God will completely destroy his power. He will continue to resist until the end of the age. But the issue was decided in the death and resurrection of Jesus.

For by being "lifted up" on the cross He will draw all men unto Himself (v. 32). This does not mean that all men will be saved. But all who come to Him, whether Jew or Greek, will be saved.

The Puzzled People (12:33-36a)

John notes that Jesus' words were relative to the manner of His death (v. 33). But they left the people about Him in a quandary. They understood Him to be talking about His death on the cross. They understood that the Scriptures taught that the Christ would abide forever. Assuming then that Jesus is the Son of man, a term used for Christ, how can He say that He will die? Is this Son of man someone else (v. 34)?

As was His custom in public address Jesus avoided a direct answer as to His identity as the Christ (v. 35). Instead He referred to Himself as "light" (cf. 1:4; 8:12). If they walk in Him as Light they shall know, for they themselves shall be "children of light" (v. 36). The answer to all of their questions will be found in an experience of faith in Him.

The Author's (John) Summary of Jesus' Ministry (12:36b-43)

With this parting word Jesus left, and "did hide himself from them" (v. 36b). Where He went is not said, but perhaps He merely faded away into the crowd. He acted out His words that the Light would not be with them always.

In a sense verses 37-43 are a summary of Jesus' ministry. He had wrought many "signs," yet the people did not believe on Him (v. 37). In truth this was a fulfilment of prophecy (vv. 38-

41). However, John notes that many, including some members of the Sanhedrin, did believe on Him (v. 42). How many, he does not say. From subsequent events we may assume that among them were Nicodemus and Joseph of Arimathea. However, lest they should be excommunicated, they did not confess Him openly. For they loved the glory of men more than the glory of God (v. 43).

Westcott comments, "This complete intellectual faith (so to speak) is really the climax of unbelief. The conviction found no expression in life." Two of these did find the courage of full commitment (19:38-39). We can only hope that others did.

The Conclusion of Jesus' Public Ministry (12:44-50)

The Synoptic Gospels record a full day of debate with His adversaries on Tuesday. But since John passes over that material, he gives at this point what may well be called a conclusion to Jesus' public ministry.

Perhaps in the temple area Jesus cried, "He that believeth on me, believeth not on me, but on Him that sent me" (v. 44). Thus He challenged men's faith. Since He is Light those who see and believe Him shall not walk in darkness (vv. 45-46). He came not to judge but to save the world. However, by His words men shall be judged (vv. 47-48). His words have not been His alone; the Father has spoken through Him. In God's words are eternal life (vv. 49-50). And with a note of finality Jesus said, "Whatsoever I speak therefore, even as the Father said unto me, so I speak."

With these words John ends the account of Jesus' public ministry. Hereafter, except for words spoken at His trial and on the cross, He will confine Himself to His inner circle. So the world has received His witness. What it will do with it is up to them. Men are free to choose, but they are responsible for their choices.

The Supper in Bethany (12:2-8)

On Tuesday night Jesus was the guest of honor at a dinner at Bethany. If we had only John's account, we might assume that it was held in the home of Martha. However, he parallels Matthew and Mark who tell us that the host was "Simon the leper" (Mark 14:3). But this is the only person, other than Jesus, that they name. By contrast John, while omitting the name

of the host, gives the names of the other principal characters involved in the event: Martha, Lazarus, Mary, and Judas.

Here then is one of the best evidences of John's purpose to
supplement the Synoptic Gospels. Since Simon's name had been
given by them, John omits it. But he also adds the names omitted
by the Synoptics, an addition which gives added meaning to
the story. Indeed, while the Synoptics quote Jesus as saying that
the woman's act of anointing Him would become a memorial
unto her, neither gives her name. This is given by John. Perhaps
Mary, Martha, and Lazarus were still living when the Synoptics
were written. By the same token Simon evidently had died. To
have given the names of the living would have endangered their
lives. However, when John wrote they doubtless were dead. So
their names could be mentioned. A comparison of the Greek
texts of these three Gospels shows remarkable similarity between
John and the others. It is entirely possible that John could have
had the other two Gospels before him as he wrote his own account.

But let us examine John's record of this event. At this dinner,
true to her character, Martha "was serving" and Lazarus reclined
at the table with Jesus. One suggestion has been made that
Martha's role indicates that she may have been Simon's wife.
However, this is pure supposition. As a neighbor she was helping
with the serving.

And what was Mary doing? Also true to her nature she interrupted the meal by anointing Jesus (v. 3). For ointment she used
"spikenard," or "nard." Literally, it was oil of nard, fragrant oil
which comes from an East Indian plant. It is described as "very
costly," or precious. Nard was considered to be a gift fit for a
king. In fact, Herodotus lists it as one of five gifts sent by Cambyses
to the king of Ethiopia. Evidently it was a precious possession of
Mary, which means that her act was one of great love.

The Synoptics say that she anointed Jesus' head. John says
that she did so to His feet, wiping them with her hair. In all
likelihood she did both. "And the house was filled with the
odor of the ointment."

The disciples seeing this were indignant, calling it a waste, or
a dead loss. But John names "Judas Iscariot . . . which should betray him" (v. 4) as the critic. Apparently he began to complain
and the other disciples joined him in it. Asked Judas, "Why was
not this ointment sold for three hundred pence [dēnarii], and
given to the poor?" (v. 5). A dēnarion was a Roman silver coin
worth about seventeen cents. So the value of the ointment was

fifty-one dollars. This sum, of course, had a greater purchasing power then than it would today. But John notes that Judas did not care about the poor. He was in charge of the treasury of the Twelve, and was stealing from it (v. 6).

But Jesus rebuked Judas and the others. "Let her alone: against the day of my burying hath she kept this" (v. 7). A better rendering from the older manuscripts reads, "Permit her, in order that unto the day of my burying she may keep it." She had expended the ointment in a deed of love. The Synoptics quote Jesus as saying that she had anointed Him for burial before His death. And the meaning of this blessed act she would *keep* long after the odor of the ointment was gone. To the poor they could always minister, but this was Mary's one opportunity to show her deepest devotion to her Lord in His hour of need for sympathetic understanding (v. 8).

With this John ends his account. But by comparing it with the Synoptic Gospels one learns that it is not the end of its meaning. While neither Matthew nor Mark names Judas in the story, they add immediately thereafter that he went to bargain with the chief priests for Jesus' betrayal (Matt. 26:14-16; Mark 14:10-11; Luke does not tell of the dinner but he joins in telling of the bargain, 22:3-6). It is from John, however, that we learn the immediate occasion for Judas' nefarious act. His resentment at Jesus' rebuke triggered him into action.

This brings us once again to face the problem of Judas. With consumate artistry John has drawn a contrast between Mary and Judas. Both had had the privilege of hearing Jesus' words and feeling the warmth of His love; in fact, Judas more than Mary. Yet in the crisis they reacted so differently. Both had come to understand about Jesus' impending death. In fact, only that afternoon Judas had heard Jesus predict His death "after two days" (Matt. 26:2 RV). This was Tuesday, so *after two days* would bring them to Friday. Apparently Mary also had heard about this.

When each knew that He was going to die, that knowledge evoked a question. Mary asked, "What can I do for Jesus?" She could not prevent His death, but she could show her sympathy and love. So she anointed Him for burial.

Judas, on the other hand, asked quite a different question. He had joined Jesus for what he could get out of Him. Interpreting His kingship as political, he thought to gain a place of prominence in His kingdom. Repeatedly he had sought to force Jesus

to declare Himself. Surely he thought that He would do so at
His Royal Entry. But He had not. To Judas, therefore, Jesus
was not a king. He was just a Rabbi who did and said wonderful
things. Now He was going to be crucified. There was nothing
Judas could do to prevent it. So he might as well try to salvage
something out of the debacle. Thus his question. "What can
Jesus do for me?" And he sold Him for thirty pieces of silver
(Matt. 26:14), less than twenty-five dollars. He tried to get fifty-
one dollars through the sale of Mary's ointment. But failing there,
he settled for less than half that amount. To Judas half a loaf
was better than none.

What shall we say of Judas? Why did Jesus choose him? Some
hold that He chose him for the very purpose of betrayal, that he
was predestined to do so. But this is contrary to God's nature.
Furthermore, Jesus said that Judas was responsible for his act
(Matt. 26:24). He was not a puppet on a cosmic string of fate.
He was a person capable of choosing and responsible for his
choice. So to try to clear Judas is to malign God.

In all likelihood as in the other disciples Jesus saw qualities
in Judas, perhaps a business ability, which if surrendered to Him
would make him valuable in His young movement. But Judas
never surrendered himself or his ability to Jesus.

Of one thing we may be certain. Judas was never a Christian.
This is seen in the upper room. When Jesus said that one of the
Twelve would betray Him, the other disciples asked, "Lord, is
it I?" (Matt. 26:22). Finally, Judas asked, "Master [Rabbi], is
it I?" (Matt. 26:25). In his act of betrayal he still called Jesus
"Rabbi" (Matt. 26:49). While to the other disciples Jesus was
"Lord," to Judas He was only "Rabbi." He was to him only
another Jewish Rabbi, not his Saviour and Lord.

Many efforts have been made to explain away Judas' act of
betrayal. Akin to the above-mentioned one is another which
holds that Judas was in the complete control of Satan, and thus
was not responsible for his deed (John 13:27). But we have
already noted Jesus' words about his personal responsibility. Another suggests that Judas was in league with the Sanhedrin all
the while, and that he joined Jesus' group in order to betray Him.
Such hardly fits the record. And the fact that the chief priests
spurned him after the betrayal belies such an idea (Matt. 27:3-4).
Two other suggestions would make Judas either a super-patriot
or else a super-Christian. The former holds that Judas saw that
if Jesus continued He would start a revolution and bring the

wrath of Rome down upon Judea. So to save his nation he betrayed Jesus. The latter holds that Judas was overly zealous for Jesus. So he betrayed Him, thinking to put Jesus in a position which would force Him to declare His Kingship.

But all of these are simply efforts to do the impossible. From the Gospel records (and Acts 1:16-20) it is futile to endeavor to clear Judas' name or to absolve him from guilt. He will ever remain a mystery. But he will always be known as "Judas Iscariot, Simon's son, which should betray him" (v. 4).

See page 136.

VIII
The Quiet Before the Storm

The Upper Room

None of the Gospels record what Jesus did on Wednesday of Passion Week. It is likely that He spent this time resting and teaching His disciples. But mingled with the joy of these last hours of fellowship must have been His sorrows over the defection of Judas.

The Passover actually began at sunset on the 15th of Nisan. This would be at sunset closing Thursday and beginning Friday. Some hold that Jesus was crucified on Thursday, His death corresponding to the time for the slaying of the paschal lamb. This was done in the afternoon on the 14th of Nisan. Other than sentiment and the provision of three twenty-four hour days for Jesus being in the tomb, there is no real basis for this position. But as will be seen later the time element may be explained otherwise. It will also be seen that the Gospels quite clearly place the crucifixion on Friday (cf. 19:42).

From the Synoptic record we know that Jesus had made previous preparations for the place and necessary ingredients for the passover meal. So late on Thursday afternoon He and His little group left Bethany to repair to the place of the meal. The place was a carefully guarded secret to prevent Judas from knowing Jesus' movements until He was ready to be taken by His enemies (cf. Matt. 26:17-19). This was a time of deep feeling for Jesus.

The Contrast of Emotions (13:1-2)

This contrast is seen in Jesus' deep love for the Twelve and His equally deep sorrow because of Judas. And, of course, through it all ran the burden of what lay before Him.

So Jesus and the Twelve came to the upper room, a guest-chamber in the home of a friend (cf. Mark 14:14). His purpose was to eat the passover meal with His disciples before He entered into His final agony and suffering on the cross.

John says that it was "before the feast of the passover" (v. 1). Some see this as a contradiction between John and the other

Gospels (cf. Matt. 26:19; Mark 14:16; Luke 22:15). However, "before" does not necessarily mean the day before the Passover. It may just as well mean just before the passover meal itself. So instead of contradicting the Synoptic record, John simply is setting the stage for the passover meal, the Lord's Supper, and the portion of Jesus' teaching which by Barnas Sears aptly has been called "The Heart of Christ" (13:2 — 17:26).

Jesus came to the upper room knowing full well that His "hour" to depart this earth to return to the Father would soon come. In this sense "his hour" involves both His death, resurrection, and ascension. "Having loved his own which were in the world, unto the end he loved them." The word "loved" renders the word for divine love *(agapaō)*. It is natural that the love which He had had for them all the while would seem even more precious as He faced the time of His departure.

But intermingled with this love was Jesus' disappointment and sorrow over Judas. He had definitely committed himself to his iniquitous deed (v. 2). However, despite this fact Jesus still loved him. Judas could not prevent Jesus from doing this. But by his obstinate unbelief he did seal himself off from God's mercy and forgiveness. It is so sad to see this tare growing alongside the wheat. But it was true then as it is ever the case.

The Example of Greatness (13:3-20)

In retrospect it is difficult to understand the crass attitude of the Twelve. But we must judge them by their light, not ours. Certainly Jesus did so.

Luke notes that upon arrival in the upper room there was a scramble among the disciples (22:24 ff.). They were contending as to which of them would be the greatest in the coming kingdom. This could have been brought on by their scramble for the chief reclining places of greatest honor about the table. The custom was to recline on couches at a meal. The Talmud says that on a couch holding three people the center place was of highest honor, the left side was second, and the right side was third. So apparently each of the Twelve sought the place on the main couch to the left of Jesus (cf. v. 25). At the time Jesus taught them the nature of true greatness in the kingdom of heaven.

But later "during supper" (the best reading of v. 2, not "after supper had ended"), conscious of His deity He demonstrated His lesson to them (v. 3). So rising from His couch and laying aside

His outer garments *(himatia),* He took a long linen cloth and with
it girded Himself around (v. 4). Then filling a hand basin with
water, He began "to wash" *(niptein)* the disciples' feet, and to dry
them with the towel about His waist (v. 5). Note the verb *niptō.*
It means to wash, or rinse parts of the body, in this case the feet.

The disciples wore sandals. Thus walking along their feet became
dusty. According to custom the host provided someone, usually a
slave, to rinse the feet of his guests upon arrival. It was considered
to be the most menial of services. Jesus had no slave, and so concerned were His disciples with personal greatness it certainly was
beneath their dignity to supply this service for their Host. Noting
that this had not been done, Jesus proceeded to do it for them.

One by one He rinsed the feet of His disciples, until finally He
came to Peter. But Peter protested. "Lord, my feet do you [propose
to] rinse?" (v. 6). "You" is in the emphatic position. No one else
had rendered this menial service to Peter. So "Lord, you of all
people, do you rinse my feet?" It was unthinkable that He should
do so. Evidently Peter was expressing the shame which all felt. The
others had permitted Jesus to rinse their feet. But, true to his
outspoken nature, Peter protested.

Replying to his protest Jesus said, "What *I* am doing *you* do not
now perceive [*oidas*], but you will know by experience [*gnōsei*]
after these things," or "hereafter" (v. 7, author's italics). Peter
cannot fully understand Jesus' actions now, but by experience he
shall know in the future. It will be a hard lesson to learn. But he
will come to render a similar service of humility. And he did
learn. For in I Peter 5:5 he says, "Yea, all of you be subject one to
another, and be clothed [gird yourselves] with humility: for God
resisteth the proud, and giveth grace to the humble." Jesus'
example made a lasting impression on him.

Nevertheless, for the present Peter protested all the stronger.
"Thou shalt never rinse my feet" (v. 8). He used the strong double
negative *(ou mē)* in the emphatic position. To this he added the
word "my" in the emphatic position. And to cap it all off he closed
with the words "unto the age" *(eis ton aiōna),* or "forever." These
words came at the end of the sentence, the place of second greatest
emphasis. *"Not never* shall you rinse my feet *forever!"* (author's
italics). He could have made no stronger protest.

But still Jesus persisted. "If I rinse thee not, thou hast no part
with me" (v. 8). This certainly does not mean that Peter would
not be a Christian. Neither does it mean that feet-washing is

necessary for spiritual fellowship. But if Peter, through mock-humility which was an expression of his pride, did not permit Jesus to do this he would never learn to humble himself unto such service.

Catching the sense of Jesus' words Peter reacted in characteristic fashion. "Lord, not my feet only, but also my hands and my head" (v. 9). Jesus' problem disciple never did things half-way. From protesting the *rinsing* of his feet he now wanted Jesus to *wash* him from head to feet. "Just give me a bath all over!" He did not use the word *louō,* to bathe the whole body, but that was the sense of his request.

And Jesus took it up. For He said, "He that is bathed [perfect tense, fully bathed] has no need except the feet to be rinsed, but is clean every whit," or "all over" (v. 10). People were supposed to take a bath before going to a dinner. Thus Jesus told Peter that if he took a bath before he came, now he only needed to have the dust rinsed from his feet. Somewhere the idea was born that Jesus was always solemn or sad, with no sense of humor. This is one of many evidences to the contrary. He probably had a smile on His face and a twinkle in His eyes as He said this to Peter.

But then Jesus did add a solemn note. "And ye are clean, but not all." From physical cleanliness He shifted the thought to spiritual cleanliness. Peter and the others are spiritually clean, save one, Judas. Judas had never been cleansed through faith in Jesus. His present purpose to betray Him was prime evidence of that fact (v. 11).

Having finished His lesson Jesus applied it (v. 12). Putting on His outer garments and resuming His place on the couch, He said, "Know ye what I have done to you?" Had they learned from this experience *(ginōskete)*? To be certain that they did not miss the lesson He explained it. "Ye call me Teacher and Lord: and ye say well; for I am. If therefore I [emphatic], the Lord and Teacher, rinsed your feet; also ye [emphatic] are indebted to rinse one another's feet" (v. 13-14). If the Lord could render this menial service for them, surely they could do the same for one another. If God can be humble, why cannot man be the same?

One cannot escape Jesus' claim to deity here. For "Lord" as used here carried the idea of Jehovah. In effect, Jesus claimed the right to be worshipped. Yet He was willing to serve as a menial slave. This scene is an apt commentary on Philippians 2:5-11. Soon He is going to the cross. Yet here He stoops to conquer the pride that still reigned in His disciples' hearts.

In this act Jesus did not give us a third ordinance of feetwashing. He called it an "example" which they should follow (v. 15). The example was humble service of whatever kind it might be. "The slave is not greater than his owner [*kurios*]; neither an apostle [*apostolos,* the one sent forth] greater than the one who has sent him" (v. 16). If a slave wants to be great in the eyes of his owner, he must be willing to render any service assigned to him, no matter how menial it may be.

Then Jesus said, "If ye know [*oidate*] these things, happy are ye if ye do them" (v. 17). In other words, if they have fully comprehended the knowledge gained from this experience, they will be *happy* in the practice of it.

The word "happy" (*makarioi*) is the word rendered "blessed" in the Beatitudes (Matt. 5:3 ff.). Barclay reminds us that it is used to describe Cyprus as "the happy isle." This island was said to contain such fertility, beauty, and natural resources as to have within itself everything necessary for a well-rounded life. Thus it was a "happy" island. This is suggestive of Jesus' meaning here. The apostles were concerned about earthly greatness as the supreme goal of life. Jesus says that this blessed estate is to be achieved through humble service. One who perceives this and does it will have within himself all that is necessary for living a rich, full life.

But Jesus hastened to add that this is true only of those who truly receive Him (v. 18). It is not true of the one who even then was eating with Him but soon would depart to betray Him. Judas, instead of being "happy" in the full sense of the word, was miserable and bereft of any sense of security or sufficiency. Jesus reminds them of this so that when it happens they will believe that He is not simply the victim of a plot. He is the "I AM" (v. 19, no "he" in the Greek text). He is God giving His life to save from sin. And those who receive His apostles on their future mission receive Him (v. 20). By the same token those who receive Him receive the Father who sent Him.

The Betrayer Identified (13:21-30)

In applying His lesson in humility Jesus touched upon the idea of betrayal. Now He dealt with it specifically. The very thought of it troubled His spirit as a sea tossed by a storm (v. 21). Recently He had spoken of Himself as God. Now the mysterious mingling of His humanity with His deity came into prominence. In such an agitated state He gave a solemn witness. "Verily, verily,

I say unto you, that one of you shall betray me" (v. 21). The word for "betray" renders *paradidōmi,* meaning to give over or alongside. It is used of handing one over to his executioners (cf. Matt. 27:26, Pilate "delivered him to be crucified").

He did not call his name. He simply said that one of this intimate group would do it. It was as though He had thrown a bomb into their midst. The disciples began to glance at one another in bewilderment (v. 22). Each doubted or was at a loss as to whom He had reference. Perhaps each wondered about all the others, even about himself! All save Judas had not thought of doing such a thing. Yet, one never knows what unsuspected sin may lurk within him.

The Synoptics note that one after another they began to ask, "Lord, is it I?" (Matt. 26:22). Each question asked for a negative answer. Finally, Judas, lest his silence betray him, asked, "Rabbi, is it I?" (Matt. 26:25; "Rabbi," not "Lord"). Again inviting a negative answer. He still hoped that Jesus did not know of his purpose.

Now one of the Twelve was in closer proximity to Jesus than the others (v. 23). This one had the place of first honor next to Jesus. Reclining on Jesus' left side, he was leaning on Jesus' bosom. Therefore, he could converse with Him without being heard by the others. He is identified as the disciple "whom Jesus loved." Of course, Jesus loved all of them (cf. v. 1). But there must have been a special intimacy between the two. This could explain his honored place at the table. It is most likely that this person is the author of this Gospel, and may be identified as John himself. His name, of course, never appears in this Gospel, but he repeatedly refers to himself thusly, by a title of which he was understandably proud (cf. 19:26; 20:2; 21:7, 20).

While the disciples were looking about at one another, Simon Peter caught John's eye. So he nodded (beckoned) to him to ask Jesus of whom he spoke (v. 24). John, therefore, leaned back and quietly asked, "Lord, who is it?" (v. 25). Just as quietly Jesus replied, "That one [emphatic] it is to whom I shall dip the sop and give it to him" (v. 26). This was a special courtesy which the host might show to one of his guests. So Jesus did so to Judas. Was this one final effort on Jesus' part to save Judas from his hellish deed? Peter did not hear Jesus' words. So he and the others thought nothing of it, unless each thought that he should have received this special attention. But had they known its meaning, each would be eternally grateful that he did not receive it. Had they known what this gesture meant, one wonders if Judas would have gotten out of the room alive.

But Judas knew. No longer could he doubt but that Jesus also knew of his purpose. So John says that "Satan entered into him" (v. 27). Satan had been toying with Judas for more than a year (cf. 6:70). Now that he knew the whole thing was known to Jesus, there was no more reason to pretend. He firmly resolved to do Satan's will.

With this Jesus said, "That thou doest, do quickly" (v. 27). Literally, "The thing you are doing [present], do more quickly" (aorist verb and "quickly"). Now that the die was cast Jesus was anxious to get on with it. Those about the table, other than John, did not understand the meaning of Jesus' words (v. 28). They were not aware of Judas' treachery. They thought that since Judas carried the purse Jesus was telling him to rush out and buy food to last during the next eight days; or else to give something to the poor.

But Judas understood. And immediately he went out of the room. John adds, "And it was night" (v. 30). This could refer to the suddenness with which darkness comes in that part of the world. Dods suggests that it could be that John wished to note exactly the time when Judas departed. However, the time element and the events involved up to this point seem to indicate otherwise. The passover meal began shortly after sunset. It would appear, therefore, that it was already dark long before Judas left. So the fact that "it was night" would be obvious. Knowing John's mystical nature we are prompted to look for a deeper meaning than merely a natural phenomenon. Was not John speaking of the *night* in Judas' soul? To go away from the light is to go into darkness. Judas fully and finally turned away from the Light of the world. And as he did so he went into the outer darkness, the darkest night in the history of the world.

Two things are worthy of note at this point. One is that the Synoptic Gospels make no mention of Judas' departure. Another is that John does not record the institution of the Lord's Supper. For this reason some hold that John's reference to this is found in 6:48-58. However, there is no real basis for such a position. Why then did John make no reference to the Supper? Apparently it was because all three of the Synoptic Gospels had done so (cf. I Cor. 11:23-26). John will record material which they omitted (14-17). So he assumed a general knowledge of the Supper from the other accounts.

But one thing the Synoptics failed to report. And that is the fact that the Supper was instituted *after* Judas had departed. This Supper is for baptized believers only (cf. Acts 2:41-42). Judas most likely had been baptized. But he was not a believer. So John is careful to note this fact by recording Judas' departure in verse 30. The Lord's Supper was instituted probably following verse 38.

The Looming Cross (13:31-35)

The departure of Judas set in motion events which within a few hours would nail Jesus to the cross. Thereby the Son of man will be glorified, and the Father will also be glorified in Him (v. 31). In turn, God will glorify the Son, "and shall straightway glorify him" (v. 32). He will do it quickly: first the cross, then the resurrection, and finally the ascension (cf. Phil. 2:8b-11).

So now that Jesus' own affairs were settled, He turned to those of His remaining disciples (vv. 33-35). Note the tenderness, "little children." How much this meant to John is seen in the fact that years later he used this same term to address those who followed him as their teacher (I John 2:1). There is a tradition that when John was an old man his pupils would set him in their midst, and he would say, "Little children, love one another" (cf. also I John 4:7 ff.). So the words which Jesus spoke in this tender scene stayed with him to the end of his life.

Soon Jesus would be taken from the Eleven (v. 33). A storm is about to break about them. The world will hate them with a venom. They can only rely upon one another — and the Holy Spirit. But even before the Spirit shall come in power, they will have need of mutual fellowship. Then Jesus said, "A new commandment I give unto you, That ye love one another; as I have loved you, that ye love one another" (v. 34). The great love with which He has loved them and still does, they are to perpetuate in their mutual love. Indeed, the badge of their Christian discipleship shall be their mutual Christian love (v. 35). It is said that one Roman remarked years later, "Behold, how these Christians love one another."

How sad, how tragic it is when this is not the case! If one loves not his Christian brother whom he has seen, how can he say that he loves God whom he has not seen (cf. I John 4:20)?

The Audacity of Peter (13:36-38)

Though these words about love were indelibly marked in John's soul, they do not seem to have impressed Peter. As at Caesarea-Philippi his mind must have frozen on Jesus' words, "and be killed," so that he seems to have missed the words, "and be raised again the third day" (Matt. 16:21; cf. v. 22), so here his mind must have frozen on the words about Jesus going away (cf. v. 33). Therefore, like a child who had not been listening he interrupted Jesus' discourse with a question: "Lord, where are you going?" (v. 36).

Jesus told him that where He was going Peter could not follow now, but in time he would do so. Did Jesus refer to Peter's own death by crucifixion (cf. 21:18-19)? At least Peter had grasped the meaning of Jesus' words. For wanting to know why he could not then follow Jesus, he said, "I will lay down my life for thy sake" (v. 37). And he meant it at the time. For later that very night he risked death on Jesus' behalf (cf. 18:10 f.).

But Jesus knew Peter better than he knew himself. Possessed of physical courage to use a sword, yet he lacked the moral and physical courage to stand true to Jesus in a spiritual crisis. So Jesus said, "Wilt thou lay down thy life for my sake? Verily, verily, I say unto thee, The cock shall not crow, till thou hast denied me thrice" (v. 38).

Peter made an audacious claim. But before we condemn him note that, "Likewise also said all the disciples" (Matt. 26:35). But even more so, let us, before sitting in judgment upon them, examine our own lives. You are willing to die for Jesus, you say? A far more penetrating question is "Are you willing to live for Him?"

John 14

The Words of Comfort

The passover meal was finished. The Lord's Supper had been instituted. As men are wont to do, Jesus and the Eleven reclined about the table in conversation. For the most part Jesus did the talking with an occasional interruption by one of the disciples. But Jesus' words were not idle chatter. They were words of profundity unsurpassed by any that He ever spoke. If Chapters 13-17 are the *heart of Christ,* in Chapters 14-17 we look into the very soul of Jesus.

The Eleven finally were made aware of what lay ahead for their Lord. Evidently the symbolism of the Memorial Supper had made it clear to them. And in that realization they were sad indeed. In such an atmosphere Jesus spoke to them words of comfort and encouragement.

The Secret of an Untroubled Heart (14:1-3)

"Let not your heart be troubled..." (v. 1). Do we need to continue? For we can quote the following words from memory. The words which Jesus used to comfort His disciples have become a pillow of faith upon which uncounted broken hearts have found rest.

The disciples' hearts were like a restless sea tossed by the wind. Jesus Himself knew the experience (11:33; 13:31). But He also knew the remedy. He said, "Stop letting your heart be troubled." How could they do this?

Jesus did not say to shrug your shoulders in a fatalistic resignation as if to say what is to be will be. Neither did He say to adopt the attitude of stoicism, freeze your emotions and endure it. Nor did He say to close your eyes to reality, refuse to recognize the gravity of the situation; eat, drink, and be merry. For in none of these ways can one truly cope with a troubled heart.

What did He say? "Ye believe in God, believe also in me" (v. 1). In the Greek text both words for "believe" are the same *(pisteuete).* They can be either present indicatives or present imperatives, state

218

a fact or issue a command. The context suggests, however, that
they are not the same. Apparently the former declares a fact
(indicative) and the latter issues a command (imperative). Jesus
stated the fact that the Eleven did believe in God; then He commanded that they should also believe in Him. No matter what
happened they were to remain steadfast in faith. Belief in both
cases carries the idea of intellectual acceptance, wilful trust, and
personal commitment.

In this sense they were to have faith in God's love, will, and
purpose. For what was soon to happen was the greatest expression
of His love, in conformity to His will, and in keeping with His
redemptive purpose. And Jesus was fully identified with the whole.

This is true also in our experiences of bereavement. God loves
us in the shadow as well as in the sunshine. Death is not a part of
God's *intentional will*. It is a circumstance brought about because
of the principle of evil which works in the present age. So God's
circumstantial will is that we shall trust Him through it. And His
ultimate will is to gather to Himself all who believe in Him. This
is in keeping with His purpose of full redemption which involves
both the spirit and the body of man.

Jesus through His death, resurrection, and ascension is the
means whereby God fully will reveal His love, express His will,
and accomplish His purpose. He was going to leave His disciples.
But His going is an errand of mercy. "In my Father's house are
many mansions [abiding or resting places]: if it were not so, I
would have told you. I go to prepare a place for you. And if I go
and prepare a place for you, I will come again, and receive you
unto myself; that where I am, there ye may be also" (vv. 2-3).

Thus Jesus gave us our most beautiful picture of heaven. One
big family dwelling in God's house with Christ our Elder Brother
(cf. Rom. 8:14-17). He is our Forerunner going ahead to prepare for our coming. And when all things are ready, He will come
for us to welcome us into the Father's house. In one sense this
coming again may be seen as the death of the individual Christian.
But in the greater, inclusive sense it refers to His return at the
end of the age.

Thus in these words Jesus tells us many things. Heaven is a
place. It is a prepared place. It is prepared by Jesus. It is a place
to which He will welcome us. Literally, "I will take you along to
my own home." And it will be an eternal home as seen in the

verbs "am" *(eimi)* and "may be" *(ēte)*. Where is heaven? It is
where the Father and Son are. And that is heaven indeed!

The Problems of the Disciples (14:4-14)

"And whither I am going ye know [*oidate*] the way" (v. 4). Peter
had asked where Jesus was going (13:36). The best Greek text does
not say that they know where He is going, but that they know
the *way*. That is the important thing. Not the destination, but
how to get there. Many people spend so much time speculating
about heaven until they miss the way to heaven. Jesus says that
to us the location of heaven is of little importance, but knowing
the way to heaven is of the greatest importance.

At this point Jesus received the first of several interruptions to
His discourse. Normally we would expect it to come from Peter.
Evidently he was subdued by Jesus' words about his forthcoming
denial (cf. 13:38). However, Thomas, the heroic one (cf. 11:16),
asked, "Lord, we do not know where you are going; how do we
know the way?" (v. 5). Not knowing where heaven is, how can
they know how to get there? Jesus still ignored the implied request
to know the location of heaven. But He spoke of the way with
emphasis. "I am the way, the truth, and the life; no one comes to
the Father except through me" (v. 6). "I" is emphatic. "I and no
other always am." He is "way," "truth," and "life."

Any one of these claims would have been staggering. But all
three — it was to compound it. Heretofore, Jesus among other
things had called Himself "life," "door," "light," "water," "bread,"
and the speaker of "truth." It is as though in this one statement
He would sum up the whole of His divine nature. He did not say
simply that He is a way, some truth, and some life. The definite
article with each sets them off as absolutes. Of no other who ever
walked the earth may these things be said. Even from the lips of
Jesus they would be absurd if He were only a man. So one must
regard Jesus either as the supreme egotist of all time even to the
point of madness, or as deity Himself. History points to the latter.
He is the Source of all *life,* the essence of all *truth,* and the only
way to the Father. Only as one is in Christ is He in the *way* to
heaven. Indeed, "the way" was one designation of the Christian
movement in the first century (cf. Acts 16:17; 18:26; 19:9, 23;
24:14).

Compounding His claim to deity Jesus continued, "If ye had
known [by experience, *egnōkeite*] me, ye should have known

[perceived, *ēidete* from *oida*] my Father also: and from henceforth ye know [are beginning to know by experience] him, and have seen him" (v. 7).

And then another interruption, this time from Philip. "Lord, show us the Father, and it sufficeth us" (v. 8). Jesus was amazed that He had been so long with Philip, and yet he did not know Him. "He that hath seen me hath seen the Father; and how sayest thou then, Show us the Father?" (v. 9). In a sense Philip had asked to see God with his natural eyes. Jesus told Him that for three and one-half years he had been seeing the Father in Him. How any one can read these words and question whether or not Jesus ever claimed deity is beyond comprehension. Like Philip, such look at Jesus without really seeing Him.

Jesus then put Philip and the others for whom he spoke to the test (vv. 10-11). Does he really believe He is in the Father and the Father in Him? Jesus both speaks and works only as the Father does through Him. Even if Philip cannot believe this without external proof, at least he should believe because of the works (signs) that Jesus had done.

But talking about His works Jesus makes an astounding statement (v.. 12). The one believing on Him shall do similar works, yea, even greater works because Jesus is going to the Father. Here he anticipates His further word about the Holy Spirit (cf. vv. 16 ff.). Because of the coming of the Holy Spirit the disciples will do greater works than even Jesus had done, greater in scope not in degree.

To this end Jesus promised an answer to prayer which they would make to Him (vv. 13-14). He invites their worship of Him in prayer! Whatsoever they shall ask in His name He will do, in order that the Father may continue to be glorified in the Son. To ask in His name, of course, means to ask within His will and purpose, by His authority, upon the basis of His work as Redeemer, and for the glory of both Father and Son.

The Promise of the Paraclete (14:15-18)

With this Jesus made a promise, a promise which will be realized in them only if they remain true to His will and purpose. "If ye keep on loving me, ye will keep on keeping my commandments" (v. 15).

"And I [*kagō*, emphatic, "and I on my part"] will pray the Father, and he shall give you another Comforter [Holy Spirit, cf.

v. 26], that he may abide with you for ever" (v. 16). Now this does not mean that only if the disciples keep His commandments will Jesus pray for the Holy Spirit. He will do this regardless. But only as they obey His commandments will the power of the Holy Spirit be realized in and through their lives.

Let us examine this tremendous promise of Jesus. He will *pray* the Father; the Father will *give* the Holy Spirit. This promise was fulfilled at Pentecost. The Holy Spirit had been in the world from the beginning. He had been at work in the life of Jesus. But at Pentecost He will come upon the church in a special way. Thereafter, He will continue to do what Jesus has begun (cf. Acts 1:1). So often we pray for God to send the Holy Spirit upon some particular endeavor. Such is unnecessary. He has already come. His power is available to all who will submit to His power. It was Jesus' business to pray for the Holy Spirit. It is ours to pray that we shall be fit instruments available for His use.

Furthermore, note the word "Comforter." It renders the Greek word *Paraklētos*, meaning the one called alongside. It was used of a lawyer, especially one for the defense, called to stand alongside one in court. In I John 2:1 it is rendered by the word "advocate," the Latin equivalent, *advoco*, to call to. So this word may be translated as Comforter, Advocate, or Divine Helper. It is transliterated into English as Paraclete. But since the function of the Holy Spirit includes so many things, perhaps the words, Divine Helper, carry the more inclusive meaning.

Still further, He is "another" Divine Helper. "Another" *(allos)* means "another of the same kind" as Jesus. Dods calls Him "Jesus' *alter Ego,*" or 'Jesus' other Self." B. H. Carroll calls Him "the other Jesus."

The Holy Spirit is to be "another of the same kind of Divine Helper" as Jesus had been. He is not to replace Jesus. But through the Holy Spirit the continuing life of Jesus is to be made evident in His church. The disciples were grieved because Jesus was going away. But He promised them an even greater privilege than His bodily presence. He had been with them; the Holy Spirit will be within them. He had spoken through their ears; the Spirit will speak in their hearts. They had felt the touch of Jesus' hand; now they will feel the Spirit's inward presence. At times they were away from Jesus' bodily presence. They will never be away from the Spirit. Jesus had been with them in body for about three and one-half years. The Holy Spirit will abide with them forever.

Jesus had just called Himself "the truth." Now He called this

Divine Helper "the Spirit of truth" (v. 17). Thus He is intimately identified with Jesus. Yet He is a Person of the Godhead in
His own right. A study of this truth in the Scriptures shows both
this distinction and this identity. While the Holy Spirit acts as
the Spirit, yet His work is so identified with that of Jesus that
often they are spoken of in the sense of identity. The Holy Spirit
is called both the Spirit of God and the Spirit of Christ.

Now Jesus said that the unregenerated world cannot receive the
Holy Spirit. For it neither sees nor knows Him (v. 17). "But ye
know him; for he dwelleth with you, and shall be in you." The
moment that one becomes a Christian he is indwelt by the Holy
Spirit. He seals him as God's own, and is God's guarantee, or
earnest money that He will go through with His promise to save
unto full redemption (soul, life, and body at the resurrection; the
sum-total of rewards in heaven) those who trust in Christ (cf.
Eph. 1:13-14).

Paul uses the word *arrabōn* (earnest-money) It is used only
three times in the New Testament, each time in connection with
the Holy Spirit (II Cor. 1:22; 5:5; Eph. 1:14). In the papyri it is
used for earnest money. One time it is used for "the engagement
ring" which a groom gave to his prospective bride. In this sense the
Holy Spirit is "the engagement ring" which the Bridegroom gives
to His Bride looking toward the marriage feast of the Lamb (cf.
Rev. 21:2).*

So for one to be "in Christ" is also to be "in the Spirit" and
for the Spirit to be in him. To this truth also Paul speaks. He says
that the Christian's body is the "temple" *(naos)* of the Holy Spirit
(I Cor. 6:19). The *naos* was the Holy of Holies in the Jerusalem
temple. Here God was said to dwell with His people in mercy. Now
the Christian is this *naos*. Man's spirit indwells his body and the
Spirit indwells his spirit. In like fashion Paul called the church
the *naos* of the Holy Spirit (I Cor. 3:16). Indwelling each believer
He also indwells the body of believers. Thus He gives the "fellowship" *(koinōnia)* of believers.

Jesus said to the Eleven that He was going away, but they would
not be alone. "I will not leave you comfortless" *(orphanous)*, or
"as orphans: I will come to you" (v. 18). And He does so through
the Holy Spirit.

---

*Cf. my *Preaching Values from the Papyri*, Baker, Grand Rapids, 1964, pp. 31 ff.

The Continuing Fellowship (14:19-25)

Shortly the world will see Jesus no more (v. 19). This was certainly the case. For after His body was placed in the tomb no unbeliever ever saw Him again. But "ye," in contrast to the blind, unbelieving world, "keep on beholding me." They did see Him after His resurrection. And because He lives, those who believe in Him shall live. As His life is eternal, so shall be that of His own. "In that day [His resurrection and continuing life] ye shall know [by experience, not just the hearing of it] that I am in the Father, and ye in me, and I in you" (v. 20). Thus He promised an abiding fellowship with the Father through Him. Having His commandments and keeping them, they will prove their love for Him (v. 21). And the one loving Him will also know the love of both the Father and the Son. Furthermore, because of this the Son will manifest Himself to them. Through their obedient love they will experience the real and spiritual presence of the risen Christ who after His ascension will be unseen by the natural eye.

At this point "Judas . . . not Iscariot" broke in with a question (v. 22). How is it that Christ will manifest Himself to His disciples but not to the world? In reply Jesus said, "If a man love me, he will keep my words: and my Father will love him, and we [note "we," Father and Son] will come unto him, and make our abode with him" (v. 23). Of course, this *abiding* will be in the Holy Spirit, who is both the Spirit of God and the Spirit of Christ. But the hating and unbelieving world will never know this blessed fellowship (v. 24a).

These blessed words are not those of the Son. They are the very words of the Father who sent Him and who has spoken through Him (v. 24b). And He has spoken them while present with them, that they may be strengthened by their assurance after He is no more with them in bodily presence (v. 25). How bereft all believers would be without them!

The Role of the Paraclete (14:26)

Later in the evening Jesus expanded on the role of the Holy Spirit (15:26; 16:7 ff.). But here in the upper room He touched upon it. For one thing He clearly identified the Divine Helper as the Holy Spirit. He it is whom the Father will send in His name. When He is come He will teach them all things pertaining to spiritual truth. And He will bring to the disciples' remembrance all that Jesus had already taught them. Much of what Jesus had said lay dormant in their subconsciousness. But illuminated by the Holy Spirit, their minds will be able to recall it beyond one's normal ability to do so.

After Pentecost they were able to relate Jesus' life and work to the Old Testament Scriptures, and to apply them to the message of the gospel. Even with the greatest Teacher they remained confused (cf. Acts 1:6). But after the coming of the Holy Spirit they were masters of the Christian message.

Furthermore, in this role of the Holy Spirit one sees the explanation of the inspiration of the New Testament. Events long forgotten came into focus, so that the Gospel writers were enabled to record their accounts of the life of Jesus. The Spirit also guided in research in this regard (cf. Luke 1:1 ff.). He was also active in the work of those who interpreted the person and work of Jesus Christ. As with the Old Testament so with the New: "Holy men of God spake [and wrote] as they were moved [picked up and borne along] by the Holy Ghost [Spirit]" (II Peter 1:21). And it is He who guides the devout scholar as well as the simplest reader in the study of the Scriptures.

The Legacy of Peace (14:27-31)

What greater legacy could the Saviour leave with His followers than "peace" (v. 27). "Peace I leave with you, my peace I give unto you." In both greeting and parting the Oriental says, "Shalom," or "Peace." As at the advent of Jesus the heavenly hosts sang of "peace" among men well-pleasing to God (Luke 2:14), so at His departure Jesus said, "Peace." It is the peace which only He can give. Therefore, those who trembled before the ominous events soon to come are to be neither troubled nor afraid. In this blessed assurance they should rejoice, not weep, for the One whom they love is returning home to the bosom of His Father (v. 28). Jesus told those things to the disciples before they happened, in order that instead of their faith being weakened it should be strengthened (v. 29).

Hereafter He will not have opportunity to speak much to them (v. 30). Even now "the prince of this world" is coming through his followers to take Jesus. "And in me he has nothing" (v. 30). His purpose is entirely different from that of the Son of God. But that the world may know that He loves the Father and obeys His will, He will submit Himself to that which evil men will do to Him (v. 31). It is in the Father's will. No man takes His life from Him. He lays it down of Himself. Thus He will accomplish God's redemptive will.

And with these words Jesus said, "Arise, let us go hence" (v. 31). Thus they left the haven of the upper room to walk through the dark streets of the city toward the rendezvous which awaited Jesus in Gethsemane.

The Words of Challenge

Jesus and the Eleven had left the upper room. In the light of 14:31 it is difficult to understand how some hold otherwise. Where Jesus spoke the words in Chapters 15-17 we are not told. Ancient teachers often did parapatetic teaching, or taught as they walked along. However, it is only with difficulty that one can see this method of teaching here. Some hold that Jesus repaired to the temple area and there continued His teaching. In so holding they relate the figure of the vine to the metal vine hanging there. It is more likely that a more private place was chosen for this intimate instruction. But where? Godet makes the likely suggestion that it was in some secluded spot outside the city wall, with perhaps a grape vine growing in the place.

But wherever it was it was somewhere along the route which led to the garden of Gethsemane. And knowing Jesus' custom to use object lessons, apparently it was in the vicinity of a grape vine. Bernard relates the figure of the vine to the fruit of the vine used in the Lord's Supper. However, this seems to be straining the imagery somewhat.

The Vine and the Branches (15:1-8)

Jesus said, "I am the true vine, and my Father is the husbandman" (v. 1). Here "I" *(egō)* is written out. and so is emphatic. "I and no one else am the true vine." And note again the familiar phrase of deity. "I am" *(egō eimi)*. So here is a contrast between the true or genuine vine and all other vines.

But with what does Jesus contrast Himself? Is it with false messiahs who claimed to be the vine of Israel? More likely He is contrasting Himself with the nation of Israel and the religious institutions pertaining thereto. Israel as a vine, or as the vineyard of Jehovah, is prominent in the Old Testament. But as Bernard points out this figure is presented as showing that Israel has failed to produce fruit or to fulfil God's purpose in world redemption (cf. Isa. 5:1 ff.; Jer. 2:21; Hos. 10:1). Nevertheless, the figure is not without meaning even in this negative sense. Dods points out that "on Maccabean coinage Israel was represented by a vine." The same is true of the coins of modern Israel.

It seems, therefore, that Jesus was saying that Israel had proved to be a false vine. He is the "true vine," the "genuine Messianic vine," as Robertson calls Him. In truth this is the teaching of the Old Testament. For all of the forms and institutions of Israel pointed to Christ as their fulfilment (cf. Hebrews). Therefore, Jesus is the true vine of which all others were meant to be but figures. It is through Him and Him alone (*egō eimi*) that God's fruitful purpose is to run. And the Father is the vinedresser. He is back of all that is happening to the Vine, and which is designed to make it fruitful in bearing the harvest of redeemed souls.

And then Jesus spoke of the work of the vinedresser. "Every branch in me that beareth no fruit he taketh away: and every branch that beareth fruit, he purgeth it, that it may bear more fruit" (v. 2). Note the two kinds of connections with the vine. Robertson calls the former the "cosmic" and the latter the "spiritual and vital." Bernard sees the former as Judas, thus implying that the latter is the Eleven. The phrase "in me" with respect to Judas should not be pressed to mean that he was a Christian. He was a dead branch attached to the vine, but with no life from the vine flowing through it. Jesus simply drew upon a common phenomenon to express a spiritual truth. Already Judas had been taken away or broken off. However, the branches which have the vital life remain. But note also that even the true branches need cleaning. Any dead twigs on them are cut away to increase their ability to bear more and better fruit. Already they are clean through having believed Jesus' word (v. 3). Westcott calls this potentially cleansed. Insofar as the sin principle is concerned they are clean. But their sins must be removed from time to time.

That they may continue to be fruitful Jesus urged them to maintain that necessary abiding spiritual relationship. "Keep on abiding in me, and I in you" (v. 4). Here the figure of the vine and branches is clearly seen. The branches are attached to the vine and the vine's vital fluid is flowing through the branches. It is true of them as it is of nature. Only thus can they bear fruit.

Applying this truth more specifically Jesus said, "I am the vine, ye the branches" (v. 5). "I . . . ye." There is a contrast of persons but a unity of relationship. Both pronouns are emphatic. "I and no one else am the vine, ye and no others the branches." Only they can bear Christian fruit, and that only as they abide in Him alone. If Jesus' followers do not bear this fruit, then no one else can or will. Even Christians are helpless apart from Christ.

Returning to those symoblized by Judas, Jesus said that branches which bear no vital relationship to Him, but which like the plant having no root (cf. Matt. 13:5-6), wither away, they will be burned up (v. 6). While this applies to non-Christians at the end of the age, even if one insists on seeing fruitless Christians here, certainly their works will be destroyed (cf. I Cor. 3:11-13). However, this latter position is hardly justified by the text. Jesus again was drawing upon a common custom to stress the importance of one being certain that His relation to Christ is vital and not simply nominal.

On the other hand, those who truly abide in Christ shall constantly draw from Him the vital fluid of life so necessary to fruit-bearing (v. 7). It is in their constant bearing of more and more fruit that the Father is glorified (v. 8). Furthermore, this is proof that they are true disciples of Jesus. By their fruit, or lack of it, they shall be known. How important it is, therefore, to be a fruitful Christian!

The Relationship of Love (15:9-15)

This vital relationship is to be one of obedient love (vv. 9-10). From the Father through the Son God's love is expressed to and in the disciples. In their obedience as bearers of fruit they shall demonstrate their love to the Son and the Father. And since we have noted that this love (agapē) involves one's absolute loyalty to its object, in these words also may be seen God's loyalty to His own and the demand of the same from them.

Jesus spoke these words with a purpose. "That my joy might remain [may be] in you, and your joy might be full," or "complete" (v. 11). The joy which Christ possesses He longs to share fully with them. Both His joy and theirs will be enhanced by their fruitful service. In verse 10 Jesus had spoken of His "commandment." Now He specified it as love for one another even as He loved them (v. 12). "Greater love hath no man than this, that a man lay down his life for his friends" (v. 13). He will soon prove His love for them on the cross. And they are to prove theirs for Him as they lose themselves in His service. He will die as their substitute (huper). In turn they are to be His subsititutes in proclaiming the gospel (cf. II Cor. 5:19:21). "Ye are my friends, if ye do whatsoever I command you" (v. 14). Not only His command to love one another, but also His command to witness to a lost world (cf. 20:21; Matt. 28:18-20). Dods says, "Self-sacrifice is the high water-mark of love."

Then Jesus announced to the Eleven a new relationship. He has called them His "servants" (*doulous*, slaves, cf. 13:16). "No longer [*ouketi*] do I call you slaves, because a slave does not really know what his owner is doing: but I from now on call [perfect tense] you friends; because all things which I heard from my Father I made known to you" (v. 15). The perfect tense expresses a permanent state of new dignity conferred upon the disciples. And they will prove worthy of it only as they are faithful in their service. Through Christ they will know the mind of the Father. It is important, therefore, that they do not betray this intimate knowledge and relationship. How true, how true it is of us also!

The Purpose of Discipleship (15:16)

This new relationship is not merely a privilege to be enjoyed; it is a responsibility to be borne. For Jesus said, "Ye have not chosen me, but I have chosen you, and ordained [appointed] you, that ye should go and bring forth fruit" (v. 16). Literally, "ye have not made the choice with respect to me within yourselves [or by their own power], but I within myself chose you." God takes the initiative in salvation but, of course, man must respond favorably to it. And He *elected* them not only for themselves but that they might be instruments in His service.

Some would make the doctrine of election to mean that God arbitrarily has elected some to be saved to the neglect of all others. This is to ignore both the nature of God as sovereign love and the nature of man as a free moral agent. Paul's great passage on election (Eph. 1:3-14) stresses that it is "in Christ." Already it has been noted that eleven times in twelve verses he uses this phrase or its equivalent. God in sovereign love elected that all who are "in Christ" shall be saved. Each man in his own will shall decide what to do with God's offer. A sovereign God set the terms. Man in his free moral agency must choose. He is free to choose, but he is responsible for his choice. The overall teaching of the Bible about election may be summed up thusly: God elected a plan of salvation; He also elected a people to propagate that plan.*

---

*See my *Fundamentals of our Faith*, Broadman, Nashville, 1960, pp. 89 ff.

In this light we may understand Jesus' words in John 15:16. He chose; the disciples responded. But He chose them not only to be saved, but to share the gospel of salvation with others. And, of course, they are free to accept or reject the second choice also. If they refuse, they will be the losers with respct to present joy and future heavenly reward. If they are fruitful, their "fruit should remain," or "abide." The Christian will meet either his fruitfulness, or his fruitlessness at the judgment. And he will be rewarded in the same proportion. Some will be saved, "yet so as by fire" (I Cor. 3:15). The soul saved, the useless life destroyed.

On the other hand, the Christian who wills to be fruitful is promised the infinite resources of the Father in his effort (v. 16b). Just remember that the Lord never told His people to be successful, but to be faithful. We should be the latter, and leave the results with Him.

The Anticipation of Persecution (15:17 — 16:4)

Because of what is coming upon Jesus' followers, it is all the more important that they should love one another (v. 17). For they will be rejected and hated by the world. If, therefore, they do not love each other, to whom shall they turn? This question is applicable to every Christian generation.

The world will hate the Christian. But he has the satisfaction of knowing that it hated Jesus before it hated him (v. 18). If he were of the world, the world would love its own (v. 19). But because he has been chosen of Christ, and has accepted that choice, he is the object of the world's hate. So rather than being a cause for sorrow, it should be one of great rejoicing (cf. Matt. 5:10-12).

Jesus then reminded the disciples of His word spoken earlier in the evening (13:16). "The servant [slave] is not greater than his lord" (owner, v. 20). Men who have persecuted Jesus will persecute them (e.g., Jewish rulers). Conversely, those who have observed His teachings will observe theirs also. They will truly have fellowship with Christ in suffering as well as in success. Those who will persecute the followers of Jesus because of their loyalty to Him, will do so because they have rejected both the Father and the Son (v. 21).

Why did the world hate Jesus? Because in His ministry He had revealed to them their sin (v. 22). Under the searching gaze of His perfect life and teaching, they no longer could hide under cloaks of self-righteousness. Furthermore, their hatred for Jesus is hatred for His Father also (v. 23). In His mighty works Jesus had revealed the Father to them. He had also made them aware of their sin (v. 24). But instead of repentance and faith they had responded with hate toward both the Son and His Father. However, this was not an unexpected reaction. It was a fulfilment of the Scripture which they proudly called "their law." "They hated me without a cause" (v. 25; cf. Ps. 35:19; 69:4).

However, in their suffering of persecution they will not be left as orphans in a storm. For when the Divine Helper is come, "whom I shall send from the Father, even the Spirit of truth, which proceedeth from the Father, he shall testify of me" (v. 26). Note that here Jesus said that He would send the Spirit (cf. 14:16). But He will go out from the Father. Thus the work of both Father and Son is intimately identified. And when the Spirit comes, He will "testify concerning me." This testimony will not be second-hand or hearsay evidence. It will be that which the Spirit knows first-hand, and so admissable legal testimony.

"And ye also shall bear witness, because ye have been with me from the beginning" (v. 27). "Ye" is emphatic. So "ye on your own" will take the witness stand on Jesus' behalf, empowered by the Spirit in doing so (cf. Acts 2:22-36). In the strictest sense one requirement to be an apostle was that one could testify personally the things concerning Jesus' life, death, resurrection, and ascension (cf. Acts 1:20b-22). So their witness would be based upon personal experience. They had been with Jesus throughout His ministry (cf. Mark 3:14). Thus the things about to happen to Jesus will be related to God's redemptive purpose. And even in their subsequent persecution they will be used of the Holy Spirit to confront men with His claims. One wonders if Peter did not recall this moment when he wrote that if one suffered persecution he should do so as a Christian (I Peter 4:16). His very suffering as such would be a testimony concerning Christ unto God's glory.

Jesus spoke these words in order that under persecution the disciples would not stumble (16:1). They will be excommunicated. Those who shall slay them will think that in doing so they will be serving God (v. 29; cf. Acts 6:13-14; 7:57 f.; I Cor. 15:9; Gal. 1:13-14; Phil. 3:6). This they will do because they do not know by experience either the Father or the Son (v. 3; cf. I Cor. 2:8).

Jesus reminded the disciples again that He is telling them these things, not to frighten them, but to prepare them for the ordeal which awaits them (v. 4). Forewarned is forearmed. So often when a Christian runs into difficulty as he tries to serve God he thinks that he is not pleasing to God. Nothing could be farther from the truth. Satan does not waste his time in troubling the indolent Christian. But when one dares to stand up for Christ, he can expect Satan's opposition at every turn. This was true of Jesus, of Paul; and it will ever be true of you.

The Necessity for Jesus' Departure (16:5-7)

Soon Jesus will be leaving the Eleven to return to the Father (v. 5). Yet no longer do they ask where He is going. They now understand, and that awareness has made them sad, not for Him but for them (v. 6).

"Nevertheless [despite their sorrow] . . . it is expedient for you that I go away" (v. 7). The word rendered "expedient" means to bear together, such as the coming together of circumstances. And this bearing together is the fact that the Divine Helper can come only after Jesus has departed. But if He departs, He will send the Spirit to them.

If the Eleven thought of Jesus' departure as a defeat for Him and them, they were mistaken. It was thereby that He would win full victory and would be glorified beyond even that glory which He had known before His Incarnation (cf. Phil. 2:9 ff.). And in the coming of the Holy Spirit Jesus would be loosed upon the world in a way that was impossible so long as He remained in the flesh. This is true because of what the Holy Spirit will mean to the world, to the church, and to Jesus.

The Paraclete and the World (16:8-11)

The Holy Spirit will have a ministry to the unbelieving world. For "when he is come, he will reprove [convict] the world" (v. 8). "Convict" *(elegchō)* means to bring to light or expose, to convict, and to refute with a view to correction. So the Holy Spirit will bring to light or expose the world's sin. He will convict it of that sin. And He will refute its claims of innocence or self-righteousness with a view to correcting it in all who surrender to Christ in repentance and faith. He will convict the world of *sin,* and of *righteousness,* and of *judgment.*

"Of sin, because they believe not on me" (v. 9). He will expose the heinousness of the sin of unbelief with respect to Jesus Christ. This involves the world's rejection of Him then and now. Shedding light upon Jesus' true nature men will know that they have crucified the Lord of glory (cf. Acts 2:22-24, 36-37). And those who subsequently reject Him will know that they are numbered among the crucifiers (cf. Heb. 6:6).

"Of righteousness, because I go to my Father, and ye see me no more" (v. 10). Jesus was/is righteousness. So long as He walked among men, He perfectly revealed God. His very life justified God's demand for righteousness. And since man cannot achieve it for himself, Jesus paid the price for sin that in Him a "just" God might also be the "justifier" of those believing in Jesus (cf. Rom. 3:26).

However, man insists upon achieving his own righteousness. Thereby he fails to achieve the righteousness that is in Christ (cf. Rom. 10:3 ff.). After Jesus no longer walks among men, the Holy Spirit will continue to expose man's lack of righteousness. He will convict him of his own lack in the light of Jesus' life and work. Thus He will refute man's claim to self-righteousness with a view to leading him to accept the righteousness of God which is in Christ Jesus.

"Of judgment, because the prince of this world is judged" (v. 11). The words "is judged" mean a full, complete judgment (perfect passive). God in Christ has rendered a final judgment upon him. And upon all who choose to serve him (cf. 3:18). If one rejects Christ and His righteousness, he can make no claim to innocence. So in the exposing light of the Holy Spirit, his claim is refuted; he can have no excuse. By his own choice he has accepted Satan and consequent judgment. And he has no one to blame but himself.

The Paraclete and the Church (16:12-13)

The Holy Spirit also has a ministry to those who believe in Jesus. We already have seen how He indwells the Christian, sealing him and guaranteeing his full salvation. Likewise, He indwells the fellowship of believers. In Acts one finds, among other things, the administrative work of the Holy Spirit.

In the passage under consideration Jesus presents a further word as to the Holy Spirit as Teacher (cf. 14:26). Jesus had taught His disciples for over three years. Still there remained many things which He wished to say. But they were unable to "bear them now" (v. 12). The truth was too heavy for them to carry. His progressive revelation has been in proportion to their ability to receive it. And some things they are not yet ready to hear. That readiness must await the illuminating work of the Holy Spirit.

But "when he, the Spirit of truth, is come, he will guide you into all truth" (v. 13). Not a scientific knowledge, but all spiritual truth. But even this will be a continuation of the teaching which began with Jesus. He had said that He spoke the things which the Father told Him.

Likewise, the Spirit will not speak "from himself" (aph' heatou). What He hears He shall speak. When the Father speaks to Him He will relay the message. This should not be construed to mean that the Holy Spirit is inferior to God. Like Jesus He is God; but He is the Spirit of God sent forth to do God's work. Furthermore, "He will show you things to come," or "the coming things." Not a chart of future history, but the outworking of God's redemptive purpose begun in Christ.

As the Holy Spirit will enlighten the apostles' memory of Jesus' past teachings and events, He also will illumine their minds to enable them to interpret those matters. Thus we can understand the source of the tremendous doctrines expounded in the remainder of the New Testament. And our ability to comprehend their meaning.

If one reads the Bible merely as a chore, it may seem to be just so many words. But when one reads it prayerfully and with a hungry soul, it becomes alive with the greatest truth ever spoken or penned. This is due to the work of the Holy Spirit in the believer and in the church.

The Paraclete and Jesus (16:14-15)

What is the purpose of the Holy Spirit's ministry? It is to glorify Jesus. "He shall glorify me: for he shall receive of mine, and shall show it unto you" (v. 14).

This very Gospel is a fulfilment of this fact. Also Colossians, to mention only two books of the New Testament. The Gnostic philosophers would reduce Jesus to the level of a demigod. But under the inspiration of the Holy Spirit these two writers exalted Him to the highest pinnacle of glory.

"He shall glorify me," or "He me shall glorify." So "me" is emphatic. "Me and no one else he shall glorify." This means that the Holy Spirit does not even seek to glorify Himself. He never calls attention to Himself. This is one reason why it is easier to understand Jesus than the Holy Spirit. For "out of the things of me [Jesus, not Himself] he takes, and shows to you." Those who magnify the Holy Spirit unduly point to the ecstatic. But the fruit of the Spirit is these quiet, inner things: "love, joy, peace, longsuffering, gentleness, goodness, faith, meekness, temperance" (Gal. 5:22 f.) .

Which leads us to conclude that any system of theology which magnifies the Holy Spirit above Jesus is not of the Holy Spirit. For His work is to glorify Jesus, not to call attention to Himself (v. 15) .

The Sorrow and the Joy (16:16-31)

Before concluding His lesson Jesus returned to the theme of His departure. "In a little while" the disciples will not see Him (v. 16). He will be dead and in the tomb. This is the reason for their sorrow. But also in "a little while" they shall see Him again. His resurrection will give them great joy. "Because I go to the Father" is not in the best texts. It probably was added by a copyist to balance this verse with verse 17 where these words are genuine.

The disciples began to talk among themselves. What did Jesus mean by their not seeing Him and then seeing Him (vv. 17-18) ? And they added, "And, because I go to the Father" (v. 17) ? This last question they recalled from 14:2-3. Perhaps overhearing them Jesus proceeded to answer their question (v. 19). Solemnly He said, "Ye shall weep and lament [both verbs suggesting loud lamentation], but the world shall rejoice" (v. 20). While the disciples are plunged into despair, the world, thinking that it has won the struggle, will joyously celebrate its *victory*. But it will be of short duration. Likewise the lamenting of Jesus' own will soon be turned into abiding joy. Their sorrow will be as that of a woman in travail (v. 21). And like it it will soon give place to great joy, even as she does when she sees her newborn baby. Now the disciples are in the throes of sorrow. But when He is raised from the dead they will rejoice again (v. 22). And unlike the world's short-lived joy, theirs will be a permanent possession.

Then Jesus made a very strange statement. "And in that day ye shall ask me nothing" (v. 23) . To what does "that day" refer? The sense is greater than simply the day of Jesus' resurrection. Bernard sees it as both that day and Pentecost when the Holy Spirit shall come, with emphasis upon the latter (cf. 14:20; 16:

26). In a sense this is true. However, between Jesus' resurrection and ascension the disciples did ask Him some things (cf. John 21:21; Acts 1:6), though not in the sense of prayer. But they did worship Him (cf. Matt. 28:17). It is of interest to note that "ask" here renders *erotaō*, basically to ask a question. But in the same verse "ask" (the Father) renders *aiteō*, basically to request, or ask favors. But in verse 26 they are used in reverse order. So we may conclude that the two verbs here may be used interchangeably. Robertson takes note of this.

Perhaps a look at the Greek text will help to point out exactly what Jesus meant. "And in that day me not you will ask anything ... but what you request of the Father, he will give to you in my name." Note that "me" is in the emphatic position. The disciples had been accustomed to asking Jesus. But He will soon be taken away. Therefore, after He is no longer with them they are to pray to the Father, and in His name the Father will grant their prayers.

Bernard is helpful at this point. "It is better to render, 'In that day, ye shall ask nothing of *me*.' The visible company of Jesus would be withdrawn, so that they would no longer be able to ask favours of Him or proffer requests to Him, face to face. But there is a greater compensation, and its promise is introduced by the solemn prelude *amēn amēn legō humin* (see on 1:51). They can henceforth have direct access to the Father, and whatever they ask Him, the due conditions of Christian prayer being observed (see on 15:16), shall be given."

So we may conclude that "in that day" includes all of the period from Jesus' ascension until He comes again. So long as Jesus remained among them, even after His resurrection, the disciples did ask Him questions. But after His ascension they prayed to the Father in His name (cf. Acts 1:14).

Up until the moment that Jesus was speaking the disciples had not prayed to the Father in Jesus' name (v. 24). But once He is gone away they are to do so. Thus they will receive answers to their prayers, and their joy shall be fulfilled or be an abiding joy. In this way they will learn that they are not left alone in the world (v. 26).

Jesus had been speaking in proverbs about His going away (v. 25). The hour comes when He no longer will do so, but will tell them plainly with respect to the Father, who loves them because they love the Son and believe that He came forth from the Father (v. 27). And then Jesus told them plainly. "I came forth from the Father, and am come into the world: again, I leave the world, and go to the Father" (v. 28). It was as simple as that. He came from the Father into the world. Now He will return to the Father from the world.

And the disciples understood His meaning (vv. 29-30). They believe that He came forth from God, as He said. But to strengthen that faith Jesus asked, "Now ye believe?" (v. 31). The emphasis is upon "now." Up until now they had believed. But is that faith strong enough to keep them in the trial which lies ahead? Will they believe when they see Him on a cross, even dead? They will pass through a raging storm. So Jesus warns them against over-confidence. He wants to anchor their faith to eternal reality in order that it will not waver in the storm.

This warning does not refer to a possible loss of salvation. That was a finished fact. But, even so, they would need assurance as they passed through the ordeal which awaits them.

The Promise of Victory (16:32-33)

That they need to shore up their faith is evident in verse 32. The hour is almost upon them when they will be scattered as sheep without a shepherd. Despite their avowal of faith they will forsake Him. Even then He will not be alone. The Father is always with Him.

But what about them? To prepare them for that hour He has been speaking to them. It is to the end that they may have peace in the storm. And then as if to fix their anchor squarely under the Rock, He said, "In the world ye shall have tribulation: but be of good cheer; I have overcome the world" (v. 33). As long as they remain in the world they will be in many tight places. But they are to be courageous. Literally, "In the world you keep on having tribulation, but keep on being of good courage."

And why? Because "I have fully conquered the world." "I" is emphatic. And the perfect tense of the verb means that He and no one else has won the complete victory over the world.

Jesus has won! And they will win in Him!

The Lord's Prayer

Even a casual reading of the Gospels reveals the great part which prayer played in the life of Jesus. And yet this is the only extended prayer of His which is recorded in the Gospels. What is sometimes called the "Lord's Prayer" (cf. Matt. 6:9 ff.) is actually the "Model Prayer." For when Jesus gave it He was teaching a lesson in prayer. So if any prayer should be labeled "The Lord's Prayer" this one bears the primary claim to such a title. It is sometimes called "The High Priestly Prayer." The High Priest was praying before the sacrifice was made.

Since the record does not say, it is impossible to know where this prayer was prayed. Some think that it was prayed in the temple area. Even if He did pray there on this occasion, that fact does not add to the high priestly nature of it. For He certainly was not standing in the Holy Place. Since Jesus was not a priest He was not allowed beyond the Court of Israel. Going back to the previously stated idea that Jesus most likely was not in the temple area as He taught John 15-16, if this be a true surmise it would militate against the temple area as the place where He prayed. The tone of the prayer suggests a place of privacy, something which would not have been true of the temple area even at this late night hour. The temple was kept open at night during the Passover for the convenience of the worshippers. We may assume, therefore, that this prayer was prayed in the same place where Jesus had been teaching. Perhaps some quiet wayside spot just outside the city walls underneath the temple area.

The prayer is divided into three parts. Jesus prayed for Himself, for His present disciples, and for all future disciples.

The Prayer for Himself (17:1-8)

The prayer was prayed aloud. As Jesus spoke He not only prayed but He *led* the disciples in prayer. And as He did so He "lifted his eyes to heaven." Some take this to mean that He prayed in the open air. While it is probably true that He did, these words do not necessarily support the idea. It is a natural posture for one who is praying.

"Father, the hour is come; glorify thy Son, that thy Son also may glorify thee" (v. 1). Note the intimacy with which Jesus prayed. Not to some far-removed Potentate, but to His "Father." The intimacy which He now expressed had been the Father-Son relationship all the while.

The "hour" toward which Jesus had been moving is here. And Jesus' only wish therein is that as He is lifted up on the cross He may glorify His Father. This had been His constant desire in life. It will be no different in the hour of death.

This glory to God will be seen in those who through Christ shall receive eternal life (v. 2). The Father has "given" Him all who will believe on Him. And to them He will give eternal life. And what is this eternal life? "That they might know [through experience] thee the only true God, and Jesus Christ, whom thou hast sent" (v. 3).

Jesus had glorified the Father on earth. He had finished the work assigned to Him on earth (v. 4). He has no sense of failure as to His ministry. And soon He will cry, "It is finished." So now He prayed that the Father would restore to Him the eternal, heavenly glory which He had laid aside during His Incarnation (v. 5).

Reciting the work which He had done, Jesus said, "I have manifested thy name unto the men which thou gavest me out of the world: thine they were, and thou gavest them me; and they have kept thy word" (v. 6). He looks on the apostles as gifts from God, apostles who have been true to Him (all save Judas who was never really one of them). They had been so imperfect in actions, but they were men with true hearts. They have received Jesus' teachings as God's own (vv. 6-9). They have come to realize that Jesus has been sent forth from God.

So in this sense Jesus has finished His work. He has revealed God to man. And this little group has believed that revelation. There are others also. But upon this little group of eleven dedicated men the future of Christ's work will rest.

The Prayer for His Contemporary Disciples (17:9-19)

So now Jesus prayed for them. "I pray for them" (v. 9). He did not pray for the unbelieving world. Not that He did not love it. But the time has come to concentrate upon those out of the world who have believed on Him. They belong to God. But God has given them to Him. "All are thine" (v. 10). Here Jesus used the singular verb *(estin)*. He is thinking of them as a group. "And thine are mine." How intimate is the relationship between Father and Son! Despite their many failures Jesus is glorified in this little group.

Jesus was about to leave the world. But this group must remain and carry on His work. So He prayed, "Holy Father, keep [guard, keep safe] through thine own name those whom thou hast given me" (v. 11). And they will certainly need guarding. (Only here in the New Testament is God called "Holy Father.") So Jesus committeed His own to the Fatherly protection, or providence. Certainly the world with its power will not guard them. Only the Father can keep them safe. But that is enough.

As long as Jesus was in the world He guarded them (v. 12). Even in Gethsemane He will ask for their safety (18:8 f.). "And none of them is lost, but the son of perdition; that the scriptures might be fulfilled" (v. 12). But He was soon to leave them. Therefore, He commended them to the Father's care, that the joy which Jesus had might also be in them (v. 13). The world hated them as it hated Jesus. Their very separation from the world, like His, marked them for the world's hatred (v. 14).

Nevertheless, Jesus did not pray that the Father would take them out of the world by some sudden translation (v. 15). But rather that He would guard them from the evil one. They are to be in the world but not of it (v. 16). So in that state He prayed that the Father would "sanctify them through thy word: thy word is truth" (v. 17). The word "sanctify" means to set apart to the service of God. And it is to be done in the sphere of "truth," the very essence of God's Word. Thus rather than withdrawing from the world with all of its sin and hatred, they were to remain in the world as dedicated heralds of God's message to that world. The Father sent the Son into the world on His mission of redemption. And the Son will send His followers throughout the world to make the offer of redemption known (v. 18).

"And for their sakes I sanctify myself, that they also might be sanctified through the truth" (v. 19). He hereby dedicated Himself to the cross, that thereafter they might be dedicated to the proclamation of the gospel of redemption which He made possible.

Some would relate "sanctify" to the idea of getting rid of sin until one is *sanctified*. But clearly Jesus had no sin of which to be freed. The thought here, and throughout the New Testament, is that of dedication, or being set apart to the service of God. The Christian is *sanctified* the second he is saved. Thus they are called "saints" (I Cor. 1:2), though at times they act unsaintly. But the Christian is set apart as an instrument in God's service. Thereafter, he should grow in his state of being sanctified (cf. II Peter 3:18).

In the sense as used by Jesus "sanctify" refers to dedication to a specific task. He was always sanctified to God's service; now He sanctified Himself to a special task, the cross. Likewise, the disciples were sanctified to God the moment that they received Christ as their Saviour. But now Jesus prayed for their sanctification to the given task of preaching the gospel.

The Prayer for all Future Believers (17:20-26)

And then Jesus looked down the centuries to that innumerable multitude which shall come to Him. "Neither pray I for these alone, but for them also which shall believe on me through their word" (v. 20). Jesus was expecting the apostles' faithfulness to be rewarded with a rich harvest. So He prayed for every last believer down through the ages, even for you and me. And this prayer contains two definite petitions: that they may be one, and that they ultimately will be with Him in glory.

"That they may be one" (v. 21). Already He had prayed this prayer for the Eleven and their contemporaries (v. 11). Now He included the fellowship of all believers.

This prayer has been variously interpreted: all the way from cooperative endeavor among churches at the local level, to national and world councils of churches, to a union of denominations into one Protestant Church. In this vein a recent invitation was issued by the Roman Catholic Church for the "separated brethren" to return to what the former calls the Mother Church.

But is this the sense of Jesus' prayer? It would seem that to read into this petition any idea with respect to denominations, or the lack of them, is an anachronism. For denominations as we know them did not exist in the first century.

Was Jesus praying for organic church union or for spiritual unity? "That they may be one; as thou, Father, art in me, and I in thee, that they also may be one in us." The norm of this oneness is that which exists in the Father and the Son. To be

sure this relationship was one of spiritual unity and essence. But
in the outward manifestation they are revealed as two Persons
of the Godhead, the Father and the Son. The disciples themselves
were individual persons with their different characteristics. Yet
Jesus prayed that they should be one. Surely He did not pray
that they should become organically one huge man. Rather He
prayed that despite their outward differences there should be a
unifying principle which bound them together in a common faith
and purpose. This same idea is seen in Paul's words about the
work of Christ in Jew and Gentile "for to make in himself of
twain one new man, so making peace" (Eph. 2:15). That for
which Jesus prayed was spiritual unity, not organic union. To
have organic union without spiritual unity would be hypocrisy
of the worst sort.

The purpose of this unity is "that the world may believe that
thou hast sent me" (v. 21). Bernard says that this unity "is not
invisible; it is to be such as will convince the world of the Divine
mission of the common Master of Christians. And He has already
explained that the badge of this unity is love, the love of Christian for Christian which all men may see (13:35)." But this can
be *visible* without organic union.

However, if the world is to believe that God has sent Jesus
as the Redeemer, there also must be a unity of faith. To disre-
gard basic elements of the faith for the sake of an outward form
of union is to betray the trust which Jesus placed in His followers.
One characteristic which Jesus gratefully attributed to His apostles
was that "they have kept thy word" (v. 6). Were they to depart
from that position for the sake of outward form? Certainly Jesus
did not subscribe to such (cf. Matt. 23). There were those who
sought to tone down the deity of Christ and all that it involved.
Neither John nor Paul ignored that for the sake of outward
form (cf. John and Colossians). There were those who preached
a gospel of works plus faith instead of a gospel of salvation by
grace through faith. And Paul most assuredly did not compromise
at that point for the sake of a visible oneness (cf. Gal. 1:6-10).

To be sure a oneness of all Christians is to be desired. But
it must be a oneness of spiritual unity of love and faith, not a
oneness of outward organic union at the expense of those things
which alone can be the basis of unity. And to obtain such unity
we must not begin where we are to follow the path of expediency.
We must not discard our differences where they involve understanding of truth. Instead we must begin at the beginning. And

that beginning is in the heart of Deity. There we must find the unity of faith and purpose which the Father has revealed in His Son. Then with the open New Testament, unfettered by those things which make for outward differences, and led by the Holy Spirit, we must find the oneness of God's revelation through His Word. There alone may we find spiritual unity. But until we achieve a unity of faith we can give visible expression to our unity of love. Admitting our diversity, we can express unity in diversity, a unity of love and understanding. And therein shall all men know that we are His disciples (vv. 22-23).

"Father, I will [wish] that they also, whom thou hast given me, be with me where I am; that they may behold my glory, which thou hast given me: for thou lovedst me before the foundation of the world" (v. 24).

His first disciples had beheld Jesus' glory on earth, the glory as of the only begotten of the Father (1:14). But even that was a glory expressed in human form. And all subsequent generations of Christians have seen that glory only through faith. Now Jesus was returning to heaven to assume the eternal glory in its full essence. He wishes that all of His may be with Him in heaven where with their eyes they may behold His glory, may see Him as He is (cf. I John 3:2).

Then, closing His prayer, Jesus addressed God as "righteous Father" (v. 25). He is both holy and righteous (cf. v. 11). The world has not known the Father by experience. But the Son so knows Him. And His disciples know that the Father has sent Him as the full revelation of His redeeming love. He has made known His Father's name (v. 26). So long as He is in the world He will continue to do so. And through the ministry of the Holy Spirit He will do so until the end of the age.

This is to the end that the same relationship of love which exists between the Father and the Son may be experienced within the fellowship of believers. This will be possible as He is in them and they are in Him.

Blessed memories! How they linger to bless our souls. As out of his own memory the old man, John, recalled so vividly these last hours of fellowship with Jesus, so we may relive them in the fellowship of the Holy Spirit. And in memory fraught with faith we may walk with Jesus as He went forth to Gethsemane.

IX
The Raging Storm

John 18:1 — 19:16

The Arrest and Trial of Jesus

With His teaching and prayer ended Jesus now entered fully into His passion. This was one part of that to which Jesus was going, and no one could follow Him. Because, indeed, only He could do that which awaited Him. We are not told the time, but it must have been near the midnight hour.

The Betrayal and Arrest of Jesus (18:1-11)

Wherever Jesus had taught and prayed we know that it was on the west side of "the brook Cedron" or *Kidrōn*. For having ended His prayer He led His disciples across this brook to the eastern side (v. 1). *Kidrōn* means "of the cedars." So it was "the brook of the Cedars." This brook was always dry except in the rainy season or after an occasional heavy rain. In all likelihood it was dry at this time.

Just beyond this brook was a garden. John does not mention its name, but Matthew and Mark call it "Gethsemane," the olive press. Evidently it contained an olive press and was filled with olive trees. Today as one walks out St. Stephen's gate such a garden may be seen just across the brook. It has several old olive trees growing in it. There stands the Church of All Nations built over what is called "the Rock of Agony." This is said to be the rock on which Jesus prayed. In the fourth century this was pointed out as the site of the Garden of Agony. It may be the location of the Garden of Gethsemane. At least it must have been in this vicinity.

Since the season of agonizing prayer had been recorded by the other Gospels, John omits it. But he notes that it was a place to which Jesus was accustomed to retire for prayer (v. 2). It may have belonged to a friend of Jesus. Judas having acquired the "band" (of Roman soldiers) and the "officers" (temple police), evidently returned to the upper room. But finding that Jesus had left, he surmised that He had gone to His usual place of prayer. Since the officers of the Sanhedrin would effect the arrest, perhaps

247

the soldiers from the Tower of Antonia came along in case there
was a riot among the people over Jesus' arrest (v. 3). So they
came to Gethsemane bearing lanterns, torches, and weapons.

By the time of their arrival Jesus had finished His prayer vigil,
and was ready to be taken. Therefore, hearing their approach He
went forth to meet them. His question: "Whom seek ye?" (v. 4).
"Jesus of Nazareth," they replied (v. 5). Surely the temple police
knew Jesus on sight. But in the dark shadows with only the
flickering lights which they carried, it was difficult to recognize
anyone. So Jesus said, "I am he." Judas was standing with the
armed band. But John omits any specific mention of his act
of betrayal. Some see this as John's purpose to ignore Judas
and to stress the voluntariness of Jesus' surrender. But since John
had stressed Judas' act of betrayal all along, this hardly seems
to be the case. He simply implied a knowledge of this act from
the Synoptic Gospels. Even though Jesus identified Himself, in
all probability Judas carried out his bargain by kissing Jesus
on the hand calling Him "Rabbi." It was customary for a pupil
so to greet his teacher.

As soon as the band heard Jesus' reply, "they went backward,
and fell to the ground" (v. 6). There was nothing supernatural
about this. Other than the fact that the band, realizing that they
were face to face with Jesus, stepped back so quickly that they
fell down. Evidently they got up only to be asked again whom
they were seeking. And when they said, "Jesus of Nazareth" (v.
7), Jesus reminded them again that He was the one whom they
were seeking. Knowing that He would be taken, He asked that
His disciples might be permitted to go unmolested (vv. 8-9).

At that point Peter went into action. He had a sword which
He had gotten in the upper room (cf. Luke 22:35-38).* He understood Jesus to mean that he was to use this sword to guard Him.
So doing as he had been told, he drew his sword and cut off the
right ear of one in the crowd which had come to arrest Jesus
(v. 10). Though this incident had already been recorded, John
alone adds the detail as to the victim's name as well as that of
Peter. The former was Malchus, a servant of the high priest.
Luke notes that Jesus healed the ear. Evidently Peter aimed for
his head. But due to expert dodging, Malchus only lost an ear.

All of the disciples understood that they were to guard Jesus.

---

*Cf. my *An Exposition of the Gospel of Luke*, pp. 307-309.

"Lord, shall we smite with the sword?" (Luke 22:49). There were two swords (Luke 22:38), the other probably in the hand of one of the group that Jesus had left at the gate as He entered Gethsemane (Mark 14:32-33). But Peter, ever the impulsive one, did not wait for Jesus to answer. He pulled out his sword and started swinging.

But Jesus told him to put up his sword (v. 11). He was now ready to be arrested, to drink the cup which His Father had given Him, and He no longer needed protecting. Peter would just get himself killed needlessly.

The Appearance before Annas (18:12-14, 19-24)

So the band led Jesus away captive. They first took Him to Annas (v. 12). Annas was a former high priest. Having been deposed by the Romans, he was in turn succeeded by his five sons. Finally, the Romans made Caiaphas his son-in-law high priest (v. 14). Annas may have occupied quarters in the high priest's residence.

Why did they take Jesus to Annas before leading Him before Caiaphas? It may be that events were moving so rapidly as to catch the Sanhedrin unprepared. Since it was night that body was not assembled. While they were being called, the time may have been spent in trying to get some charge to present to the Sanhedrin.

But still another matter may have prompted this preliminary hearing before Annas. Even though he no longer was high priest in fact, he still maintained quite a hold on the people. Also, he was well liked by the Romans. A charge brought by him would carry great weight with both the populace and the Romans.

For the sake of continuity it is necessary to rearrange the order of John's account at this point. It seems that he injects a portion of the account of Peter's denial (vv. 15-18), and then relates what happened to Jesus before Annas (vv. 19-23).

In verse 19 John says that the "high priest" asked Jesus about His disciples and teaching. Bernard suggests the possibility that this "high priest" was Caiaphas who also was present at this time. But he assumes most likely that this title here referred to Annas who was still called "high priest" in the popular sense. He was the real power behind the office, even though he no longer occupied it.

The nature of Annas' questions was designed to ascertain the basis upon which Jesus taught and made disciples. Was He simply a Rabbi or did He claim to be the Messiah? In reply Jesus ignored the question about His disciples. Previously He had asked for their safety, and did not wish now to involve them. But as to His teaching He said, "I spake openly to the world; I ever taught in the synagogue, and in the temple, whither the Jews always resort; and in secret have I said nothing" (v. 20). Of course, He had taught in private groups (cf. Nicodemus, Jacob's well, and John 13-17). But He had also taught openly. So instead of asking Him, Annas had only to inquire of those who had heard Him (v. 21).

With this one of the temple police slapped Jesus, asking, "Answerest thou the high priest so?" (v. 22). Here Jesus did not turn the other cheek. Instead, He remonstrated, "If I have spoken evil, bear witness of the evil [prove it]: but if well [if what I have said is a fair statement], why smitest thou me?" (v. 23). So seeing that he would get nowhere by questioning Jesus, Annas "sent" (aorist) Him to Caiaphas (v. 24).

John does not relate Jesus' appearance before Caiaphas, since it had already been fully recorded by the other Gospels. But he does tell of Peter's denial of Jesus. It is natural that he would do so. Already he had noted Jesus' prophecy of the event (13:38). And he will return to this in Chapter 21.

The Denial of Peter (18:15-18, 25-27)

John does not tell about the disciples' fleeing when Jesus was arrested. But he implies it in the statement that Peter "was following" (imperfect) Him on the way to the house of Caiaphas (v. 15). "Another disciple," probably John, was doing the same. He was known to the high priest, not necessarily a friend, but known well enough to be admitted to the palace by the doorkeeper. So he went into the palace with Jesus.

But Peter was not known. So he was standing outside, probably even outside the courtyard (v. 16). Seeing this, John went out and persuaded the portress to let him come into the courtyard. The portress asked Peter if he were not one of Jesus' disciples (v. 17). Her question invited a negative answer. Robertson suggests that she probably knew, but wished to make Peter's answer easy. Wishing to remain unnoticed Peter curtly replied, "I am not." Those in the courtyard had made a fire for warmth in the cool night air. Peter, perhaps feeling that he was safe after his first denial, joined the group about the fire. He probably was facii g it so that the light fell on his face (v. 18). As has been p. 'nted out in many sermons, he was warming himself at the enemy's fire.

As Peter stood there those about the fire asked him, "Art not thou also one of his disciples?" (v. 25). Again they invited a negative answer. The devil was making it easy for Peter to deny Jesus. And he took the bait. Apparently his second denial was a little stronger. For "he denied it, and said, I am not."

Finally, one of the servants of the high priest and a kinsman of Malchus asked, "Did not I see thee in the garden with him?" (v. 26). The form of this question invited an affirmative reply. This question was getting too close to home for Peter. The implication is that this man was certain that he had seen Peter, maybe remembered that it was he who had tried to kill Malchus. Peter could see himself being arrested for attempted murder, or even worse, for resisting the officers. So the Synoptics report that he began to swear (Matt. 26:73; Mark 14:71). Thus for the third time he denied Jesus (v. 27). "And immediately the cock crew."

Jesus had said that this would be the case. Peter instinctively looked at Jesus, and saw that He was looking at him (cf. Luke 22:61). And Peter went out and wept bitterly (cf. Matt. 26:75). The look of Jesus and his own sense of guilt broke his heart. Despite his boasting he had failed in the crisis. In a moment of heroism he risked his life for Jesus, but now, cursing, he had denied Him. How little Peter understood himself! As, indeed, how little do we understand ourselves. But Peter wept his sin. Do we do the same? There is hope for such a man.

The Appearance before Pilate (18:28 — 19:16)

28-32

The third denial by Peter came at the end of the preliminary trial of Jesus before the Sanhedrin. After dawn, therefore, that body held its formal session at which time they agreed that He should be put to death. This agreement had been reached in the preliminary hearing. To give it a semblance of legality they reassembled after dawn for the formal condemnation. However, even this was illegal, since their law forbade a capital sentence to be given on the same day as the trial. But the Jewish rulers did not bother with this fine point of law. After all, for weeks now they had been determined to put Jesus to death (cf. 11:53).

The Roman government permitted the Sanhedrin to exercise

authority in religious and civil matters. But they reserved to themselves the right to inflict capital punishment. So no matter how distasteful it was to them the Sanhedrin took Jesus to appear before the Roman governor, or procurator Pilate (v. 28). It was early in the morning.

The place to which they took Jesus was the "hall of judgment," or the Praetorium. In Rome the Praetorium was the camp of the praetorian guard (Phil. 1:13). But in the provinces it referred to the palace, or residence in which the governor lived (cf. Acts 23:35). The exact location of the Praetorium in Jerusalem is a matter of dispute. A fourth-century tradition places it in the Tower of Antonia, the garrison for Roman soldiers, just north of the temple area. The traditional Via Dolorosa is figured from this point. Those who hold to this place claim that Pilate would have stayed here while in Jerusalem in order to be near his troops. However, there is no real evidence to support this position.

The other suggested place for the Praetorium is the palace of Herod the Great, located in the western part of Jerusalem. Some of the original portions of this palace are still standing. At the time of the destruction of Jerusalem in A.D. 70 it was preserved as a place to quarter a band of Roman soldiers left there to guard the site.

It is held by the champions of this building as being the Praetorium that it was here that Pilate resided when in Jerusalem. Bernard cites Philo as evidence that on one occasion the procurator did live here. Furthermore, he cites Josephus as the authority that another procurator of Judea, Gessius Florus (about thirty-five years after Pilate) also lived here. Thus it seems most likely that this was the residence of Pilate on this occasion. Knowing his proud nature it is unlikely that he would live in the troops' quarters. And besides, he had officers to do his bidding in handling the soldiers. Other than tradition there is no evidence to support the Tower of Antonia as the place. But there is documentary evidence (cited above) to suggest that it was to Herod's palace that Jesus was brought to appear before Pilate.

Pilate served as procurator of Judea A.D. 26-36. Since Judea was a sub-division of the province of Syria, this means that Pilate served under the authority of the Roman propraetor of Syria. In the Roman provincial system peaceable areas were ruled over by proconsuls under the authority of the Roman Senate (cf. Acts 13:7; 18:12). But where troops were required to keep order the provincial ruler was a propraetor under the direct authority of the emperor. Syria, including Judea, was such a province.

Pilate had a bad record in his relations with the Jews. Shortly after coming to Judea he sent troops into Jerusalem bearing their standards on which were images of Caesar. The Jews regarded this as idolatry. It was only after a delegation to Caesarea, the governor's Judean residence, made a severe protest that he removed them. Again, Pilate placed on the walls of Herod's palace shields bearing the names of pagan deities. Only on orders from the emperor Tiberius did he remove these. In an effort to improve the water supply of Jerusalem Pilate used sacred money from the temple treasury to build an aqueduct. In the riot which ensued his soldiers slew many Jews, including innocent by-standers. Luke 13:1 records how his soldiers killed some Galileans while they were worshipping in the temple. Their blood being mixed with the blood of their sacrifices was a serious profanation of the temple and its altar. Philo relates Pilate's murders without a trial, his acceptance of bribes, his pillage and plunder, and many other outrages against the Jews. It is no wonder that the Jews, even the Sanhedrin, hated and despised him. And he returned the compliment. Only when duty required did he journey from Caesarea to Jerusalem. Such a duty was his at the Passover season when the threat of Jewish rebellion was always at its peak. This was especially true this particular year.

When the Jewish rulers arrived with their prisoner, they refused to enter the residence of a Gentile (v. 28). To have done so at this season would have made them unclean for a month. Thus they would have been prohibited from *eating the passover*. Some insist that this was the actual passover meal, which would place this event on Thursday morning. But this may mean otherwise. For instance, II Chronicles 30:22 speaks of eating the festival for seven days. Robertson notes that John uses the word "passover" *(pascha)* eight times, all of them referring to the entire feast, not to the supper itself. It would appear, therefore, that the supper had been eaten the night before (cf. Matt. 26:17). The problem here is that the rulers could not have participated in the remainder of the festival. Note their meticulous hypocrisy. They were about to lie the Son of God to His death, but they would not violate one of their ceremonial laws.

So Pilate went out of the place to stand before them. He asked, "What accusation [formal charge] bring ye against this man?" (v. 29). Note the hostility in their answer. "If he were not a malefactor [evil-doer], we would not have delivered him unto thee" (v. 30). They did not bring a charge. But the word "delivered" means that they were bringing Jesus to Pilate for execution. Assuming that the case involved nothing more than a religious matter, the governor told them to handle it themselves. But they reminded him that they had no authority to execute a man (vv. 31-32).

33-38   The matter was more serious than Pilate had first assumed. So re-entering the palace he called Jesus to him. "Art thou the King of the Jews?" he asked (v. 33). John has made no mention of such a claim. But Luke 23:2 records that the Jews charged that Jesus was guilty of attempted revolution, forbidding the people to pay tribute and claiming to be Christ a king. Jesus replied with another question. "Sayest thou this thing of thyself, or did others tell it thee of me?" (v. 34). Was this Pilate's own belief ("from thyself," *aph' heautou*), or was he just reporting the words of others? "Others" *(alloi,* others of the same kind) suggests that Jesus recognized a cynical note in Pilate's question. Did he ask this of himself, or was it just the cynical words of others like him?

Scornfully Pilate replied, "Am I a Jew?" (v. 35). The "I" is emphatic. That, plus the strong negative *mēti,* gives a strong negative flavor to his question. He had no personal interest in this squabble among these despised Jews. And he certainly did not want to be classed with them and their religious or nationalistic pretensions. Jesus' own "nation" and the chief priests had turned Him over to Pilate. So He must be guilty of some crime. "What hast thou done?" he asked. What was the nature of His crime?

Ignoring the specific questions, Jesus said that His kingdom was not an earthly one (v. 36). Had it been so, His "servants" *(hupēretai,* same word used for the temple police, 18:3), or officers would have fought to protect Him. (One had tried to do so, but Jesus had stopped him.) And Jesus would not then have been a prisoner before Pilate. This showed that His kingdom was not of this world.

Pilate then asked ironically, "Art thou a king then?" (v. 37). His question invited an affirmative reply. It was asked in scorn. Jesus ignored the irony. But taking up the form of Pilate's question as inviting an affirmative reply, He said, "Thou sayest that I am a king." A better rendering of the Greek text reads, "Thou sayest [you just admitted], because I am a king." And then Jesus explained the nature of His kingdom. To this kingship was He born; for this reason He came into the world in "that I should bear witness unto the truth. Every one that is of the truth heareth my voice" (v. 37). If Pilate were "of the truth" he would have believed Jesus. But because he was a slave to pagan error, he replied only with a cynical question.

"What is truth?" (v. 38). Evidently he asked this with a sneer. Philosophers might debate this question. But as a practical man he had neither time for, nor interest in, "truth," even though he stood before Truth Himself. He demonstrated his attitude with his actions. For turning on his heel he went outside to announce to the Jewish rulers, "I find no fault [*aitia*, crime] at all in him." He was not guilty of revolutionary tactics as they charged. He was merely a Rabbi who prattled about "truth." Having said this about Jesus, he should have released Him on the spot. But he did not do so. Three times he pronounced Jesus as innocent (cf. 19:4, 6). Yet he weakened before His accusers.

Luke records that at this point the rulers charged that Jesus stirred up the people in Judea, Galilee, and Jerusalem (23:5). And hearing the word "Galilee" Pilate thought that he saw an escape from his dilemma. Since Herod Antipas, ruler in Galilee, was in the city, Pilate sent Jesus to be tried by him. But He was soon back before Pilate (cf. Luke 23:6-12).

Pilate still had Jesus on his hands. But at this point he remem- 39-40 bered a custom which the Romans practiced among the Jews at the Passover. To placate them they would release a prisoner of their own choosing (v. 39). Other than the Gospel accounts there is no other record that such was done in Judea. But Bernard notes that Livy reports this as being done by the Romans elsewhere. So there is no reason to doubt the report here.

Thinking that this custom would give him his out, Pilate asked the entire crowd, "Will ye therefore that I release unto you the King of the Jews?" (v. 39). Even in so desperate a strait as this Pilate taunted the Jews with Jesus' Kingship. But they refused his suggestion. Instead the mob cried out, "Not this man, but Barabbas" (v. 40). And then John adds the note that Barabbas was a "robber." He was a brigand, possibly the leader of a band of robbers.

Origen of Alexandria at the beginning of the third century reports having seen a manuscript of Matthew 27:17 which gives the robber's name as *Jesus Barabbas*. Whether this be a true reading or not, it is certainly suggestive. This man could have been a false political-military messiah, the very role that Jesus refused. If so, as in so many cases, he had degenerated into the leader of a band of robbers who killed and plundered. He may have been arrested for these very crimes. As a false messiah he could have assumed the name "Jesus," Jehovah is salvation.

Now following this line of thought a very remarkable contrast appears. *Barabbas* means "son of father." So we see "Jesus, Son of His Father" and "Jesus, son of his father." The One offered Himself as a spiritual Messiah: the other offered himself as a political-military messiah. The One offered deliverance through salvation; the other offered deliverance through revolution. The One proposed to save men by the shedding of His own blood; the other proposed the same through the shedding of their own blood. And the Jews made their choice. They accepted *Jesus Barabbas* and rejected *Jesus Christ!*

Pilate figured that the people would prefer that he release this innocent Rabbi rather than this murdering brigand. And he probably was right about the *people*. But he did not reckon with the wily Jewish rulers. Matthew tells us that at the very point of Pilate's offer his wife came to him troubled over a dream that she had had about Jesus (27:19). During this interruption of the proceedings, the Jewish rulers seized upon the opportunity to persuade the people to ask for Barabbas' release and Jesus' death (Matt. 27:20).

Pilate was astounded at this turn of events. But he still hoped to appeal to the sympathy of the crowd and to show how ridiculous it was to charge Jesus as claiming to be a king. So he took Him inside and had Him scourged (19:1); scourged an innocent man! He was fastened to a post, and His bare back was beaten unmercifully with a whip. The end of each thong had on it a small piece of metal or bone, so that the lashes, perhaps thirty-nine, dug out pieces of flesh. A king needed a crown (v. 2). So the soldiers made one with branches from a thorn bush. As it was placed on His head the thorns dug into His flesh, adding to the pain of His lacerated body. A king must have a royal robe. Since no royal purple was available, they probably bedecked Jesus with a scarlet cloak belonging to one of the soldiers. And a king must receive obeisance (v. 3). So the soldiers mockingly said, "Hail [Greek, *chaire*; Latin, *ave*] King of the Jews!" They cried, *Ave!* as they would to Caesar (Bernard). *But* they also *slapped* Him with their hands!

Pilate then went out to the crowd, saying, "Behold, I am bringing him out to you, that ye may know [by seeing] that I find no crime whatever in him" (v. 4). This was Pilate's second avowal of Jesus' innocence. With this, Jesus came forth in His pitiable condition, wearing the thorn-crown and the scarlet cloak. Then in derision Pilate cried, "Behold the man!" (v. 5). *Ecce homo!* Look on this poor, pitiable man that your rulers accuse of claiming to be a King! Even if their charge were true, this sight should prove that Jesus was no threat to Rome. Mingled scorn and pity were in Pilate's words.

But there was no pity in the hearts of the chief priests. For they thundered back, "Crucify, crucify" (v. 6). With this the whole scene degenerated into a shouting debacle. For Pilate cried back, "Take ye him, and crucify: for I find no crime in him." His third avowal of Jesus' innocence. Yet the representative of proud Roman justice told them to crucify Him. It would have been mob law, a lynching, since they could not do this legally. The vaunted Roman justice never appears in a worse light.

Seeing that they could not achieve their nefarious goal by falsely accusing Jesus of a political crime, the Jews changed their charge to a religious one. And that right in the middle of the trial! By their own Jewish law Jesus should die, "because he made himself the Son of God" (v. 7). At least they were now stating a semblance of truth. Jesus had made such a claim, even though they had rejected it. In effect, they wanted Jesus put to death for what they called the sin of blasphemy.

Pilate should have thrown the case out of court at this point. After all, claiming to be the Son of God was no crime against Rome. But being of superstitious nature, as were most Romans, the words "Son of God" frightened him more than ever (v. 8). Added to his moral cowardice was his spiritual dread.

Upset by his wife's dream, he was even more unnerved by Jesus' claim to deity. He had no concept of the Jewish Messiah, but he was familiar with the ascription of deity to the Roman emperors.

Thus unnerved Pilate again went into the palace. There he asked Jesus, "Whence art thou?" (v. 9). He already knew that Jesus was from Galilee, so the question involved more than geography. Impressed by Jesus' kingly bearing throughout the trial and His claim to deity, evidently he wanted to know of Jesus' origin. "But Jesus gave him no answer."

This refusal has caused much speculation. For instance, one suggests that His silence was caused by exhaustion. His ordeal was taking its toll. True, He is recorded as speaking only one time after His scourging (v. 11). But this one statement does not sound like an exhausted person. Actually this silence was not a new thing. From the beginning of His trial Jesus had spoken little. He gave no replies to insincere or *loaded* questions. All along Pilate had shown that his only object was to get out of his predicament. When he asked this question as to Jesus' origin, Jesus refused to reply. After all, why should He? Pilate would not have believed Him had He spoken of such things as His pre-existence and virgin birth.

But there is even more to Jesus' deliberate silences. He spoke only when necessary. Even though the chief priests, Antipas, and Pilate thought that Jesus was on trial before them, in truth they were on trial before Him. Not they, but Jesus was in charge, directing the progress of the trial. He would die. But He would do so as the Divine King. And His periodic answers were designed to establish that truth, whether His adversaries believed it or not.

Pilate was exasperated. Why would not Jesus talk? "To me you do not speak?" (v. 10). "To me" is in the emphatic position. "To me you are not speaking? Do you not really know [*oidas*] that I have authority [*exousia*] to release you, and I have authority to crucify you?" (v. 10). He was Roman authority in Jerusalem that day, with the power of life or death over Jesus. And yet He ignored him.

In part Pilate received his answer as to Jesus' origin. For He said, "You would have no authority whatever against me, except it were given to you from above" (v. 11). Strangely some see this to mean authority from the Sanhedrin. That was the last thing in Jesus' mind, or Pilate's. Pilate might think of the propraetor of Syria, or of the Roman emperor; but not Jesus. His thought in "from above" (*anōthen,* cf. 3:3) only can mean "from God." Paul says, "Let every soul be subject unto the higher authorities [*exousiais huperechousais,* the supreme authorities]. For there is no authority except from God: the existing authorities are ordained by God" (Rom. 13:1). In other words, the institution of government is ordained of God. This does not mean that God approves of any one government or its acts; but that He has ordained *government* as such. And Pilate was the appointed official of a constituted government. In this sense he had his authority "from above," or "from God."

"Therefore he that delivered [handed over for execution] me unto thee hath the greater sin" (v. 11). Does this mean that Caiaphas is simply a greater sinner than Pilate? Or is there an even deeper meaning? The answer is found in the words *dia touto* rendered here as "therefore." They mean, "because of this." Because of this what? Because of this authority which Pilate has from God.

But how does Caiaphas fit into this picture? As the high priest he also had a spiritual *authority* from God. Like kings, he might abuse it. But he still was representative of constituted religious authority. Had Caiaphas merely killed Jesus he would only have been a murderer or an irresponsible executioner. But as the high priest he was using his spiritual authority from God to cause the governmental authority from God to put the Son of God to death. He was manipulating these God-given authorities to achieve his own selfish and base goal. Thus his was a greater sin than had he acted merely as an individual person.

This solemn word from Jesus should be a warning to every conniving ecclesiastic or politician who seeks to use his authority to manipulate the authority of the other for nefarious ends. And history has produced many of both.

From this moment on Pilate "kept on seeking" (imperfect) to release Jesus (v. 12). But as he did so he was met by the fury of the Jews. They cried out in fury, "If thou release this one you are not Caesar's friend: anyone making himself a king is speaking against Caesar" (v. 12). This did it! Despite the fact that Pilate knew that Jesus had no political pretensions, he could not stand up against this implied threat to report him to Caesar. If they proved to Caesar that Pilate had released a pretender to a throne it would mean his own death. Also Philo tells of Pilate's fear of any appeal to Tiberius by the Jews lest they tell of his "acceptance of bribes, plunderings, outrages, and wanton insults, continual and most grievous cruelty." Pilate's chickens had come home to roost. And in the greatest crisis of his life he was putty in the hands of those whom he despised.

12–16.

Hearing this threat he capitulated (v. 13). Bringing Jesus forth from the palace he sat down on the "judgment seat" *(bēmatos).* The *Bēma* was a raised platform (cf. Acts 18:12) on which a judge sat to pronounce sentence. Bernard suggests that this was an improvised *Bēma,* since it was outside the palace. At any rate, despite his disgraceful behavior Pilate meant to perform this function in all Roman dignity. The *Bēma* was placed on a mosaic pavement where the governor could be seen. And he mounted it. But before he pronounced sentence he said, "Behold your King" (v. 14)! This was a final jibe at the hated Jews. But they immediately cried out, "Away with him, away with him, crucify him" (v. 15). Almost as if he were begging, Pilate asked, "Your king shall I crucify?" Note the emphatic position of "your king." And the chief priests answered, "We have no king, but Caesar." Note that the chief priests, Sadducees, not the Pharisees, said this. In so doing they denied not only any Messianic hope, but also the basic idea of the Jewish nation as a theocracy, to them (the nation) Jehovah was King (cf. I Sam. 12:12). *So the Sadducees rejected Jehovah Himself!* And that in favor of a pagan emperor! Truly sin had driven them mad.

With this, Pilate gave up. He handed Jesus over to the soldiers who were to crucify Him. "And they took Jesus, and led him away" (v. 16). How sad! How tragically sad! Not for Jesus. He was laying down His life of Himself. But for those who that day had committed the crime of the ages.

As Pilate took his seat on the *Bēma,* John makes another note of time. "And it was . . . preparation of the passover, and about the sixth hour" (v. 14). Both of these time elements are important. For here John tells us both the day of the week and the hour of the day when Jesus was sentenced to die.

Some see "preparation of the passover" to mean the day before the Passover, or Wednesday. If so this would mean that He was buried late that day, and was in the tomb three whole days. However, when later we examine this idea (20:1), it will be seen that the length of Jesus' stay in the tomb permits another interpretation. As to the day Bernard notes that if John had meant Wednesday he would have used the definite article before "preparation." But the Greek text has no article. John does not say "the preparation of the passover," or the day before, when preparation for the feast was made. He says "preparation of the passover." It was the day of the week when *preparation* regularly was made for the Sabbath. So "preparation" *(paraskeuē)* had come to be a technical name for Friday (cf. Luke 23:54). In fact this very word is used in modern Greek for Friday. John clearly says that Jesus was crucified on Friday of Passover week.

But what about the hour of the day? We have already noted the question as to whether or not John uses Jewish or Roman time (cf. 1:39). It was shown that in other instances he probably used Jewish time, which in any case would also correspond to the popular reckoning of Roman time. However, in this instance under consideration a problem is encountered between John's time, if it be Jewish, and Mark's time for the beginning of the crucifixion, for he says that it was the "third hour," clearly Jewish time, or 9:00 A.M. So if we insist upon John using Jewish time here his hour for the sentencing of Jesus would be about noon. Quite obviously then there would be a conflict.

However, we recall that *official* Roman time was figured from midnight. So if John here were following that time pattern, he says that Jesus was sentenced at about 6:00 A.M. Which would coincide with Mark. At the same time we run into problems in John's other references to time, especially at Jacob's well. In view of the Jewish nature of his Gospel, however, it seems wise to say that in these other references he was following Jewish time, which incidentally would also coincide with the popular Roman time method. (Recall that on the Roman sun dial noon was marked by VI.)

However, the problem as to 19:14 is resolved if we see this reference as *official* Roman time. This was the time used in official matters such as this court. Therefore, we conclude that, whereas in other cases John followed Jewish time, in this case he gave the official time as recorded in the court record. Jesus, therefore, was sentenced to die at about 6:00 A.M. on Friday morning. We are indebted to John, an eyewitness, for this very careful detail. He considered it of great importance to note the official time of the most infamous court decision in the history of jurisprudence.

The Blackest Day in History

Language cannot express, neither can the mind of man fully comprehend the meaning of the crucifixion of Jesus Christ. History may record that He was crucified under Pontius Pilate, but it does not say why. Yet it is only in the light of the death and resurrection of Jesus that history can find its true meaning. For these events were at the heart of God's redemptive purpose, the achievement of which is the goal of history.

Those who were involved in this historic event were ignorant of the role that they played. Yet history itself judges them either for good or bad according to the part which they played. But most of all they are judged by Him who was the recipient of either their rejection or their love.

The Place of a Skull (19:17-18)

In keeping with custom Jesus was required to bear His cross, at least the horizontal part, to the place of crucifixion (v. 17). The Synoptic Gospels tell how Simon of Cyrene was forced to bear Jesus' cross. The ordeal through which He had been had taken its toll. His strength was not equal to the task.

Finally, the grim procession arrived at the place of crucifixion. It was a place outside the northern city wall called "a place of a skull" (*kraniou topon*). The Aramaic name was "Golgotha." It is also called "Calvary," the Latin equivalent of *kranion*. Why it bore this name is uncertain. One tradition says that it was the place of execution, and got its name from the skulls of criminals left there after their execution. This is unlikely for two reasons. In the first place, dead bodies were not left there to decay. In the second place, if this were true it would be called "the place of skulls (*kraniōn*) rather than "the place of a skull" (*kraniou*). A more likely tradition is that it got its name from its appearance. It was a hill whose shape resembled a human skull.

Neither can we be certain as to its exact location. This is partly due to the fact that archaeologists are not sure where the north wall of the city was located in the time of Jesus. Tradition says that the Church of the Holy Sepulchre is built over the site. However, it is debatable as to whether or not this site was outside the wall. Some years ago General Charles Gordon discovered a site which was definitely outside the wall. It is called "Gordon's Calvary. Even today it is a hill with two caves which give the appearance of eye sockets. It does have the shape of a skull.

But wherever it was located there Jesus was crucified (v. 18), and with Him two thieves or robbers, one on either side. Truly Jesus was put on the list of those to be executed along with the transgressors (cf. Luke 22:37). It is possible that they were companions in crime of Barabbas. And but for the choice of the mob he probably would have been nailed to the center cross. In a very real sense, therefore, Jesus died as a substitute for him. We can only hope that he realized the full impact of this and believed in Him unto salvation.

Crucifixion was perhaps the most painful method of execution ever devised. It probably originated among the Phoenicians, but it became of widespread use. Roman law forbade it to be used for a Roman citizen.

From knowledge as to the method of crucifixion we may imagine what was done to Jesus. He was stripped naked and caused to lie flat on His back on the ground. To render Him helpless His arms and legs were jerked out of joint. His arms were then stretched out along the cross piece which had been placed on the ground. After His hands had been nailed to this piece it was then fastened to the upright piece which previously had been placed in a hole in the ground. It is possible that His feet were placed on a small shelf about two feet above the ground. Or He may have been suspended by the nails (cf. Ps. 22:17). In either case His feet were crossed and then nailed to the wood. There Jesus was left to hang for hours. Sometimes it took days for the victim to die. In Jesus' case He was on the cross for six hours, 9:00 A.M. until 3:00 P.M., before death released Him.

Hanging there He was so stretched out as to enable one to count His rib bones (Ps. 22:17). Every point in His body was in agony. His nerves throbbed in pain. The sunbeams like hungry leeches sucked the fluid from every pore in His skin. Thirst became unbearable. Fever mounted, His lips were parched and cracked, His tongue became dry and swollen, and His vocal cords became so inflamed that the voice became raspy. The flow of blood was hindered, causing excruciating agony. Gradually the body stiffened and the strength ebbed. And in Jesus' case, mental and spiritual suffering was almost beyond endurance. No mortal can fully understand His suffering. But a reading of Psalm 22 and Isaiah 53 helps to see that which the Saviour suffered for our sin.

The "Crime" of Jesus (19:19-22)

Roman law required that above the head of one crucified there should be placed a "title" (Greek, *titlos;* Latin, *titilus*), or board on which was written the crime of which the victim was guilty (v. 19). It was designed as a warning to others. In Jesus' case, the title read, JESUS OF NAZARETH THE KING OF THE JEWS.

John notes that it was written in Hebrew (Aramaic), Greek, and Latin (v. 20). There was a practical reason for making it trilingual. *Hebrew* was the language of the Jews. *Greek* was for the benefit of those who could not read any other language. It was a near-universal language in the first century. *Latin* was the official language of the Empire.

However, since the other Gospels make no mention of the three languages, one wonders if John did not have a deeper purpose than simply to supplement their accounts. In his mystical nature may be found his deeper meaning. Three great streams of ancient life were represented by those languages: Hebrew, Greek, and Latin. Hebrew was the language of religion. Greek was the language of culture. Latin was the language of government. And these three streams flowed together at Calvary. Institutional religion rejected Jesus. Institutional culture ignored Him. And institutional government crucified Him. Thus it is that no one group can be accused of His death. The whole of life brought Him to the cross. And each of us shares in the guilt. Yes, we were there when they crucified our Lord!

This title was an affront to the chief priests (v. 21). So they rushed off to Herod's palace to protest to Pilate. They "kept on saying" (imperfect) to him, "Write not, The King of the Jews; but that he said, I am King of the Jews." After all, the mob about the cross was unpredictable. The chief priests had used them to accomplish their purpose. But seeing this title the mob just as easily could turn on them.

But Pilate finally became adamant before these wily rulers. They had used him long enough. Some see the wording of the title as Pilate's mockery of the Jews. Perhaps so. But, after all, this was the primary charge which they had made against Jesus. According to Roman law on no other basis could Pilate have based his decision. And even though he had not believed their charge, still to preserve his dignity in following due legal processes he had written this charge as the legal "crime" of Jesus.

So he curtly said (aorist), "What I have written I have written" (v. 22). This is most picturesque in Greek. *Ho gegrapha, gegrapha.* Despite the rulers' much insistence, Pilate's curt reply, plus the dual perfect tenses, had the ring of finality in it. And he was in his right in refusing to alter it. He wrote it as a legal decision. And it could not be changed.

The Gambling of the Soldiers (19:23-24)

In the meantime back at Calvary a familiar scene was taking place. The detail of soldiers was gambling at the foot of Jesus' cross (v. 23). According to Roman law they were permitted to divide among themselves the clothes of the victim. Four soldiers comprised a crucifixion detail, in addition to an officer, a centurion. Jesus' clothes consisted of headgear, sandals, girdle, and a *tallith* or outer garment, and a *chitōn* or inner garment. So the four soldiers each took one of the first four. However, John notes that the *chitōn* was woven throughout with no seam. Rather than to tear it into four pieces, they decided to gamble for it (v. 24).

They neither knew nor cared that they were fulfilling Scripture. For Psalm 22:18 said, "They parted my raiment among them, and for my vesture did they cast lots." As revolting as this scene may seem to us, we must not judge the soldiers unduly. After all, they were pagan soldiers assigned to a duty, and were only doing what the law permitted. A far more grievous sin is for lost men to gamble before the cross — and for infinitely greater stakes — their immortal souls.

The Island of Love (19:25-27)

Jesus died in an ocean of hate. But in that raging ocean there was a tiny island of love. Matthew 27:55-56 and Mark 15:40 mention a little band of women who watched the crucifixion from a distance. They make no mention of Jesus' mother. Matthew lists them as Mary Magdalene, and Mary the mother of James and Joses, and the mother of the sons of Zebedee, James and John. Mark lists Mary Magdalene, Mary the mother of James the less and of Joses, and Salome. Some would see Matthew's Mary the mother of James and Joses as Jesus' mother. But it is hardly likely that he would indicate her so obscurely. Mark clearly shows that this Mary's sons were James the less and Joses or Joseph. Apparently the Salome of Mark is the same person whom Matthew calls the mother of the sons of Zebedee.

But John mentions a small group of women who stood by the cross of Jesus (v. 25). They were Mary, Jesus' mother, "and his mother's sister, Mary the wife of Cleophas, and Mary Magdalene." As this reads it appears that, in addition to John, there were only three women at the cross. But when we compare this with the Synoptic accounts, it appears that there were four women at the cross. As punctuated, Mary the wife of Cleophas seems to be the sister of Jesus' mother. But apparently from the Synoptic records she is the mother of James and Joses. It is unlikely that two sisters would bear the same given name. Both Matthew and Mark mention three women. We have noted that the Salome of Mark could be the mother of the sons of Zebedee in Matthew. Neither of these mentions the mother of Jesus. And yet, according to John she is present at the cross with at least two of the women who stood afar off, a Mary (the wife of Cleophas) and Mary Magdalene. It would appear that Mary the wife of Cleophas is the mother of James and Joses. But where was the mother of Zebedee's children as the women came to the cross? It would appear, therefore, that John 19:25 should read "his mother, and his mother's sister, [and] Mary the wife of Cleophas, and Mary Magdalene." Bernard notes that the *Peshitta* version does place an "and" before "Mary the wife of Cleophas." This is probably a correct reading, since it balances the uses of "and" in the sentence.

If this be a true reasoning it accounts for the three women of the Synoptics. It also means that in addition to the mother of Jesus there were three other women at the cross. Furthermore, this means that Mary's sister is Salome the mother of the sons of Zebedee. And it also means that her sons, James and John, were first cousins of Jesus. In keeping with John's purpose to remain anonymous in his Gospel, this suggests his subtle way of combining his account with the Synoptics to show his relationship to Jesus. And it would also explain why he was the disciple whom Jesus loved and who leaned on His bosom. It also sheds light on the request of these brothers and of their mother that they be given places of preference in Jesus' kingdom (cf. Matt. 20:20 f.; Mark 10:35 ff.).

Looking down from His cross Jesus saw this little island of love. One can imagine the comfort which it gave to Him. Therefore, in that tender atmosphere He bequeathed a blessing upon both His mother and His beloved disciple. He looked at Mary. And evidently His eyes moved from her to John as He said, "Woman [gunē], behold thy son" (v. 26)! Then as His eyes moved back to His mother, He said, "Behold thy mother" (v. 27)!

In so doing Jesus in His dying hours thought of the two people who probably were nearer and dearer to Him than any others. And He gave to each a source of comfort. To John He showed His absolute trust and gave to him a mission of love. These two things would be a source of comfort to that disciple to the end of his days. And to His mother He gave a sense of security. Since her children did not yet believe in Jesus, that very fact may have brought about a strained relationship with their mother. Certainly they could not be relied upon for sympathetic understanding in the days ahead. But John, who both loved and understood Jesus, perhaps more than any other man, could supply her need. So Jesus bade His mother from henceforth to look to His beloved disciple, His cousin and her nephew, who will take His place insofar as such would be possible. Bernard notes that these were not mere suggestions from Jesus. They were commands to them from Him who was their Master and Lord.

But a further thought should be noted in Jesus' command to His mother. As in Cana so here He called her "Woman" (gunē). With love and respect He reminded her again of the separation between them. He is not to be regarded merely as her "son." He is her Saviour and Lord dying for her sin as for the sin of John, yea, for the sin of the world. This was the final lesson in the course which began in Cana. Gently but firmly and finally He used the "sword" to sever all earthly relationships. He is the divine Lord, soon to be exalted at the right hand of God. But Mary and John are to continue living on earth. And in this new relationship to each other and to Jesus they shall find peace.

"And from that hour that disciple took her unto his own home" (v. 27). He took her as his own and to his own things, or home. One tradition says that John had a home in Jerusalem, and that Mary lived with him there until her death some years later. Another says that Mary finally went with John to Ephesus where she died at a ripe old age. There is no real evidence to support either tradition. Also whether or not John had a home in Jerusalem is only surmise. One wonders, however, that if he did, why it was not used as the Jerusalem meeting place for the early Christians. It seems that they used another home for this purpose (cf. Acts 12:12).

"From that hour" need not mean that within the hour he took her to his dwelling place. In that event John could have used *oikos,* house. Instead he said that he took, or received her *eis ta idia,* unto his own. This could mean that he assumed the responsibility placed upon him by Jesus. Of course, this would mean to take her into his home and into his life. But whatever this means it is clear that he proved worthy of the trust that Jesus had placed in him.

The Agony of Thirst (19:28-29)

At this point once again John used the phrase "after this" *(meta touto).* He does not mean to imply that the event of verse 28 followed immediately that of verse 27. Or else the *fulfilment* in verse 28 would have little meaning. There is no Scripture which prophesied that Jesus would intrust the care of His mother to His disciple. By this phrase once again John noted that he was inserting additional information not found in the Synoptics.

All three Synoptic Gospels record that there was a strange darkness for three hours from the sixth hour (noon) until the ninth hour (3:00 P.M.) (Matt. 27:40; Mark 15:33; Luke 23:44). It was at the ninth hour that Jesus gave His cry of dereliction (Matt. 27:46; Mark 15:34). In this cry we see the Holy Place of Jesus' suffering for sin. And immediately thereafter both Matthew and Mark note that someone gave Jesus a drink of vinegar, or sour wine. Since this was the drink provided for soldiers on such a detail as this, we may assume that a soldier did this But neither of these Gospels tells why he did it. It is to John that we must look for this detail of information.

He says, "Jesus knowing that all things were now accomplished, that the scripture might be fulfilled, saith, I thirst" (v. 28). So the soldier acted in response to this statement of Jesus.

The words "accomplished" and "fulfilled" call for attention. They translate two kindred words *teleō* and *teleioō* respectively. Even to one unskilled in the Greek language it is clear that they belong to the same general family of verbs. *Teleō* expresses the final act of doing something (cf. v. 30). *Teleioō* speaks of the process of doing so. Throughout the trial and crucifixion various Old Testament prophecies had been fulfilled. The latest one in this series was the cry of dereliction (cf. Ps. 22:1). Only one remained unfulfilled before Jesus' actual death, and that with reference to His thirst (cf. Ps. 22:14-15). Jesus' cry of thirst was the final act (teleō) of fulfilling (teleioō) the Scripture with reference to His suffering on the cross. (Note that verses 36-37 came after His death.) *

Knowing this, Jesus said, "I thirst." This was not a mechanical act merely to fulfil Scripture. It was spoken out of His experience of suffering. He did this no more mechanically than did the soldiers as they gambled at the foot of the cross. And yet both acts were fulfilments of Scripture.

We have noted that thirst was one of the greatest of agonies endured on the cross. It was most evident in one's mouth, making it difficult for one to speak. Just before Jesus was nailed to the cross He had refused drugged wine offered for the purpose of dulling the pain of crucifixion (Matt. 27:34; Mark 15:23). He proposed to endure that suffering in the full awareness of all His faculties. But now at the close He asked for a drink of this sour but undrugged wine. He did so with a purpose. He was now ready to give His cry of victory. And it must be as clear as a trumpet, not in a raspy note.

In response to Jesus' word of thirst a soldier dipped a sponge in the sour wine, fastened it to a reed of the hyssop bush about three or four feet long (this suggests how high off the ground Jesus was suspended), and pressed it to Jesus' mouth (v. 29). Obviously He did not receive a great deal of the beverage. But it was enough for the purpose.

The Cry of Victory (19:30a)

Having received the wine Jesus said, "It is finished." The Synoptic Gospels say that Jesus uttered this in a loud voice (Matt. 27:50; Mark 15:37; Luke 23:46). But none of them tells what Jesus said.

John records that Jesus said, "It is finished." Like "I thirst" (dipsō) it is only one word (tetelestai). But it is one of the greatest words ever uttered. It is the perfect tense of teleō. This is the tense of completion. "It stands finished." And it will remain so forever.

Now what did Jesus mean by this word? That the suffering was over? That certainly was true. That the last Old Testament Scrip-

* See my *The Crucial Words from Calvary*, Baker, Grand Rapids, 1958, 61 ff.

ture prior to His death was now fulfilled? This was also true. That the redemptive work of Jesus was finished? Most certainly this was true. He had made the "once-for-all sacrifice" (*ephapax;* Heb. 7:27; 9:12; 10:10). There will never be another. But is this all of the picture contained in this word?*

In interpreting the New Testament we often say that we must go back to the *original Greek*. But what do we mean by this? To go back to the Greek text? Yes. Or to examine the various Greek lexicons? Yes. But even there we often find that the Greek words have picked up the theological debris of the centuries. Where are we most likely to find the most original Greek? We suggest that it is to be found in the Greek papyri.

Now the Greek of the New Testament is not classical Greek, the language of the Greek scholars. It is *koinē* Greek, or the language of the common people. It is the form of Greek spoken by the housewife, the man on the street, the business man, or a soldier away from home at war. Fortunately a wealth of light has been thrown upon the New Testament by archaeological discoveries of the *papyri,* the plural of the Greek word *papyrus* whence comes the English word "paper." Among the papyri have been found letters, receipted bills, legal documents, and many other items of everyday living. And in this wealth of material have been found all but about fifty of the Greek words used in the New Testament. Thus from this source we learn what these words meant to the ordinary people of the first century and in their daily concourse of life.

Words are but pictures of ideas. To one versed in a given language one word may contain many pictures. And hearing that word one simultaneously will see many pictures flash through his mind. If we are to get back to the *original Greek* we must learn what those words said to the person who first read or heard them in the Christian context. And applying this test to the word *tetelestai,* what does it say in the *original Greek?* There were many pictures contained in this word. But let us examine only three of them. Two of these examples reveal that it was used in commercial life.

For instance, an example has been discovered of a promissory note. "I will pay you this sum." In connection with this, note that the very word *tetelestai* is used in the sense of introducing a receipt. In such usage it would mean "it has been paid, the payment is still in force, and it will never again be demanded."

Ibid, pp. 75 ff.

In eternity the Son gave to the Father a promissory note that He would pay the price for man's redemption (cf. Heb. 10:5-7). And on the cross just before He died He said, *Tetelestai.* "I have paid it in full. The promissory note stands paid, and it will remain so forever."

Furthermore, the verb *teleioō* was used in the papyri in the sense of executing a deed by inserting the date and signature. Until this was done the deed was not in effect.

Now Jesus said, "I have finished the work which thou gavest me to do" (John 17:4; cf. John 4:34). Here the verb *teleioō* is used. This expresses the idea of accomplishing the act of completing the deed. But the final act of doing so would be expressed by *teleō.* So in eternity the Son made out a deed to salvation for all who should believe in Him. But until the deed was dated and signed it was not in effect. On Calvary, therefore, He dated and signed the deed. It was dated 15th of Nisan A.D. 30. And it was signed in His own precious blood. When He did this He cried, *Tetelestai.* "It is dated and signed. It is in effect and will continue to be so" (cf. Heb. 9:15-17).

The third example of *teleō* cited in the papyri is that of a father sending his son on a mission. As the son departs the father says, "Until you accomplish this for me." Here this verb is used. It means that the son is not to return until he has performed the final act of the mission. We may assume that upon his return from a successful mission, he said to his father, *Tetelestai.* "It is fully accomplished."

In like fashion the heavenly Father sent His Son into the world on a mission of redemption. Now as He is preparing to re-enter the Father's house He says, *Tetelestai.* "The final act of the mission has been performed. It is finished, and will remain so forever."*

The Death of Jesus (19:30b)

When Jesus had given this report to the Father "he bowed his head, and gave up the ghost," or "he handed over his spirit" to the Father (cf. Luke 23:46). Mark and Luke say that He "expired," or breathed out His spirit. But Matthew says, "He dismissed his spirit," or He "permitted" His spirit to depart.

Though the Gospels used different words to express the fact of

---

* See my *Preaching Values from the Papyri,* pp. 118 ff.

Jesus' death they are agreed as to the manner in which He died. They all express the idea of voluntariness. He *breathed out* His spirit (Mark and Luke) rather than to try to hold on to a last gasp of life. He *dismissed* His spirit. As the King He said to His spirit, "You may go now." But John says that He *handed over* His spirit. Bernard notes that this word *paradidōmi* means to give up voluntarily. John here used the same verb form that he used in 19:16 for Pilate turning Jesus over to the soldiers for crucifixion. So as he handed Jesus over to His death, now in death Jesus handed over His spirit unto the Father in life. No man took His life from Him. He laid it down of Himself (cf. John 10:18). Thus He did not die as a criminal or as a helpless martyr. He died voluntarily, and was in command of the situation unto the very end. He died as the Saviour!

The Cause of Jesus' Death (19:31-37)

The day that Jesus died was the *Preparation,* or Friday (v. 31; cf. 19:14). It was the day before the Sabbath. It was "an high day," or "a great [*megale*] day." This means that it was the Sabbath day during the Passover. Bernard notes that it was a Sabbath which syncronized with "the first day of unleavened bread" which was a "high," or "great" day (cf. Exod. 12:16). In that sense this Preparation, or Friday had a double significance.

For this reason the Jewish rulers requested that Pilate hasten the death of Jesus and the two thieves by breaking their legs. According to Jewish law a criminal's body should be buried before sunset (Deut. 21:23; Josh. 8:29). Josephus says that the Jews were careful to bury before sunset the bodies of those who had been crucified. This would be true especially on the day before the Sabbath, and even more so since this Sabbath was a "great day."

Ordinarily the Romans left bodies on the crosses as an example to the people. However, no Roman law forbade the removing of them. So Pilate was free to decide the issue. He had had enough trouble with the Jews for one day. Therefore, he granted the wish of the rulers.

Thus soldiers were sent to break the legs of the three victims (v. 32). This they did to the two thieves. But when they came to Jesus this was unnecessary, since they saw that He was already dead (v. 33). Pilate was surprised that He had died so quickly (cf. Mark 15:44). But as Bernard says, "A highly strung nature is less able to endure physical agony than one of coarser fibre; and Jesus was the Perfect Man."

However, John seems to go a step farther. He notes that a soldier, thinking to make sure that Jesus was dead, ran a spear into His side. "And forthwith came there out blood and water" (v. 34). In his work *Physical Cause of the Death of Christ* Dr. Stroud concludes that this indicates that Jesus' death was caused by a rupture of the heart. This view has been challenged by some who point out that blood would not flow from a dead body. But the Greek text simply says that blood and water *came out*. If they were collected there, the force of gravity would have been sufficient to cause this. John may have pointed this out to refute the Docetic Gnostics by showing that Jesus did have a real flesh and blood body. However the mixture of blood and water was significant to John who evidently saw this happen.

Of one thing we may be certain. Jesus did die quickly. And since crucifixion usually was a lingering death, it is evident that Jesus' death was out of the ordinary. Regardless of differing opinions about the "blood and water," we may assume that Jesus did die of a broken heart. It was the heart that was broken for you and me.

John gives his eye witness testimony that the phenomenon was true (v. 35). And he adds that it was a twofold fulfilment of Scripture (vv. 36-37; cf. Exod. 12:46; Zech. 12:10). From beginning to end Jesus' death was as the Old Testament Scriptures had said that it would be. He died in the manner and for the purpose that God said that He would. The manner is a matter of secular history. The manner and purpose also are the teachings of *holy history,* God's *history within history.* And His death is made personal for all who believe in Him. For such it is truly salvation history.

The Burial of Jesus (19:38-42)

Had the body of Jesus not been claimed it would have been thrown into the vale of Hinnom, the garbage dump of Jerusalem. This was the place called *Gehenna,* which Jesus used repeatedly as a symbol of hell as a place of punishment. But such was not to be the fate of the body of the Saviour.

John had added material not found in the Synoptics (19:31-37). Then with his usual method (*meta tauta,* "after these things") he joins with their report of Jesus' burial in order to relate it and also to add at least certain details, including the part which Nicodemus played in it.

Joseph of Arimathea and Nicodemus joined in providing a decent burial for Jesus. None of the Gospels have mentioned Joseph up to this point. He is called a "disciple of Jesus, but secretly for fear of the Jews" (v. 38). He probably was one included in the reference in John 12:41-43. The other Gospels refer to him as "an honorable counsellor" (or member of the Sanhedrin) (Mark 15:43), "a rich man" (Matt. 27:57), and "a good man, and a just" (Luke 23:50). Luke adds that he had not consented to the death of Jesus (v. 51). Since that decision was unanimous, it is evident that Joseph and, no doubt, Nicodemus were not present when the Sanhedrin condemned Jesus to death. Since their attitude toward Him was known, evidently they were not called to the meeting, or else, being called, they did not attend.

Though his fear of the Jews had kept Joseph from openly avowing his faith in Jesus, he boldly came forth in His behalf after He was dead. This latter act is commendable for three reasons. It was performed at a time when it could have meant great personal danger to him. It involved being discredited before his fellow-rulers. And it was performed in the context of the death of Him in whom he had believed. Judging by the attitude of the other disciples, he must have thought that this was the end of Jesus and His work. Yet out of love he was determined that Jesus should have a proper burial. If this was the end, like Mary of Bethany he at least could demonstrate his love for Jesus, despite the cost to himself.

And he was not alone. For Nicodemus, another member of the Sanhedrin, joined him in this service of love (v. 39). For over three years Nicodemus had carried the profound impression of that night visit in his heart. At one time he had dared to speak out in the Sanhedrin on Jesus' behalf (7:50-51). True, he had only raised a point of law. But it was a gesture nevertheless. We may well imagine that he also was one of those to whom John made reference in 12:41-43. But now, like Joseph, despite the cost he came forth boldly to give a final token of his faith and love.

These two friends of Jesus prepared his body for burial in keeping with Jewish custom (v. 40). Nicodemus brought about "an hundred pound weight" of spices (a little less than our one hundred pounds), a mixture of myrrh and aloes. Evidently Nicodemus was a man of wealth to bring so costly an amount. Bernard notes that John does not state that he bought these spices for this particular purpose, concluding that he may have had them in his home. If this be true, it is most suggestive. Did he have them prepared for his own burial? So great a sum would indicate that he did have them for some purpose. As a man who could afford it, he may have intended that his own body should be thoroughly *spiced* for burial. Such would have been a burial of great honor (cf. II Chron. 16:14). And if this be a proper surmise, he, like Mary, gave to Jesus something that he had treasured for himself.

Myrrh, a sweet-smelling gum, was mixed with the powdered aromatic wood of aloes. Some of this probably was placed next to the body as well as being scattered within the folds of linen cloth with which the body was wrapped. Then the body was placed in the tomb.

This tomb was located in a garden near the place of crucifixion (v. 41). Only John mentions the garden. But all four Evangelists call the tomb a new one. Matthew says that it was the new tomb of Joseph of Arimathea (27:60). Luke joins with John in noting that it had not previously been used for burial (v. 41; Luke 23:53). It was a tomb hewn out of rock something like an artificial cave (cf. Matt. 27:60; Mark 15:46; Luke 23:53). John omits this detail, probably because it was recorded in the Synoptics.

Pursuing a previous thought, it is worthy of note that Joseph had prepared this tomb for himself. Which suggests again something of great importance and value to him. Yet, like Mary and Nicodemus, he gave it to Jesus. Mary of Bethany, Nicodemus, and Joseph of Arimathea stand united in hands and hearts. They did what they could to demonstrate their love for Jesus in His hour of death. And as with Mary so with these two men. What they did has become a memorial to them wherever the gospel has been proclaimed.

Where was this garden tomb located? We do not know. In view of John's word as to the proximity of the two — Calvary and the tomb — their location stands or falls together. One tradition places the tomb within the Church of the Holy Sepulchre. The same problem as to the location of the city wall at that time applies to both Calvary and the tomb. Likewise, there is a tomb located hard by Gordon's Calvary. It is hewn out of stone, and was closed by a stone being rolled across the entrance (cf. Matt. 27:60; Mark 15:46). The groove for such a stone may still be seen there.

In comparing these two possible tombs certain things are worthy of note. Since Joseph was a member of the Sanhedrin, he was a married man and may have had children. It is reasonable to assume that in preparing a tomb he would have provided for

his family also. The tomb in the Church of the Holy Sepulchre
has a place for only one body. But Gordon's Tomb has two
sections divided by a wall. On either side there are places for
two bodies, or four in all. Furthermore, on one side of this
tomb the unfinished stone suggests that it was incomplete. This
would suggest a new tomb that was used before it had been
finished. For some reason it was used prematurely. Could it
be because it was used for an unexpected burial and thus was
never finished? Such a thought would fit into the Gospel account
of Jesus' burial. Just outside this tomb recent excavations have
uncovered a small chapel of the Byzantine period. Evidently at
this time, possibly as early as the middle fourth century A.D.,
this spot was considered to be a Christian shrine. To be sure,
this does not prove that this is the location of the tomb of Jesus.
But it is of interest nevertheless. If this writer were required
to name a spot on the basis of present evidence, he would choose
Gordon's Calvary and Gordon's Tomb as the most likely places
of Jesus' death and burial.

But wherever the tomb was located, there tender, loving hands
placed the body of our Lord (v. 42). It was late on Friday
afternoon (cf. Luke 23:54). Their desire to inter the body before the beginning of the Sabbath at sunset is given by John as
the reason for using Joseph's nearby tomb. Some hold that Joseph
planned later to remove the body for permanent burial elsewhere.
There is no evidence to support such an idea. The very manner
in which the body was prepared for burial seems to indicate
otherwise. It is more in keeping that Joseph intended that his
new tomb should be the permanent resting place for the One
whom he had loved and trusted in secret, but for whom he now
declared his love for all to see.

A permanent resting place? But God had other plans!

X
The Rainbow of Assurance

The Greatest Day in History

If "Black Friday" was the blackest day in history, the Sunday following is the greatest day in history. For it affirmed that Jesus truly was the Son of God. It marked His complete triumph over Satan, sin, and death. It assured salvation to all who receive Jesus as Saviour. And it is the foundation stone upon which rests our confidence in our final resurrection from the dead at the Lord's return.

The Christian gospel rests upon three giant pillars: Jesus' virgin birth; His redeeming death; and His triumphant resurrection. Remove any one of these and the entire structure falls. It is little wonder, therefore, that the seasons of the year which commemorate these events are of the highest sacredness in every Christian's heart.

The Empty Tomb (20:1-10)

The empty tomb stands as a bulwark against all denials of the bodily resurrection of Jesus. When skeptics have exhausted their ingenuity in efforts to deny it, they still must explain the empty tomb. All four Gospels tell of Jesus' burial on Friday. They all agree that the tomb was empty on Sunday morning. And they are credible historical documents, despite the denials of doubting men.*

John tells us that on "the first day of the week" Mary Madgalene came to the sepulchre (v. 1). The Greek reads "the first day of the sabbaths" (plural, cf. v. 19). The "sabbaths" so used denoted "the week." Matthew mentions another Mary also (28:1). Mark 16:1 mentions these and also Salome. But this verse says that "when the sabbath was past," or after sunset on Saturday, they went and bought spices. They did this in preparation for a further anointing of Jesus' body. Then early on Sunday morn-

---

*See my *Exposition of Matthew*, pp. 413-418.

ing they started to the tomb. John's mention of Mary Magdalene alone may be explained in that he singled her out for a later reference (cf. vv. 11 ff.). This was a commonly used literary device. John notes that Mary Magdalene started out to the tomb before dawn. By the time she arrived it would be "at early dawn" (Luke 24:1, RV). Upon her arrival she found the stone rolled from across the entrance to the tomb. So Jesus had risen by early dawn on Sunday.

This time element has posed a problem for some. Noting Jesus' own words about being in the heart of the earth "three days and three nights" (Matt. 12:40), they insist on three twenty-four hour days for His stay in the tomb. In order to arrive at this figure, they measure time back from Jesus' resurrection to arrive at a time for His death and burial. In so doing they came to either Thursday or Wednesday. But the Gospels are explicit that Jesus died and was buried on Friday, the Preparation. However, this problem vanishes when one recognizes the Jewish, Roman, and Greek method of figuring time. Any part of a day was considered as a whole day. When Jesus spoke of the time that He would be in the tomb He used the popular way of saying three days. So He *was* in the tomb three days: Friday before sunset (one day), Saturday until sunset (two days), Sunday between sunset and sunrise (three days). Seven times Jesus said that He would rise on "the third day." So the above reckoning of time is in keeping with His words.

As soon as Mary Magdalene saw the open tomb she ran to tell the apostles (v. 2). She did not remain with the other women to see the empty tomb (cf. Matt. 28:5-8).

But when she found Simon Peter and John she said, "They have taken away the Lord out of the sepulchre, and we know not where they have laid him" (v. 2). The "they" is indefinite. But apparently she thought of a grave robbery. In "we" Mary included the other women. But she only assumed their ignorance of what had happened. By remaining at the tomb they had learned otherwise.

Upon hearing Mary Magdalene's report Peter and John "were going" (imperfect) and "came" (aorist) to the sepulchre (v. 3). These tenses vividly express their journey and arrival. They "were running" (imperfect). But since John was the younger, he arrived before Peter (v. 4). He stooped down and looked in the empty tomb (v. 5). But he saw no body, only the empty grave clothes. At once he knew that this was no grave robbery.

Else the clothes would not have been there. However, because of his retiring nature he did not enter the tomb.

About that time Peter arrived, probably out of breath (v. 6). True to his nature he brushed past John and immediately "went in" (aorist) and "sees" (present), or keeps on seeing. He took a thorough look. But what did he see? He saw the linen clothes just as John had seen at a glance from the outside (v. 7). He also saw the napkin which had been around Jesus' head. It was lying apart from the other clothes. Also it was rolled up or arranged in an orderly fashion. And it was "in a place by itself." Apparently it was lying where Jesus' head had been. There was no evidence of haste as would have been true if it had been a grave robbery. But while Peter saw all of this, it evidently made no particular impression on him.

Influenced by Peter's boldness John also entered the tomb. And "he saw, and believed" (v. 8). The word "saw" (eiden) is different from the word used for Peter's seeing (theōrei). This latter word means to see with the eye. But the former word means to see with understanding. Peter saw no more than John did as John glanced into the tomb. But when he entered and saw what Peter had seen, he saw it through the eyes of understanding. Thus he believed that this was no grave robbery but a bodily resurrection. John was the first of the Eleven to believe the resurrection, and the only one who believed before He saw Jesus alive. Indeed, he was the first person to believe it without some supernatural demonstration. The other women had seen the angels. John's believing without seeing may be reflected in 20:29. Jesus spoke these words. And John was careful to record them. He cherished the fact that he had believed without seeing Jesus outside the tomb.

Even though John believed, he was charitable toward Peter's lack of understanding. For he noted that the apostles did not really know or comprehend (ēideisan from oida) the Scripture that Jesus must rise from the dead (v. 9). Jesus had repeatedly told them. But they had heard without understanding. This is within itself one of the strongest arguments for Jesus' bodily resurrection. Psychologically the disciples could not have fabricated this story. It was contrary to all of their expectations.

Then Peter and John went away again "unto their own home," or to wherever they were staying (v. 10). Doubtless Peter went away wondering. But John went to tell the glorious news to Jesus' mother.

The Reward of Love (10:11-18)

Meanwhile Mary Magdalene remained at the tomb weeping (v. 11). She, like Peter, had not yet believed that Jesus was raised. And as "she was weeping" (imperfect) she suddenly stooped (aorist) and glanced inside the tomb. She saw two angels in white sitting, one at the head and the other at the feet, where Jesus' body "had been lying" (imperfect, v. 12). It had been lying there, but was there no longer.

In reply to their question as to why she was weeping, she said, "Because they have taken away my Lord, and I know not [do not really know, *ouk oida*] where they have laid him" (v. 13). She apparently was not frightened at the angels' presence as the other women had been (cf. Matt. 28:5). Due to her tear-blinded eyes, she evidently thought that they were only two men.

With this she turned away from the tomb (v. 14). And there before her stood Jesus! But she did not recognize Him. Was this because of a changed appearance? Apparently not. Again we may assume that it was because of her tears. Jesus asked, "Woman, why weepest thou?" (v. 15). Still Mary did not recognize Jesus' voice. Perhaps in her grief she was hardly listening. Supposing that He was the gardner, she said, "Sir, if thou have borne him hence, tell me where thou hast laid him, and I will take him away." Hoping against hope she thought that maybe the empty tomb was not a grave robbery after all. Perhaps for some reason the gardner had simply moved the body. If only he would tell her where, she would take the body away and give Her Lord a permanent burial.

Such love could not be denied. So Jesus then spoke her name. "Mary." He evidently did so with great tenderness as He had been wont to do. And Mary recognized His voice. Apparently after her words to the "gardner" she had turned away from Him. But when she heard that voice she whirled toward Him. This is seen in the aorist participle *strapheisa,* meaning "turning about suddenly." And as she whirled about she said, "Rabboni." "My Teacher!" For the benefit of his Greek readers John interpreted this word as "Master" or "Teacher" *(didaskale).*

With this Mary evidently threw herself at Jesus' feet and embraced them (v. 17). For Jesus said, "Stop clinging to me." "For I am not yet ascended to my [the] Father: but go to my brethren, and say unto them, I ascend [am ascending, present tense] to my Father, and your Father; and to my God, and your God."

The familiar rendering of the King James Version "Touch me not" causes some difficulty in interpretation. For later Jesus permitted, even invited, the disciples to touch Him. By the words which follow we can hardly suppose an *ascension* to the Father between this and later appearances.

Robertson renders Jesus' prohibition as "Cease clinging to me." And since the verb form is a present tense this seems to be a good translation. She was not to continue clinging to Him, but was to bear His message to the apostles. This is suggestive to us. We are not simply to linger about the shrine of the resurrection, but are to go declaring the fact of it. Before His ascension Jesus will give several commissions to this effect. Indeed, the substance of the angels' message immediately after the ascension is that instead of standing gazing after Jesus they are to go and proclaim the gospel, including the assurance of His promised return (Acts 1:10-11).

Jesus added to Mary that He had not yet returned to "the Father" (v. 17). And this Father He identified as "my Father ... my God" and "your Father ... your God." Of course, the relation of Jesus to the Father is different from that of the apostles. He is eternally the Son; they have become sons of God (cf. John 1:12; 2:16).

Mary Magdalene went and told the disciples that she had seen the Lord. The perfect tense "I have seen" expresses both her certainty and the fact that she will retain the vision all of her remaining days.

There are many mysteries connected with the resurrection body of Jesus. But several facts are clearly stated. His dead body was placed in the tomb. Three days later the tomb was seen with no body in it. And at intervals for forty days various individuals or groups of disciples saw the body of Jesus alive. And some of them saw Him ascend bodily into heaven. No unbeliever ever saw Jesus after the resurrection, which He said would be the case. Likewise, no unbeliever, save the soldiers on guard before the tomb, had any first-hand information about the empty tomb. According to the Gospel record the foes of Jesus never went to see that it was empty. After Mary Magdalene saw Jesus alive no believer is recorded as ever going there again. The enemies of Jesus did not go because they feared that they would find the tomb empty. The believers never returned there because they knew that the tomb was empty.

But, even so, the disciples, save John, did not fully believe until they saw Jesus Himself. According to John the first one to see Him after His resurrection was Mary Magdalene. But even she did not *believe* until she heard His voice calling her name. After the others had left the tomb she was held there not by faith but by love. Her faith was not yet equal to the trial. But her love persisted. And Jesus first revealed Himself to love.

The Appearance on Resurrection Sunday Night (20:19-23)

On resurrection Sunday evening a group of disciples was gathered together in some room in Jerusalem (v. 19). This may have been the same place where the previous Thursday evening Jesus had eaten with the apostles. Perhaps it was the home of John Mark's mother (cf. Acts 12:12). From Luke 24:33-35 we know that in addition to the apostles the group included the disciples of Emmaus. It is possible that others were present also.

Robertson points out that the time element "the first day of the week" indicates that John was using Roman time. According to strict Jewish time the second day would have started at sunset. Perhaps Robertson is right at this point. However, this time element admits to another interpretation. This was after the resurrection. And thereafter "the first day of the week" was used of Sunday. This could be the case here.

Nevertheless, it was Sunday night. And the disciples were gathered behind closed doors. The word for "shut" is a perfect passive participle. The perfect tense suggests that the doors were shut and locked. The disciples were fearful of what the Jewish rulers might do to them.

Many things had happened that day. After Jesus' appearance to Mary Magdalene He had also appeared to the other women who had gone to the tomb (Matt. 28:9-10), to the disciples on the road to Emmaus (Luke 24:13-32), and to Simon Peter (Luke 24:34; I Cor. 15:5). It is possible that the disciples had heard of the guard's report to the chief priests (Matt. 28:11-15). This could be one reason why the doors were locked.

As the disciples were rehearsing these matters, Jesus suddenly appeared in their midst. John does not say whether or not the door was opened. But the implication from the two aorists ("came ... stood") is that it was otherwise. Apparently Jesus suddenly appeared among them. We do not know the nature of Jesus' resurrection body. But we do know that on this occasion He invited the disciples to handle His body to show them that it was real and not a phantom. Furthermore, He ate some broiled fish, not that He needed it but to demonstrate that His body was real (Luke 24:39-43). At the ascension His body was not subject to the law of gravity (Acts 1:9). He suddenly disappeared from sight in the house in Emmaus (Luke 24:31). This suggests also the manner in which He appeared in the room in Jerusalem. We may conclude, therefore, that His body was not subject to the degrees of time, space, or density.

Luke tells us that Jesus' sudden appearance frightened the group (24:37). John implies this in Jesus' greeting. "Peace be unto you." This was also the customary oriental greeting. Having said this He showed them His hands and side which still bore the evidence of the crucifixion (v. 20). Luke adds that He showed his feet also. And thus seeing the Lord the disciples were glad.

Then repeating His word of peace Jesus gave the first of four commissions. "As my Father hath sent me, even so send I you" (v. 21). This is the only one recorded by John (cf. Matt. 28:18-20; Luke 24:44-51; Acts 1:3-11). With this He breathed on them, saying, "Receive ye the Holy Ghost [Spirit]" (v. 22). Robertson calls this "a foretaste of the great pentecost." But Bernard does not agree. He sees this as John's record of the fulfilment of Jesus' promise to give to them the Holy Spirit. Dods comments, "The breathing upon them was meant to convey the impression that His own very Spirit was imparted to them."

However, the word "receive" is an ingressive aorist tense. So it could mean "Begin to receive ye the Holy Spirit." In view of His commission they were to begin even then to prepare themselves for the Holy Spirit's power when He should come at Pentecost. In Luke 24:49 Jesus tells them to remain in Jerusalem "until ye get yourselves clothed with power from on high" (middle voice, something they were to do to themselves). The Spirit will come. But they must be submissive to His power if they are to be used by Him. They are to begin to receive the Holy Spirit as they repent of their sins of cowardice and disloyalty to Jesus, repair their marred fellowship, and lay themselves upon God's altar of service. Bernard is in general agreement with this position.

Then Jesus spoke words which have been the subject of sharp disagreement. "Whose soever sins ye remit, they are remitted unto them; and whose soever sins ye retain, they are retained" (v. 23). Some see this as Jesus giving the apostles power to forgive or not to forgive sins. But it should be remembered that other than apostles were present.

Perhaps these words should be interpreted in the light of Matthew 16:19. Again, some hold that these words were spoken to Peter alone. Thus they gave to Peter as the first pope, and to his successors, the right to forgive or to retain sins. And, of course, this is enlarged to include all priests. However, there is no real evidence that Peter was the first pope.* True, Jesus spoke these words to Peter. But an examination of this passage reveals that as Peter spoke to Jesus for the Twelve, Jesus spoke to the Twelve through Peter. Almost the same words Jesus later spoke with reference to a local church (Matt. 18:18).

But what did Jesus actually say? "I will give unto thee the keys of the kingdom: and whatsoever thou shalt bind on earth *shall have been bound* in heaven: and whatsoever thou shalt loose on earth *shall have been loosed in heaven*" (author's italics). The keys of the kingdom are the gospel. The disciples shall bind or loose it by either not preaching or preaching it. Heaven has already decreed that if we do not preach it there is no other way by which men may be saved. But if we preach it men will hear it, some will believe it, and those who do so will be saved.

This seems to be the sense of Jesus' words in John 20:23. By carrying out Jesus' commission they will make it possible for men to be saved. If they fail to do, then men are still lost in sin. This would apply to all who were in the room that evening, not to the apostles alone. Truly, proclaiming the gospel is "every Christian's job."

The Doubt of Thomas (20:24-25)

Thomas was not present on this first Sunday evening (v. 24). Later when he learned that the others had seen the Lord, he said, "Except I shall see in his hands the print of the nails, and put my finger into the print of the nails, and thrust my hand into his side, I will not believe" (v. 25). He used a strong double negative. "I not never will believe."

For this statement Thomas has been called "Doubting Thomas." It has wiped from most people's memory his act of heroism (cf. 11:16). But should Thomas be so severely condemned?

In the first place, he only asked for the same evidence which

---

*See my *Exposition of Matthew,* pp. 216-222.

Jesus had already given to the others. They did not believe until Jesus did this (Luke 24:36-37). Thomas as yet had not seen Jesus after His resurrection. And this idea was too vital to accept without proof. Incidently, his demand has furnished us with one of the greatest proofs of the bodily resurrection of Jesus.

In the second place, he did not say flatly, "I will not believe." He prefaced this with "Except...," showing that he was open to proof. Charles Kingsley reminds us that one need not be afraid to doubt so long as he has a disposition to believe. And Thomas had such a disposition.

Doubt is not necessarily a bad thing. It is a protective device given to us of God. If you tell me that drinking a solution of arsenic will not hurt me, I shall doubt it. If you insist that Jesus is not the virgin-born Son of God, I shall doubt you. It is only when one allows Satan to pervert this God-given ability into cynicism and agnosticism that it becomes an evil. When one doubts, he should not be content to let the matter end there. But he should pursue all evidence with an open mind — and with a disposition to believe — if the evidence demands it. Thomas did just this. And the result was most wholesome indeed!

The Appearance to the Eleven (20:26-29)

The next Sunday evening the disciples were back in the room, this time with Thomas present (v. 26). And again Jesus appeared to them through locked doors. He greeted them with the oriental blessing of peace.

Without delay Jesus accosted Thomas with the evidence which he had demanded (v. 27). He urged him to be "not faithless, but believing" (mē...apistos alla pistos). That was all that Thomas needed. Without doing any of the things which he had said he must do, he said, "My Lord and my God" (v. 28). Truly, in his doubt he had a disposition to believe.

And in this attitude he made the greatest confession of all. Many had called Jesus "Teacher," "Son of God," "Christ," and "Lord." But Thomas is the only person recorded in the Gospels as calling Jesus "God!" So instead of calling him "Doubting Thomas" we may more fittingly call him "Thomas the Great Confessor."

Jesus did not protest when Thomas called Him "God" (v. 29). Instead, He acknowledged his belief. Then He said, "Blessed are they that have not seen, yet have believed." Thomas had made

a noble confession. But he had missed the higher faith and blessedness which comes without the evidence of the senses. One may
see in this the note of pride on John's part that he had believed
in the resurrection before he had seen Jesus after the event (cf.
20:8). But this was no more a rebuke of Thomas than it was of
the others who had not believed without seeing.

However, one may see a further thought in this. It could be
a blessing upon all future generations who without seeing Jesus
with the natural eyes yet believe on Him. The aorist tenses of
"have seen . . . have believed" simply express the historical facts.
So ours may be a greater blessedness than those of the days immediately following the resurrection. For through the Holy Spirit
Jesus is with us as He was with them.

The Purpose of the Fourth Gospel (20:30-31)

John has now finished his Gospel. And it ended on the highest
note of faith. Later, before releasing it he will add Chapter 21.
But for the moment he brings it to a close.

He does not claim to have written a complete record of all of
Jesus' deeds (v. 30). None of the Gospels makes such a claim. For,
says John, "many other signs truly did Jesus in the presence of
his disciples, which are not written in this book." The Synoptics
are an evidence of the truth of this statement. And doubtless
many of the things which Jesus said and did are not recorded in
any of the Gospels (cf. Acts 20:35). In recent years certain papyri
have been discovered which contain sayings attributed to Him.
And some of them have the ring of genuineness in them.

But John says that he has selected certain *signs* for his record
which are designed to the end "that ye might believe that Jesus
is the Christ, the Son of God; and that believing ye might have
life through his name" (v. 31).

These are not all of Jesus' *signs*. But they are enough. For count-
less multitudes reading them have believed, and have found life
through His name.

John 21

The Epilogue

Despite the fact that John 20:30-31 comprises a definite ending to the Gospel of John, there is strong evidence that Chapter 21 was written by the same author. Insofar as we know no copy of the Gospel was ever issued without this chapter. It is quoted by Tertullian and is treated by Origen in his commentary as on a par with the other twenty chapters. There are some scholars who attribute it to another author (Pfleiderer, Moffatt, and Stanton). But by far the majority hold to the same authorship as that of the body of the Gospel (Godet, Harnack, Sanday, W. Bauer, Bernard, Dods, and Robertson). The evidence seems to support the latter group.

Why was this chapter added? Since it deals largely with Simon Peter we naturally look at him for the answer. This Gospel was written many years after Peter's death. It was also written long after the other three Gospels. All of these leave Peter in a rather bad light. They tell of his three denials (John also). After that little mention is made of him. Mark 16:7 says that the angels told the women to tell the disciples "and Peter" to meet Jesus in Galilee. Luke 24:12 records his hesitancy to believe in the resurrection (also John). And then Luke 24:34 mentions that Jesus had appeared to Peter (cf. I Cor. 15:5). The overall effect was to leave Peter under a cloud.

And yet he was one of the giants of the early church. So John, putting all of this together, evidently decided to add the event in Chapter 21. Even his Gospel through Chapter 20 left Peter puzzled about the resurrection of Jesus (20:2-10). And yet John knew that Jesus had forgiven Peter and had given him a special commission. So to clear the atmosphere he added this event to his record before it was sent forth. Thus we are in his debt for one of the most beautiful stories in the Gospel records. It is thoroughly Johannine in style. It is true to Jesus' own nature. And it shows Peter in the same light as he appears elsewhere in the ministry of Jesus.

The Fruitless Fishermen (21:1-3)

As in other instances where John gave additional material, so here he began with his words "after these things" *(meta tauta)*. This within itself should be a tip-off as to the authorship of this chapter. He was inserting in the record material not related by the other writers, and which he also had failed to tell. Specifically he notes that this material involved a hitherto unrelated appearance of Jesus after His resurrection (v. 1). John says that it oc- curred at the sea of Tiberias, his name for the sea of Galilee (cf. 6:1). Apparently this took place prior to the appearance mentioned in Matthew 28:16-20.

Evidently some of the apostles had arrived back in Galilee prior to the appointed time for their scheduled meeting with Jesus. In this group were Simon Peter, Thomas, Nathanael, James and John, and two other disciples (v. 2). Where the other four were we are not told. But while they were waiting with time on their hands, Peter said, "I am going to fish" (v. 3). The others said that they were going to do the same. Sermons have been preached about Peter forsaking his calling to go back to his old life and leading others with him. However, this is to miss the point. After all Peter was formerly a fisherman by trade. And it is natural to suppose that in his time of waiting he would return to his former means of livelihood. They certainly could use the money that might be derived from a fishing expedition. So instead of wasting his time waiting, Peter proposed to occupy it profitably.

Night was the best time for fishing. But after a night of work they had caught nothing.

The Great Catch (21:4-8)

But when morning came, probably about daybreak, Jesus was standing on the shore. However, apparently because of the dis- tance and the early morning mist, the disciples did not recognize Him (v. 4). They saw someone, but did not know *(eideisan* from *oida)* that it was Jesus.

Then Jesus said to them, "Children, have ye any meat?" or, anything to eat? (v. 5). And they called back, "No." He said, "Cast the net on the right side of the ship, and ye shall find" (v. 6; cf. Luke 5:4). Did Jesus from the shore see a school of fish, or was this due to supernatural knowledge? At any rate they did as He said. And they caught so many fish in their nets that they were unable to draw them into the boat. This was beyond the expectations of the fishermen. Perhaps they recalled a similar experience when at Jesus' word they had made a great catch (cf. Luke 5:4 ff.).

At any rate it suddenly dawned upon John that the man on the shore was Jesus (v. 7). Maybe the mist had lifted by now, so that he could see more clearly. So he said, "It is the Lord!"

That was all that Peter needed to hear. He was naked except for a waist-cloth, as would be true of one who was fishing. So putting on his upper garment, he plunged into the water and either waded or swam ashore. He could not wait for the slow boat which would be made even slower by the bulging nets. The other disciples came in "a little ship" (v. 8). This was a small boat attached to the larger fishing vessel. They too were anxious to get ashore. It was only about one hundred yards. So they rowed ashore dragging their filled nets behind them. This is a vivid picture of the scramble for shore when they knew that Jesus was there.

The Breakfast Scene (21:9-14)

When they arrived on shore they found that Jesus already had a fire of coals with a fish being cooked on it. Also Jesus had bread (v. 9). Since Jesus was cooking the fish we may assume that it was fresh, possibly having been caught by Jesus Himself. It was not one of the fish that had just been caught in the nets. They were brought ashore after the fish had been placed on the fire. John does not say that Jesus ate on this occasion. But the evidence suggests that the one fish and the bread were for Jesus' own breakfast. When the disciples came ashore Jesus told them to bring some of their own fish (v. 10). It was an invitation for them to join Him at breakfast.

Peter, therefore, went to fetch some fish (v. 11). He found that although the net contained one hundred and fifty-three fish, the net itself was not broken. Note this eyewitness detail of the author. Nothing is said about cooking any of these fish. But it is implied. So finally Jesus said, "Come and dine" (v. 12). They were subdued in Jesus' presence. Nevertheless, they accepted bread and fish from the hands of Jesus (v. 13). It must have been an impressive scene. These hungry fishermen being fed by the Lord who evidently had served as the *Chef* here, even as He had served as the *Foot Rinser* at a previous meal.

John notes that this is the third time that Jesus had shown

Himself to the apostles after His resurrection (v. 14). This means
to the apostles as a group. He had done so twice on succeeding
Sunday nights in Jerusalem. John points out that this event preceded the appearance on a mountain in Galilee (Matt. 28:16 ff.).

The Testing and Commissioning of Peter (21:15-17)

As in the upper room after the passover meal, so here, the
group sat around talking. Suddenly Jesus addressed Simon Peter
with a question. "Simon, son of Jonas [note that He did not call
him "Peter"], lovest [agapais] thou me more than these?" (v.
15). To what does "these" refer. Some see it as referring to Peter's
boat and other fishing gear. While others relate it to the other
ten apostles. Since the word translated "these" (touto) may be
either masculine or neuter, it could refer to either. However, one
thing should be noted. Peter had long since forsaken his fishing
gear in order to follow Jesus. It is mere supposition to see in
this one night of fishing a permanent return to his former trade.
We have noted the likelihood that he was doing this while waiting for the appointed meeting with Jesus.

The entire dialogue between Jesus and Peter seems to take on
added meaning if "these" is seen as referring to the other disciples.
In fact, Godet translates this, "Lovest thou me more than these
do?" Furthermore, there is significance in the fact that Jesus called
him "Simon, son of Jonas" and not "Peter." Of late he had been
acting more like unstable mud than like a rock. In this light let
us examine this question.

On the night before His crucifixion Jesus had said, "All ye
shall be offended [be caused to stumble] because of me this night"
(Matt. 26:31). But in characteristic fashion Peter had replied,
"Though all . . . shall be offended because of thee, yet will I never
be offended" (26:33). The pronoun "I" is emphatic. Peter, in
effect, said that even if all the others were caused to stumble,
he most certainly would not. He claimed to be superior to all
the others, which involved his love for Jesus. The next few hours
demonstrated how utterly wrong he was. He not only stumbled;
he fell flat on his face.

So now in the early morning about the breakfast fire Jesus
probed into Peter's heart. In the light of all that had happened
since his boasted superior love and loyalty, did Simon still say
that he loved Jesus more than these other apostles? And since
he had claimed such great love, Jesus naturally used the word

for the highest kind of love *(agapaō)*, the love akin to God's divine love.

It is evident that Peter was subdued. Somewhat like a little child wishing to avoid an unpleasant subject, he made no reference to "more than these." Instead, he simply said, "Yea, Lord; thou knowest that I love [*philō*, the love of a friend] thee." Jesus replied, "Feed [*boske*] my lambs."

Again Jesus asked, "Simon, son of Jonas, lovest [*agapais*] thou me?" (v. 16). Note that Jesus dropped the "more than these." He asked Peter if he loved Him at all. And Peter replied as before. But here Jesus said, "Feed [*poimaine*] my sheep [both young and old]." The word *boske* (v. 15) simply means "to feed," in this case with spiritual food. But *poimaine* refers to all of the duties of a shepherd toward his sheep: e.g., feeding, guarding, guiding.

The third time Jesus asked, "Simon, son of Jonas, lovest [*phileis*] thou me?" (v. 17). Peter was grieved because Jesus said "the third time," Lovest [*phileis*] thou me?" So this time he said, "Lord, thou knowest [*oidas*, hast insight into] all things; thou knowest [*ginōskeis*, knowest by experience] that I love [*philō*] thee." Again Jesus said, "Feed [*boske*] my sheep."

The question naturally arises as to the cause of Peter's grief over Jesus' third question. Was it because He asked three questions corresponding to Peter's three denials? Certainly one cannot separate the two. With design Jesus probably matched His number of questions with the number of denials. But there is more than this involved when one reads this dialogue in the Greek text.

The reason for Peter's grief is seen in the Greek verbs used for love. *Agapaō* is the verb whence comes the word *agapē* used in I John 4:8, "God is love." The verb form is used twice along with the noun in verse 10, showing that this love is divinely expressed in God's gift of His Son as the basis of the forgiveness of sins (cf. John 3:16). So this obviously is the highest kind of love. This is the verb used by Jesus in His first two questions. On the other hand, Peter each time used the verb *phileō*. This expresses the warm love of friendship. But is not as high a love as that expressed by *agapaō*. Even though these verbs are different in nature, at times in the New Testament they are used interchangeably. However, there is a basic difference. And that distinction is preserved in the passage under consideration.

Now the point of the "third time" is that in His third question Jesus used *phileō*. Twice He asked Peter if he loved Him with this highest love. Twice Peter said that he loved Jesus as a friend, or with this lower kind of love. Then Jesus asked if he loved Him as a friend. When Peter twice failed to rise to Jesus' level of love, the third time Jesus came down to Peter's level of love.

This cut Peter to the heart. It humbled him and made him a more suitable instrument for the Lord's service. John recorded this incident to show that Peter was both forgiven and commissioned to be a shepherd of the Lord's sheep. And this he did. He came to love Jesus with this highest love, and to exhort the "sheep" to do the same (cf. Peter 1:3).

The Curiosity of Peter (21:18-23)

Peter was humbled, but he retained his curiosity and forward nature. Jesus followed this dialogue with a solemn statement to Peter. "Verily, verily, I say unto thee, When thou wast young, thou *girdedst* thyself, and *walkedst* whither thou *wouldest:* but when thou shalt be old, thou shalt stretch forth thy hands, and another shall gird thee, and carry thee whither thou wouldest not" (v. 18). The italicized words are all imperfects, showing that Peter had had the habit of doing these things in the past.

Now this could mean that when Peter was a young man he had had the habit of dressing himself and walking about wherever he wished. But when he shall reach old age he will be dependent upon others to dress him and to take him places. However, the words "whither thou wouldest not" suggest an entirely different meaning. They suggest that he will be taken forcibly. And this is suggestive of his death.

This is the meaning given by John in verse 19. "This spake he, signifying by what death he should glorify God." And since the word "glorify" is used repeatedly in John to refer to Jesus' death on the cross, this idea seems to apply here.

There is an early tradition that Peter suffered martyrdom by crucifixion. The first mention of such is by Tertullian who makes reference to John 21:18. Later Origen said that he was crucified head downwards. This was said to be at Peter's own request, since, having denied his Lord, he did not deserve to die as He did with his head upwards. However, this latter idea of his being crucified head downwards is not to be derived from John's explanation. But it does seem to corroborate that Peter died by crucifixion.

When Jesus had finished His words to Peter He told him, "Follow me" (v. 19). On the surface this could simply mean that for the rest of his life, until death, he is to "go on following" Jesus (present imperative, a command). But taken in this context it says otherwise. For some reason Jesus seems to have started walking away from the group. And He told Peter to follow Him. This is suggested by the next verse. "Then Peter, turning about, seeth the disciple whom Jesus loved following." As Peter started to walk away with Jesus, he evidently heard someone else following. So suddenly "turning around" (aorist), he saw John following behind. The close relationship between Jesus and John (v. 20) would lead John to feel that he was not intruding.

If curiosity killed a cat, it certainly kept Peter in hot water. For, seeing John, and remembering Jesus' words about his own death, he asked, "Lord, and what shall this man do" (v. 21)? Literally, "Lord, this man, what?"

So once again Jesus had to deal with His problem disciple. He said, "If I will that he tarry till I come, what is that to thee? follow thou me" (v. 22). In simple terms Jesus said that what was to happen to John was none of Peter's business. He did not say that John would live until His second coming, even though some did so construe His words at the moment. He simply said that if He should so will that was His concern, not Peter's (v. 23). Peter had all that he could handle just to go on following Jesus. This is evident in the emphatic position of "you" and "me." Literally, "You me go on following." That was Peter's responsibility; John's fate was the responsibility of Jesus.

Bernard notes that this command, "Follow thou me," is the last precept of Jesus recorded in the last of the Gospels. It is a fitting *finale* which encompasses the whole of the Christian life for all who propose to become disciples of Jesus.

The Affadavit of the Elders (21:24)

This verse is a definite break in the narrative which is concluded in verse 25. The words, "we know," clearly show that this verse is not from the pen of the author.

This statement definitely identifies the author of this Gospel as "the disciple whom Jesus loved ... which also leaned on his breast at supper, and said, Lord, which is he that betrayeth thee?" (v. 20; cf. 13:23-25). "This is the disciple which testifieth of these things [the entire Gospel], and wrote these things: and we know [*oidamen*, know for a certainty] that his testimony is true" (v. 24).

To understand these words one must recall the basic meaning of the word for "testify," or "witness." In the papyri the primary idea of *martureō* is that of giving legal testimony of what one has seen or experienced. It was a common practice to write this word after a signature in the sense that we write "witness." For instance, a will is so witnessed: "I, Serapion, am witness" (*Serapiōn marturō*). The word *marturia* was used in the sense of the thing witnessed or evidence.

Now verse 24 reads literally, "This is the disciple, the one giving eyewitness testimony of these things, and the one who wrote these things: and we know that his evidence is true." The "we" evidently was a group of trusted disciples in Ephesus, probably Ephesian elders. So in essence they wrote, "We, the Ephesian elders, are witnesses to the truthfulness of the one who wrote his eyewitness testimony as contained in this Gospel."*

The Abundance of Jesus' Works (21:25)

The "Epilogue" closes on the same note as did Chapters 1-20. And it forms a fitting finish for the entire Gospel.

"And there are also many other things which Jesus did, the which, if they should be written every one, I suppose that even the world itself could not contain the books that should be written."

So once again John does not claim to have written a complete account of the life of Jesus. Indeed, he sees such as an impossible undertaking. What a wonderful thing it would be if we did know every thing that Jesus did and spoke. But also how wonderful that we do know what we know. The blessed Holy Spirit inspired men to recall and recount that which is necessary.

For thus we know that the eternal Christ who always was equal with God, who always was God Himself, who was the Creator of every single part of the universe, and who is the Source of Life and Light — the Same came into being as flesh, and for a little while tabernacled among us full of grace and truth. Those who walked Palestinian streets and paths with Him "beheld his glory, the glory as of the only begotten of the Father." And those then, as now, who received/receive Him, to them He gave/gives

---

* See my *Preaching Values from the Papyri*, pp. 84-88.

power to become the sons of God, even to them who believe on His name.

And God grant that those of us who do now believe in Him may hear and heed His abiding command, "Follow thou me."